# My Children, Listen

Catherine Helene Toye, M.D.

Published by Caritas Communications, Inc.
P.O. Box 2460
Lenox Hill Station
New York, New York 10021-0058
Website: http://www.caritasinc.com

See acknowledgments and bibliography.

Printed in the United States of America
Printed on acid free paper.

Publisher's - Cataloging-in-Publication
(Provided by Quality Books, Inc.)

Toye, Catherine Helene.
    My children, listen / Catherine Helene Toye. -- 1st ed.
    p. 384  cm.
    Includes bibliographical references.
    Preassigned LCCN: 98-70377
    ISBN: 0-9663088-0-8

    1. Chronically ill--Religious life.  2. Toye, Catherine
Helene--Health.  3. Spiritual journals.  4. Meniere's disease
--Patients--Religious life.  5. Suffering--Religious aspects--
Catholic Church.  6. Physicians' writings, American.  I.
Title.

BX2373.S5T69 1998                        242'.4
                                         QBI98-291

This book is dedicated,
with love,
to my children...
and
to all God's children.

"I give you a new commandment:
love one another.
As I have loved you,
so you also should love one another.
This is how all will know
that you are my disciples,
if you have love for one another."
John 13:34-35

# WITH LOVING GRATITUDE,

Souls are drawn to me of love.
Seeing and feeling love
makes them more receptive to my call.
This is man's role
to make manifest—
directly visible to their bodily eyes—
my love to all.
How else can man (more readily) see me?

March 14, 1996

It is with deepest appreciation that I thank my family, from my earliest days to the present, for bringing these words to life around me. Family is, for most of us, our initial experience of love and nurturing, the first manner in which our hearts are primed to be receptive to God's love. To deny one another love, especially a child, is mankind's self destruction.

I am further grateful for my family's help in doing for me what illness has taken from me. My scattered notes would not have been brought together as they are in these pages or published were it not for my family.

I am thankful for the love and caring of friends. I am dearly grateful to all who took their time to review this manuscript and offer comments, critique, editing, and encouragement.

I am especially appreciative of my cousin, Daniel O'Sullivan, whose artistic talent and patience so faithfully brought the beauty and spirit of my vision to canvas. How elated I am to see it again; what pleasure it is to share it on the book's cover.

As he passed by he saw a man blind from birth. His disciples asked him, "Rabbi, who sinned, this man or his parents, that he was born blind?" Jesus answered, "Neither he nor his parents sinned; it is so that the works of God might be made visible through him."

John 9:1-3

# CONTENTS

The LORD is my shepherd, I shall not want;
    he makes me lie down in green pastures.
He leads me beside still waters;
    he restores my soul.
He leads me in paths of righteousness
    for his name's sake.

Even though I walk through the valley
      of the shadow of death,
    I fear no evil;
    for thou art with me;
      thy rod and thy staff,
      they comfort me.

Thou preparest a table before me
    in the presence of my enemies;
thou anointest my head with oil,
    my cup overflows.
Surely goodness and mercy shall follow me
    all the days of my life;
and I shall dwell in the house of the Lord
    for ever.

Psalm Twenty-three, RSV

# Prologue

*"I will not leave you desolate; I will come to you."*
John 14:18, RSV

This book is about the personal experience of God in my life. Faith is a gift—not the product of reason, need, or choice. There are no words to prove God's existence; the secret is in listening to the silence.

Dire circumstances brought me face to face with my own helplessness. I had lost my marriage, then my health, and with it my ability to practice medicine. Powerless, and with my own mortality glaring back at me, I was brought to the true source of strength and life. In the despair and darkness of the abyss in which I lay, I grew still enough to simply "listen," and in so doing I received the most precious gift. That gift was a deep awareness of God's presence in my life.

Gently cradled in the grace of God, my broken body and spirit were carried across the fathomless chasm between hoping or believing there is a God—and knowing there is a God. It is only through accepting the gift of God's grace that this chasm can be bridged.

With faith came an awareness of God's intimate and personal presence, not only in my life, but in the lives of others and in the world around me. I was allowed to feel this Presence with such force that God is as real to me as anything I have known through seeing with my eyes, hearing with my ears, or touching with my hands.

My journey is not yet complete. It was and remains imperfect. It is my wish to give you the gift that I received in my hours of desolation—but I cannot. The gift is in the experience. We must find our own way, listening and allowing God to direct our individual paths to the Truth. Herein lies discovering the unique meaning and joy of our own lives—the purpose for which we were created and chosen by God—and thence appreciating God's call to each of us to share in divine eternal life.

# LEGEND

It is true that the voice of God, having once fully pen-
etrated the heart, becomes strong as the tempest and
loud as the thunder, but before reaching the heart it is
as weak as a light breath which scarcely agitates the air.
It shrinks from noise, and is silent amid agitation.
St. Ignatius Loyola 1491-1556

Locutions are communications "heard" not with my ears but within
my heart. I have experienced these in two ways. The first is through individual words. The second is through the instantaneous comprehension of
thoughts or insights without intervening words. They are set apart as follows.

**Boldface:** communication with words.

***Boldface Italic:*** communication without words.

At times communication has come faster than I could record, and in
these instances I have paraphrased the content within parentheses. To
respect others' privacy, most names have been replaced by pronouns and
verb conjugations have been adjusted as needed. At times greater privacy
is preserved at the expense of accurate pronouns or singular and plural
pronoun agreement, using they or them instead of him or her. All these
changes are not in boldface. Transitional words (the, a, and, etc.), which
were skipped to keep up with recording the locutions, are added for clarity. These are also in nonbold type. Word and wordless communications
were sometimes mixed, and several words separated by slash marks have
been used to preserve the fullest meaning. Quotation marks have not been
used in the locutions, since they are set apart in bold type.

Repetition in the locutions has not been edited out entirely in order
to preserve the gradual unfolding and development of the words as they
were given me. This evolution illustrates God's gentle patience, waiting for
us to accept the love he pours upon us, as we are ready to receive it.

# INTRODUCTION

I am the good shepherd. A good shepherd
lays down his life for the sheep.
John 10:11

I have other sheep that do not belong to
this fold. These also I must lead, and they
will hear my voice, and there will be one
flock, one shepherd.
John 10:16

The ultimate comfort is from God. It is the comfort of giving
meaning to our daily lives, its struggles, joys, losses, successes, suffering,
loneliness, duties, fears, doubts and questions. It is the comfort of knowing there is a spiritual realm of truer, fuller life beyond the blindness of
our human sight. It is the comfort of immortality—the invitation to
divine eternal life in God's presence.

Drawing my scattered notes together in this book was for my children.
I wanted them to have a record of my greatest treasure to accompany them
in all the ages of their lives, to inspire them, guide them, and give them hope.
In the process this book gained a life of its own.

For many reasons I have been reluctant to publish this journal—the
privacy and anonymity of my life in part lost. Sharing this book, saying
"Yes," and trusting that this is God's will for me is like stepping off a cliff in
free fall. I still ask myself, "How could it be?" There is no one more incredulous than I am, that I should be the one to have witnessed the events and
words herein, yet it gives me great joy to share my experience of God's love.
The encouragement of early readers in sharing how deeply it touched their
lives has helped me to let the book go. The common thread in their remarks
was an element of healing—a healing of the spirit. It was a quality of
response to the book's message which went beyond the book and had

occurred within their own hearts. Out of this healing emerged the small miracles of daily living: finding meaning, hope, acceptance, peace, strength to persevere; an inclination toward greater love and forgiveness, consolation in loss or betrayal, and more openness to God's presence in their own lives.

> Your (story/book) will comfort many:
> those with illness...those bereaved.
> Your pain and suffering is with a purpose.
> You will lead others to me in your writing
> and I will comfort them.
>
> November 15, 1994

## One Creator

We all share one Creator, whom we call by many names. My experience of God is not pure, but my description of it is as accurate as words allow me. It is not pure because it is colored by many things like my culture, religious background (Roman Catholic), temperament, life's experience, and more. My experience of God is through the person of Jesus Christ, and the Blessed Trinity (God the Father, God the Son, and God the Holy Spirit). The Blessed Trinity is a conceptualization of one God in three distinct but indivisible divine Persons, inseparable in absolute union of their wills. The full nature of the Trinity cannot be understood by man but only accepted as divine mystery.

The God I have experienced, however, speaks to us all regardless of our religious affiliation or non belief.

> There are many religions in the world;
> they all come to me.
>
> October 17, 1994; February 27, 1996

Referring to the world's many religions:

> Respect your differences,
> love one another
> and live together peacefully.
> Leave the mystery
> of bringing all men to salvation to me.
>
> March 14, 1996

> I am not a God of exclusion.
> All come to me...
>
> December 4, 1995

# Gender

God is not limited by gender, race or any criteria; it is only man's thinking that is. God is beyond all description. I have used traditional gender pronouns to preserve the personal quality and accuracy of my experience, but not because our Creator is any more masculine than feminine.

# Authenticity

I do not have a theological background. Until the day I had a spiritual experience myself, I did not believe in their existence. There had been no room in my analytical, scientific, medical thinking for such an occurrence. I did not deny that others believed such experiences were real to them, but I fully dismissed these as originating in their own imaginations. Now I see it is not so simple. Yes, some people create things in their imaginations. Yes, some people may experience unusual phenomena perhaps influenced by dark or paranormal forces. Yet there are bona fide mystical phenomena of truly divine impetus, and I believe this is the source of my experience.

To those skeptical of what I relate, I can only say, "I understand." I have long stood in your place. I have seen the world through your eyes. Despite my own transition from skeptic to believer, I have nothing to convince you otherwise. It would be foolhardy to try.

How do I know my experience is authentic? I can only satisfactorily answer that question to myself. I know because it is. I know because of its permanent transforming effects upon me—none of which I can prove outside myself. My experience stands alone. That is what I have to offer you—sharing my experience. The value is not in convincing you that it is real or true, but in hoping some aspect of it leaves your own heart more open to experiencing God's healing love, forgiveness, and peace. Faith by its nature is belief in the unseen, that which is unsupported by material evidence or logical proof.

## From The Raising Of Lazarus

So the sisters sent word to him, saying, "Master, the one you love is ill." When Jesus heard this he said, "This illness is not to end in death, but is for the glory of God, that the Son of God may be glorified through it."

John 11:3-4

# Part I

# From Despair To Faith

Then the LORD addressed Job out of the storm and said:

Who is this that obscures divine plans
   with words of ignorance?
Gird up your loins now, like a man;
   I will question you, and you tell me the answers!
Where were you when I founded the earth?
   Tell me, if you have understanding.
Who determined its size; do you know?
   Who stretched out the measuring line for it?
Into what were its pedestals sunk,
   and who laid the cornerstone,
While the morning stars sang in chorus
   and all the sons of God shouted for joy?

And who shut within doors the sea,
   when it burst forth from the womb;
When I made the clouds its garment
   and thick darkness its swaddling bands?
When I set limits for it
   and fastened the bar of its door,
And said: Thus far shall you come but no farther,
   and here shall your proud waves be stilled!

Job 38:1-11

# December, 1990

Because God did not make death,
  nor does he rejoice in the destruction of the living.
                                              Wisdom 1:13

I was thirty-eight years old, happy, successful at least by many worldly standards, and full of life. My two children were my greatest joy. Our lives had seen the trauma of a marriage failed—its end divorce. I persevered in its wake, striving to put the comforting rituals of life in place about us. I made as great a sense of permanence, family, and continuity as circumstances allowed. My work as a physician was fulfilling and challenging, making the long arduous years of school and training pale in memory.

Suddenly it was all over. One December morning I simply could not get out of bed. Each time I tried, I fell back. I could not plant my feet on the floor. I could not find the floor, as I realized I could not tell up from down. The room was spinning round and round. As the spinning become more violent, I held tightly to the bed for it seemed I would otherwise be thrown from it. By comparison it was relief when this vertigo subsided into continuous dizziness and nausea—punctuated by periods of uncontrolled vomiting. The high-pitched ringing and intense pressured pain deep within my ears distracted me. Later that morning my attention was otherwise fully seized, when I realized that intermittently I could not hear those around me. My body was drained of energy. An oppressive fatigue shackled me—my body felt four times its weight.

That was my first episode of Meniere's disease, an inner ear disorder, and it heralded my entry into a world of chronic illness. Initial testing confirmed the diagnosis: bilateral Meniere's disease, cause as yet undetermined. My prognosis was laid before me. I could expect repeated episodes of Meniere's with progressive hearing loss, and in five to fifteen years be deaf in both ears. I sat frozen in stunned silence upon hearing my physician's words. I thought, "This couldn't be real...there must be some mistake."

He continued, "Some patients are actually grateful when they are deaf, because they have some relief from the bouts of vertigo, vomiting, and dizziness."

"Grateful? Was that supposed to be consoling? The good news, the silver lining?" I thought. Being unable to relate to this at all distanced me further still from the reality of the moment. Beneath my outward composure, I wanted to scream as long and loud as I could, "NOOOOOOO!"

An intensive search for the cause was begun in hopes of tailoring any form of treatment to stem the inevitable progression of the disease. Weeks of testing followed, but nothing more definitive emerged. Though ninety-nine percent of Meniere's many causes had been excluded, what brought about mine remained a mystery. Only a handful of rare etiologies remained, stones not yet turned.

The first two months of my illness were quite severe, spent almost entirely lying still in a darkened quiet room, seeking any modicum of relief from the unremitting motion sickness. I was blessed by having my mother and grandmother interrupt their lives to come help my children and me.

Some days I could not raise myself out of bed to even care for my own needs. At times I felt panic and confusion over the body which I held motionless because even the slightest movement of my head was accompanied by suffocating waves of sea sickness rolling over me. I felt useless, worthless. Who was I? What was left of me? Was there any spark of the vibrance I once had? I was indignant at confronting an identity crisis.

I was affronted by the lack of permanence offered by so many things we anchor ourselves to in this life—transient moorings to distract us from thoughts of our mortality. For me, now, nothing seemed permanent. Reduced to my present circumstances, there were few distractions to cling to. I envied those who continued in the reassuring routines of daily living, though I knew firsthand how precarious their illusion of security was. It was a hoax awaiting inevitable exposure, if not by an early fate, then by time. In the havoc illness wrought I slipped beneath the veneered semblance of life's order onto its raw, fragile edge. A solitary thread held me from being swallowed into the nothingness engulfing me on every side. That fine thread was my children—needing me and depending upon me.

We three were together. Now, in the wake of my illness, our lives had been turned upside down once again. It was even less certain what lay ahead.

Angry and frustrated at my losses, I slipped into despair. Overwhelmed, I felt the full burden of my illness as failure. I was alone and without hope. I was frightened for my children and myself. I was their sole provider. All that I had hoped and wished, worked, struggled, and dreamed for lay wasted around me. I was desolate—except for my children, and it grieved me to wonder how I would protect and care for them. The tomorrow of our lives had become a growing uncertainty. I could no longer see a path or clear direction, nor did it much matter; there was barely a shred of me remaining with which to take the first step.

"What is your opinion? If a man has a hundred sheep and one of them goes astray, will he not leave the ninety-nine in the hills and go in search of the stray? And if he finds it, amen, I say to you, he rejoices more over it than over the ninety-nine that did not stray. In just the same way, it is not the will of your heavenly Father that one of these little ones be lost."

Matthew 18:12-14

# January, 1991

He heard this and said, "Those who are well do not
need a physician, but the sick do. Go and learn the
meaning of the words, 'I desire mercy, not sacrifice.'
I did not come to call the righteous but sinners."
Matthew 9:12-13

As had become our new morning routine, my daughters, six and
nine years old, came to my room together to kiss me good-bye before
school. Their faces were bright, their hair shiny, neatly combed, and their
jumpers and blouses pressed. The usual sparkle in their eyes was dimmed
by unspoken questions, not to be thought, much less asked. Brown eyes
wide and limpid, they approached my bed with the apprehension of fawns
nearing the injured doe. Propping myself up on one arm, I made my best
effort to look and sound like the mother they had known five weeks
before. Their eyes searched mine for reassurance. I thought my heart
would break as I watched their pain and fright, leaving me overcome at my
helplessness. I would have moved a mountain for them—but I could not
stand up to see them to the front door.

They walked away from me, anxiously turning for a last glimpse and
wave before I heard the front door open and shut. I closed my eyes and
rested my head on the pillow. A tear welled at the corner of my eye.

What immediately followed their departure was not a dream or a
hallucination. I was fully awake, my mind sharp and focused. I had a
heightened clarity of perception beyond anything I knew possible.

At first my mind was completely blank. I was enveloped in a soothing, soft, velvety, indescribable blackness that was more than black. At the
same time the steady, intense pain and continuous, noisy, high-pitched
ringing deep in my ears, and the marked nausea and dizziness totally abat-
ed. I felt no physical sensations. It was like floating effortlessly, weight-
lessly. A living, rapidly moving stream of light in the shape of an inverted

V appeared around me. The apex of the V was far above and ahead of me, and I could not see where the two arms of the V joined. The arms of the V enclosed the space I was in and beyond. The light had a quality I had never seen before. It was radiantly beautiful and alive as it streamed from the V's apex. At about the same time that I became aware of the light, I heard the most beautiful, soft musical chimes.

Then I "heard" a voice, but I did not just hear it. I saw and felt the words spoken. The letters forming the words had three dimensions and were made of light. It was a similar, beautiful, live, white-golden light as in the V. The words all originated from the apex of the V and as they came down to me they became larger in size. I did not see the words stop short of me, nor was I aware of having the physical border a body provides. I could feel the words, as if gently bathed in them. I cannot at all describe what they felt like. It was more pleasurable than our bodily senses would allow. The voice was not like one I have ever heard. It was magnificently resonant, harmonious, deep, and extraordinarily soothing. But there was something ineffable about that sonorous voice. Immediately, in a familiar, entirely commonplace manner, and without fear, I recognized the Presence speaking to me as God.

**My child, you have had a difficult life...**

I felt undeserving of so much compassion, and thought how many others have suffered so much more and for longer than I. In that moment, I knew that God was there for them too, matched to their needs. I found infinite solace in the depth of pure, unconditional love, acceptance, and understanding from the One who knows my every fault.

In rapid succession scenes from my life were before me, beginning with the more recent. It was in no way akin to memory. It was rather like actually being there again, with all the accompanying details, sensations, and feelings. The one difference, however, was viewing my life with crystal clear perception and a knowledge superior to hindsight and experience alone. The two most painful areas were revisiting my father's death, when I was four, and the dissolution of my marriage.

The death of my father when he was thirty-three, and the loss of the person I thought I was married to had been the most tragic and deeply saddening events in my life. I saw these events in brutal clarity and appreciated rippling aftershocks from each into many other scenes in my life.

I had not mourned my father's death until I was twenty-three years old, when I shed my first tears of grief for him. I knew he was dead, but

I could not let him rest as only a memory. I had made him part of my daily life. As a little girl I would think of him in heaven, at various times throughout my day, and I would imagine his reaction: praise, encouragement, support, and sometimes gentle scolding. Most of all I carried the memory of his love inside me, playing it over and over as if it were in the present. At day's close my ruse never worked as well because all I really wanted was to feel his reassuring hug wishing me a goodnight and sweet dreams. There were times I was bitterly disappointed and angry with him for not truly being there. There were times I was frustrated at his silence when I grew tired of my monologue with him. But his silence was less painful than letting him go from my life would be, and I grew more and more accustomed to a very one-sided relationship with the most significant man in my young life. Unwittingly, I shaped my future expectations of a spouse.

Viewing my life in retrospect, I became more compassionate and forgiving toward myself. I appreciated how my inability to face the pain of my father's death had led me to choose a spouse who I came to feel interacted with me in a manner as remote, self-absorbed, and unfeeling as if he were dead; I, through this choice, doomed the relationship to end in loss. I mistook the familiar for the normal.

Flowing from my life review, I became exquisitely aware that when we sin, that sin always hurts people, and the injury does not remain contained in isolation. As one raindrop falls on a quiet lake, there is an ever-widening disruption of the serene water. Sin is like the raindrop that ripples its effects over the lake of life to an ever-widening circle of people. Injured, they in turn generate new raindrops, till the lake's calm is obliterated and the water can no longer reflect the beauty around it, the beauty of God's love and creation. In this heightened state of perception I also became acutely aware that sin is not accidental, but always involves choice given us through the gift of our free will.

In these scenes before me I witnessed how I had perpetuated this chain and in turn hurt other people. I not only saw but felt, from the vantage point of others, the consequences of my actions or lack of them. I was overcome with regret, remorse, guilt, sorrow, shame, and a deep sense of being unworthy of the many gifts I had been given in my life. The manner in which I was able to see and think laid all things bare, without any possibility of deception, dissembling, or forms of excuse. Nothing was allowed to be hidden; all was apparent. The stark truth alone made judgment obsolete. Absolute truth was judgment.

This awareness would have been unbearable were it not for the incredible Presence I felt with me, holding me, gently guiding me. Instead of fault, blame, judgment, reproach, condemnation, or accusations I felt the most indescribable, incomparable, boundless, absolute love support-ing me. It was filled with a depth of compassion, and there were no con-ditions. Forgiveness was implicit. Instead of demoralization at having now starkly witnessed my own sins, from the active through the acquiescent, I had hope and confidence that I could do better.

I felt incredible peace. Again I became aware of floating in the soothing blackness pierced by the inverted V-shaped arms of light and the chimes around me. In the same manner more words, which I could see, hear, and feel, appeared. The interval between these and the first seemed no more than a mid-sentence pause. I heard the next phrase as if it had been a smooth continuation and completion of thought.

**...but there is a plan.**

This was explained to me in the following words, which I heard but did not see or feel.

**There is a purpose for the pain and
suffering in your life,
as there is for everything in your life.**

Without words I was made aware of several personal events that would one day occur. What was revealed to me illustrated the above expla-nation. I was shown what I could uniquely bring to these circumstances as a direct consequence of the suffering I had in my own life. I was there-in shown how purpose could underlie pain and be brought to fruition.

Again without words I understood that there was always a purpose to our lives even when we could discern none. It was God directing the overall plan and so all-powerful as to harness even evil, drawing good from it, such that his will alone prevails. So too it is when we use the gift of our free will to turn from God in sin. God does not forsake us but continu-ally seeks to draw us back to his plan. God's boundless love and merciful forgiveness await those who are prepared to receive it.

I was filled with a profound faith and trust in God as my all-power-ful, loving, and kind Father. I experienced a deep sense of peace, and again floated in the blackness, cradled by the arms of light and soothed by the chimes. I saw, heard, and felt the following.

**Your body is the Temple of the Holy Ghost.
Do not let anyone, including
yourself, or anything abuse it.**

This was explained to me, as it applied to my life. Simultaneously I was vividly immersed in relevant past scenes. "Anything" was demonstrated as working to excess, with its attendant improper sleep, nutrition, and relaxation. "Anyone" was exemplified by those who took advantage of my regularly responding to the needs of others without proper regard for my own needs. The contribution of "self" was illustrated throughout all scenes in that it was I who had not set the appropriate limits. It returned the ultimate responsibility to me.

There was never judgment or reproof from the enveloping consoling Presence, only deep compassion, overwhelming love, and the most gentle guidance leading me to see the truth. In this manner I was taken back again to scenes from my early childhood.

I was four years old, unable to make sense or find comfort in the incomprehensible—my father not coming home. I did not know I stood at a crossroads: letting him go and accepting and mourning his death, or progressively deadening the awareness of my own needs, dulling my disappointment and anger in order to tolerate his silence—his absence. It was never a choice. I took the only comfortable path, the one in his "company," and there I remained throughout childhood and yet a little longer.

It pierced my heart to watch and re-experience the fragile vulnerability of childhood. It was all the more poignant knowing where that path led. Compassion and love from the enveloping Presence obliterated all else. I had been shown the source of my weakness in setting limits, having learned to ignore some basic needs.

I was shown how to do yet more, in proper balance. We are to regard our bodies with a reverence due the Temple of the Holy Spirit. To most fully love and care for others, we must begin by loving and caring for ourselves. In this there is more strength; in this there is more to give.

I was left with a wellspring of hope, empowered to change with a sense of completeness beyond the insight of mere understanding. I felt extraordinary peace and perfect contentment, beyond words. I felt more love than I can begin to describe. Once again I drifted off into the soothing blackness, bounded by the arms of light and bathed in chimes. Then, I heard, felt, and saw the following:

**I am the head of every household,
married or single.**
This was explained to me in words that I did not see or hear:
**Do not be looking for a husband
or father for your children.**

I was then given understanding into my lifelong yearning to have my own father back and recreate an intact family, and the similar wish I now had for my children. I saw how this deep need, which had been too painful for me to face, had sabotaged my life's choices, and thus I created exactly what I tried to escape. It was reaffirmed to me that my daughters and I were a complete family, with God in our midst—head of our household, and our ceaseless, dominant, governing constant, whether I was married or a single parent.

Again I was at great peace, and my being was permeated with joy. At once I felt I had been filled to overflowing with a father's love, gone from my life too soon, and always desperately wanted back. Simultaneously, another gaping void was also healed—feeling abandoned by the man I had loved and committed my life to. I was brought to terms with the calamity of my own self-deception. The person I thought I married was a figment of what I could imagine, rationalize, excuse, or deny.

The first question I initiated to the Presence about me was my prime concern: "What about my children?" I saw, heard, and felt the following words in response:
**Your children will be fine,
if you let them know me.**

This was explained to me twofold. The first was didactic: teaching them about God. The second was by my living example, and in my relationship with them—to simply love them as purely and as much as I was able. By loving them as I had experienced God's love for me, I would help them be more readily able to find God in their lives and be open to his grace and love.

The next interchange is difficult to relate. Being enveloped by this Presence was somewhat like the ease of being reunited with your dearest long-lost friend, now unexpectedly found. It was the delight in picking up exactly where you had been, as if twenty years, thirty years, or even a lifetime were two days. I felt an overpowering, comfortable oneness, something missing made whole, a deep longing fulfilled. In this familiarity I felt totally free to express myself, despite full knowledge of my absolute insignificance. Simultaneously, I appreciated the awesome power, yet gentleness beyond words, of this Presence, imbuing my entire being with boundless, infinite love. Another quality of this magnificent Presence was the warmest, kindest sense of humor, further inviting me to share in light-hearted mirth. Responding to this and with the deepest reverence, the tone of the following was one of affectionately shared jest. I suddenly remembered the reality of the Persian Gulf War looming, and said, "Oh, and while I have you here; please grant us world peace." I paused, conscious of the enormity and privilege of these precious moments, then remembered my prognosis: the prospect of one day not hearing my children. It startled me in nearly forgetting—nearly forgetting to ask. I quickly added, "And, oh yes, I'd really like to hear!" In response I saw, heard, and felt the following:

**Rest your body, and heal.**

Filled to overflowing once more with the gifts of faith, trust, hope, peace, joy, and love, I floated in the soft blackness cradled between the arms of light, soothed by the chimes. I wanted to stay there and never, ever leave. From a state more awake and aware than any I had ever known, I fell swiftly and gently into a deep sleep. When I awoke later that day, my life was forever changed.

From the Prodigal Son

"His son said to him, 'Father, I have
sinned against heaven and against you; I
no longer deserve to be called your son.'
But his father ordered his servants,
'Quickly bring the finest robe and put it
on him; put a ring on his finger and
sandals on his feet. Take the fattened calf
and slaughter it. Then let us celebrate
with a feast, because this son of mine
was dead, and has come to life again; he
was lost, and has been found.' Then the
celebration began."

Luke 15:21-24

# Awakening

Jesus told her, "I am the resurrection and the life;
whoever believes in me, even if he dies, will live, and
everyone who lives and believes in me will never die.
Do you believe this?"

John 11:25-26

As sleep's veil lifted, I found myself back in the familiar reality of
my quiet, dimly lit room and broken body—but there was a dramatic
difference. I no longer felt imprisoned by them. My new outlook was at
first disorienting, particularly as I tried to quickly shake the remainder
of sleep from my eyes, and make sense of this. The vivid memory of so
wondrous an experience was jarring against accustomed surroundings.
My first coherent thought startled me: "Ohhh myyy! There really is a
God!" I repeated this over and over and over to myself, awestruck.
Consumed in wonder, I tried to absorb its ramifications for the first
time, elation soaring within me.

I wanted to tell my family. I wanted to tell everyone. I wanted to tell
my grandmother first—I could not wait to tell her. She had prayed fervently for me for many years, and I wanted to share my good news with
her first. My mood was not the least dampened at the prospect of telling
old news, myself not the first to discover the real existence of God. My
thoughts raced ahead of me, commanding full attention, and pre-empted
any notion of breaking my solitude.

My astonishment and exuberance at having glimpsed the reality of
God were in sharp contrast to the serenity of the experience. Those
moments had seemed natural—not the least out of the ordinary. Now it
was difficult to contain myself, though I continued to lie still in my quiet,
curtained room.

My thoughts cascaded in a lightning torrent of amazement. Not
only was there a God, but a God of pure love, who had breathed a unique

and great value into each and every life he created. Each soul is valued so greatly by God that he has ever remained present in us—waiting for each of us with infinite love, kindness, gentleness, compassion, mercy, and forgiveness. Patiently waiting for us as he allows our free will life, regardless of our choices. He allows us to turn away or flower in his light and be drawn to greater life in alignment with his all-powerful will. One God, existing in every man, calling each of us to him, for all time, regardless of our beliefs, or lack thereof. A God wanting each of us to be with him—to be a part of him and live forever—gently waiting for us to say "yes" by accepting him.

I quickly realized the experience had touched and altered me in ways words could not, affecting what I felt and believed from my heart. "It was all true!" I thought, nearly incredulous at this transformation; mere words had crystallized into meaning. God really had sent his own divine Son to live among us in the human form of Jesus Christ; and he really did suffer, die, and rise from the dead for our salvation. This truly was an actual man, Jesus Christ, a person with both divine and human nature, who with the Holy Trinity knew me, my thoughts and every act, better than anyone, including myself, and despite it cared about me and loved me so much he suffered extraordinary human pain and death for me. That Christ had done this for all, across time, did not diminish the personal bond I felt.

My revelry of discovery was abruptly arrested. Words from the Mass, first spoken by Christ at the last supper, hauntingly echoed in my mind:

"Do this in memory of me."*

Recalling my past responses had replaced wonder with stark embarrassment. In this moment I became aware just how real and present Christ had become in my life. It was as if Christ were physically beside me, as real as another person. My thoughts filled: "Oh, I am so sorry! I didn't know you were real. I mean, I didn't know it was actually true—who you are, what you did. Oh, I am so sorry!" I was mortified at the years I had fallen away from the Church, barely attending Mass, the years I had occupied a pew at Mass strictly out of obligation, the times I had gone only for myself, searching in the scriptures or homily for guidance, direction, consolation, or meaning. I was embarrassed that in all my attendance at Mass I had never given back to Christ who loved me so much. I had never gone just out of love for him or as he

* These words are said by the priest in the Eucharistic Prayer during Mass.

asked, in memory of him. I did not feel an extraordinary presence but I knew Christ was there. I knew I was forgiven.

My thoughts turned to Communion and I realized another profound change of heart—the Eucharist. At seven when I received First Holy Communion I believed, as I was taught, that the consecrated Host was literally the "Body of Christ" and I managed with difficulty through that one ceremony. On the following four Sundays I found the concept so disturbing that I could not physically consume the host. In retrospect, now for the first time, I understood why. I remembered, on several occasions at the ages of six and seven, looking at the crucifix over my bed, in particular Christ's hands and feet nailed to the cross, and crying myself to sleep, thinking of the suffering he had endured. I recognized he must have seemed a very real person to me, even though my sense of him was not living in our midst, but having lived two thousand years ago. I could not reconcile the act of ingesting Christ's body with thinking of him as a real person. Our parish priest counseled me, and out of respect for his authority I wanted to comply with his instruction, but I could not. I came to view the Eucharist as a most sacred symbol of Christ and in this way I was able to receive Communion, never questioning it again. As a child I quickly learned to keep my inability to fully conform to the Catholic faith to myself.

Now, with a start, I caught my breath, astounded at the wellspring of conviction within me: the Eucharist is the Body of Christ, the real presence of Christ, not a symbol, regardless how sacred. Enlightenment in this truth replaced my lukewarm regard for the Eucharist with passion, and with it compelling urgency to attend Mass. I felt an unquenchable desire to draw closer to Christ. The vitality of new life burned within me; its flames fanned by hope, warmth abounding. I had come full circle. How much more there was than the physical world! The bodily presence of Christ in the Eucharist paled beside his living spiritual presence. Now I understood; it was food for our soul. The Eucharist was the living pure presence of Christ—sustenance for that within us which must choose to accept or reject his presence in all mankind, and throughout all creation.

My thoughts finally slowed enough for me to shape their direction. I recognized I was not the same person. I thought differently. I felt differently. I perceived the world differently. I tried to get my bearings. I could see it would take me a while to become fully reacquainted with myself and the changes that were unfolding within me—living changes begun that day. My enthusiasm was difficult to contain, and I wanted to run with joy, though still I lay quietly in my bed.

I took stock of my physical self. I had the same aches, pains, and physical discomforts, but they did not seem as important or to bother me as much. This oddity reminded me of my earlier disorientation—at no longer feeling imprisoned by my sickroom or illness. Fully awake now, I better identified the sensation as detachment. There was a subtle change of emphasis in my view. The physical, my body included, and material world around me did not have the same importance. There were no negative connotations. It was not that the physical or material were bad or undesirable, but my detachment was in knowing that there was much more than our physical bodies and the world with its hierarchy of power, privilege, wealth, possessions, status, physical beauty, mental or muscular prowess, and assorted trappings. I knew there was a soul within each of us that existed and would live beyond the physical demise of our bodies. I had experienced a flash of this soul's consciousness, unfettered by body. The spirit within me glimpsed a realm not constrained by the dimension of time, as we know it, and not limited by our bodily senses or mental capacity. Therein I experienced the indescribable, things beyond human senses or mental capacity—lightning fast comprehension, effortless grasp of facts without words, and concepts for which no words or worldly frame of reference exists.

In spite of my ills I had a tremendous sense of well-being. I felt complete and more whole than even prior to my illness. Something deep within me had been healed. How good it was to be so happy, content, and at peace. I felt real joy at having experienced the Father's love—lifting a weight of burdens, some near life-long. That dull, constant ache of something missing, a full life's memories that should have been, but were not, childhood's carefree security too soon gone, the gaping wounds of my father's absence never given a chance to mend—all were now made whole. Now I knew the pain had purpose. In the same restorative breath, the anguish of divorce took perspective and paled.

I felt great comfort and reassurance for my children and myself. I was elated at no longer feeling alone, solitarily holding terror at bay with shoulders bowing under the weight of responsibility. I knew God was with me even though I could not feel the Presence as I had in those moments I now cherished. It was comforting to know there was a plan with purpose, and an all-loving, all-powerful God in absolute command, providing the source of meaning for our lives. Pain and suffering were for a reason, as were our good fortunes. We were not just randomly shifting on the tides from one tragic loss to the next till our meaningless death.

Given my physical circumstance, I was quite taken aback at feeling so light-hearted, carefree, and more childlike than even during most of my youth. I felt a willingness to let go and be open. I was newly aware of my total dependence on God, and comfortable with it rather than fearful of it. Though I was well aware of the predicament my illness made, and still saw no way clear, it concerned me significantly less. I felt confident that God would provide a path for me to tread. I could not understand this childlike trust I now felt. I continued to be surprised at the changes within me.

I had a profound sense of purpose, although I did not know what the purpose was. I felt there was meaning in my present circumstance, that what had occurred was for a reason, from which some good was to flow, but I did not know what reason. I could now begin the difficult path of accepting my illness and the new limitations it brought into my life because I knew that it was God's will for me and that God, in infinite wisdom and love, knew better what I needed than did I. I wondered what lay ahead but had less concern. Having the same physical discomforts, with less suffering, I likened to childbirth. I fondly remembered how much more bearable, even sweet, labor became when I focused on the new life discomfort would bring.

As a child blindly trusts his parents, now I was able to accept the mystery of God with faith and further marvel at the awe and wonder of God. In the past trying to make sense of the incomprehensible was not only a source of frustration but prompted me to doubt God's very existence. Now, carefree as a child, I was unbothered, accepting what I could not understand in God's name.

It was as if my life, or more accurately a new life, had been given back to me. Only it was different. I knew it was not mine; it belonged to my Creator. Whatever strength, ability, and talent returned, if any, were not mine to do with as I pleased, reaching for my goals and aspirations. The remainder of my days belonged to the One who created me from nothingness and pulled me back from the brink of nothingness yet again, imbuing my soul with vitality, renewing my life in Christ. I wanted to conform my will to God's.

Despite this inspired rush of commitment I had no illusion I would ever fully succeed. I only knew I would have to try and try again in the face of my own failings and imperfections. I fervently prayed, "If I am not to succeed in doing good, please let me do no harm." I longed to be more pleasing before God in my next life review. I yearned for this out of love, not fear of punishment or reproach. I wanted to have done more with the gifts given me.

Lifted from the depths of uselessness, despair, and helpless depression, I felt empowered and filled with purpose and hope. Repeatedly I relived the moments of epiphany, wanting to experience them again, wishing to preserve them in my memory. I prayed that the gift of faith and trust in God with its hope and new life would not slip away from me.

I did not want to do anything that would tarnish or fade my cherished experience. I momentarily reconsidered telling anyone, unsure whether inviting reaction might cast a cloud. I dismissed this when I thought of my grandmother. I decided to get up and find her. I sat up slowly, by degrees, to accommodate the postural light-headedness accompanying so much bed rest. Remaining seated, I very deliberately turned my body, then methodically planted both feet on the floor. The room rocked and swirled nauseatingly about me. I stretched my arms out wide behind me and leaned into them, as if trying to stabilize a precarious tripod. I waited for the degree of motion to abate sufficiently for me to rise to my feet. Cane in one hand, with the other I reached from bed to chair, to walls, to furniture, to walls; and so slowly I worked my way, looking for my grandmother. My outward appearance was the same: a drunken sailor staggering about in rough seas; but if you looked closely, my step was lighter and the sparkle was back in my eyes.

# First Steps

"Which is easier, to say, 'Your sins are forgiven,' or to say, 'Rise and walk'? But that you may know that the Son of Man has authority on earth to forgive sins"—he said to the man who was paralyzed, "I say to you, rise, pick up your stretcher, and go home." He stood up immediately before them, picked up what he had been lying on, and went home, glorifying God.

Luke 5:23-25

I found my grandmother as she was happiest—working. For a brief moment I watched her from the end of a long hall. Her strong muscular arms belied her eighty-eight years, as she deftly moved the broom about. Her slight stoop and hearing aid were the only hint of her true age. Watching her in this simple act evoked the lifetime of love and appreciation I held for her. She had opened her home to my sisters, mother, and me, sharing what little she had, when my father died. There we all remained, growing up surrounded by the luxury of an extended family as my mother of necessity changed reins from home to work-force. Now, when it seemed age would have the tables turned, she was still performing acts of kindness for me, bringing a thoughtful word, a bowl of chicken soup, a glass of ginger ale to my bedside. She had always been there for us. She had lived a life of generosity to both us and many others.

I leaned up against the wall and called, "Hi, Nanny." She looked down the hall's length, clearly surprised at seeing me. "I have to tell you something!" I said, bubbling with excitement. Her face lit with a smile as she registered the old familiar strength in my voice and noted my joyful demeanor.

"What, what is?" She quickly responded, sensing my urgency, and already walking towards me. She watched me with puzzled expression as I in turn hastened my faltering steps to meet her.

Touching her arm I said, "The God you've been praying to all these years is really there!"

"Oh yes..." She said, raising her eyebrows and with the lilt of her speech asking how I knew this.

"He spoke to me!" I said. She looked directly into my eyes and in several silent moments we exchanged questions and answers with a closeness requiring no words. Having read my veracity, she reached her arms about me and we embraced.

She asked, "Tell me, what did he say?" Noticing my wobbly stance had increased, she took my arm as she suggested, "Maybe you should sit down first." We settled back, just the two of us, and I recounted my experience. She listened intently, her clear blue eyes becoming moist as I spoke.

When I finished, she clasped her hands together and brought them close to her chest saying, "I am so very happy you have found God in your life! I have prayed so hard for you—for this, and that God would see you through all the hardships you have had these many years. I continue to pray for all of you, your mother, your sisters, and all of your families that all turn to God."

"Thank you, Nanny," I said, "I guess it must have worked." She joined in, and we were like two school girls giggling over a secret.

In a more serious tone she entreated me, "Please tell your mother." Before I could respond she said, "I will go get her."

"Wait," I said and paused, before I hesitatingly continued. "I am not sure I can. I don't know." My grandmother looked quizzically at me. Stammering, I tried to put my reluctance into words. I knew why, and my search for words was only an effort to cover my fear of possible ridicule. Unsuccessful, I just blurted out the truth, "She won't believe it and I don't know if I want to hear what she might say." I looked at the floor wondering what my grandmother must think of such cowardice.

My grandmother regained her seat and said, "Please tell her. She needs to hear. She needs to soften her heart towards God and turn to him."

I took in a deep breath, knowing I could not refuse her. "OK," I said.

My mother was as quick, sharp-witted, and incisively perceptive as she was fair, strong, and self-reliant. Behind her stoic, sometimes gruff, exterior were an expansive, warm, generous heart, great sensitivity, and selflessness when it came to her family and the downtrodden. She had lost much in her life, and yet she voluntarily sacrificed more to better provide for those she loved. I had the greatest love, admiration, and appreciation for her. It was her habit to be forthright, not couching her thoughts in apology or euphemism. While there may sometimes have been more diplomatic alternatives, there was never any confusion or doubt about her position. It was exactly this that I mentally prepared myself for as I waited and thought, "How would I begin?"

My mother was clearly wondering what this was all about when my grandmother brought her into the room. I did not give her much opportunity to ask, as I quickly began to speak before I had time to change my mind. They both sat down as I spoke. I felt the need for some sort of introduction, feeble though it was. "What I will say might sound unusual..." I said tentatively; my courage waning, I quickly added, "even unbelievable!" I thought, "So much for an introduction," and just said, "Mom, please listen." Again I repeated my experience, and she listened quietly without giving away her reaction, much as an impartial, learned judge would give the matter full deliberation.

"Do you believe me?" I asked. My mother's brow wrinkled in perplexity. What seemed like a long silence followed. I wondered what she must be thinking. I mused, "Could this actually be my rational, analytical physician daughter, or have I flipped on an afternoon TV talk show?" I could not resist and said, "Are you afraid the house has been invaded by an outrageous TV talk show guest who just looks like your daughter?" We laughed, tears coming to our eyes and the room's tension dissolved.

"It really does sound incredible!" my mother said.

"It's really true, Mom, no matter how incredible it sounds."

"I don't know what to make of it..." her tone bewildered. She hesitated, at a rare loss for words, then continued, "...but clearly something has happened to you!" Even this degree of acknowledgment was an unexpected surprise. Though I felt a deep transformation, I did not know how apparent, if at all, it would be to someone else. I knew in her response that she had caught at least a glimmer of the change. Seeing it with her own eyes defied her natural skepticism, holding it at bay.

Instead of offering critical analysis, she inquired more about the experience, trying to better understand. Then, referring to life's future adversities, she said, "It must be nice to feel someone is holding your feet out of the fire."

My natural inclination was to shake my head no, but I caught myself in time, evading additional waves of motion sickness. "No, I didn't get that impression. There was no promise my life would be easy, just that the pain in it had a purpose, just as the pain and good fortune does in everyone else's life—all part of a bigger plan." I said.

"This purpose you speak of, what do you think your purpose is? What is it you are to do?" my mother asked.

"I don't know," I replied.

Then she asked every mother's question, her child's health a prime concern, "Are you going to get better to do whatever this is?"

"I don't know," I replied again. "This may be it—just living with my illness and trying to be as present to my family as I am able. Maybe one day there will be more, I don't know. It's not just me—we are all here for a unique purpose."

Still trying to make sense of all this, she asked, "Why do you think this happened to you?"

"I don't know," I replied, and continued, "It is an extraordinary gift. I feel very blessed and fortunate, but I don't know why me. There are many others more deserving—many with far greater suffering than I've ever known, and many with far fewer faults. It's such a great privilege to have received this gift; but I just don't know why." I paused, momentarily look-ing down at my hands beginning to fidget, then continued, "A part of me feels a bit anxious."

"Why?" my mother asked.

Matter of factly and without self-deprecation I replied, "Every priv-ilege has proportional responsibility, and I am afraid I will not rise to the occasion, that I will be more unworthy of the gift than when I first received it. It's a bit overwhelming to think about like this." Again I paused, trying to put my feelings into words, then continued, "I hardly feel invincible. I am overjoyed at knowing God is there, but I don't have absolute confidence that I can meet every test life offers me with unfail-ing faith and trust in God. That even part of me should entertain these doubts after so compelling and wonderful an experience is difficult to rec-oncile. It seems only proof of my weakness, and that I am not worthy of this blessing. It makes me the more dumbfounded as to your question— 'Why did this happen to me?'"

My grandmother interjected the wisdom of her many years of faith: "God doesn't give us crosses greater than we can bear. We must all remem-ber to live one day at a time, placing our faith and trust in God, and he will do the rest."

"There's something else which bothers me," I volunteered. I paused then continued, "It is particularly unnerving because I wonder whether I am just plain unworthy or outright hypocritical." I hesitated. My mother and grandmother each looked at me with concern. I continued, "Though I know my illness is God's will for me, and I am willing to take great comfort from this, I know equally well that if it were within my power, I'd choose otherwise and be healthy. That's a bit like wanting it both ways, right? It's not exactly submitting my will to God's, is it?" I asked rhetorically. I began to laugh at myself, and said, "that should clear up any misconceptions that you'll be living with any saint or hero—I am nothing but a captive audience!" They both joined in laughter.

"It's so good to hear you laugh again!" my grandmother said.

"Yes, it is!" my mother agreed.

At that time the disciples approached Jesus and said, "Who is the greatest in the kingdom of heaven?" He called a child over, placed it in their midst, and said, "Amen, I say to you, unless you turn and become like children, you will not enter the kingdom of heaven. Whoever humbles himself like this child is the greatest in the kingdom of heaven."

Matthew 18:1-4

# Reunited

But to those who did accept him he gave power to become children of God, to those who believe in his name, who were born not by natural generation nor by human choice nor by a man's decision but of God.

John 1:12-13

Now by myself, still seated on the family room couch, legs resting on the ottoman, I heard the front door open. Two sets of footsteps tapped out their quick short strides, their sound trailing off in the direction of my bedroom. I heard several faint, distant calls:

"Mom? Mom? Where are you?" And a second voice, "Mom? Mom? Where are you?"

"Right here." I responded, though they could not hear me. Before I could get myself up, I heard their footsteps approaching, at a quickened pace. They continued calling, an edge of panic now in their voices. They burst into the room at each other's heels.

"Mom you're up! Mom you're up!" the girls echoed one another, big smiles gleaming across their faces, as they found me sitting up. Perceptive as children are, they knew something had happened. Their eyes danced with the delight of a Christmas morning.

They nestled alongside me, and with an arm around each I drew them to me, as they curled into my hug. I sensed their pleasure—securely warm, safe, and protected, encircled by my arms. Holding them to me, I was reminded of the first time I had ever held each of them, immediately after birth. Now, as then, I burst with joy along with hope and optimism for the future. I knew the children could sense the strength emanating from my transformation, but I also knew it had hardly begun to erase their apprehensions.

The simplest things, my children's presence, their affection, elated me; my exuberance in having discovered God intensified the beauty of all else. It was perfect contentment, the joy of that moment, and knowing God was in our midst. This is what was important. Life was becoming simpler. So much else did not really matter.

"How are my little ones today?" I asked. They giggled and cuddled closer, reassured at the routine of their reception, even though I was seated and not walking through the door after work. Their giggles gave way to deep belly laughs, the more contagious to me in my already ebullient state. Emotions of the past two months released, and we were reunited in a flood of laughter; all became a blurry swirl through tears of joy. When I could speak, I asked, "Have you had a fine day at school?" Yes, they each nodded and snuggled closer. "Tell me, what did you do?" I asked. They were simultaneously off, each speaking at once, trying to command the floor.

It was like not only having my children given back to me but my children receiving back their mother. Illness had removed me, but my reaction to illness, in anxiety and finally despair, removed me further still. I marveled at this change—the impenetrable wall of fog between myself and others had been lifted—as I gratefully appreciated once again being able to listen and enjoy the music of their voices. How normal and familiar! Again, I became aware of my new-found sense of detachment. How freeing it was to be aware but no longer drowning in worries about health and our future. This detachment was not being removed and distant. It was the contrary. I was more fully alive in the moment and available to those around me. Detachment restored the space, time, and energy to love and be present to my family.

# ANCHORED

"Peace I leave with you; my peace I give to you. Not as the world gives do I give it to you. Do not let your hearts be troubled or afraid."

John 14:27

I never realized that I had been drifting as if anchorless without God in my life. I had not recognized that my own yearning for God had become misplaced striving in so many other directions—all ambitions achieving empty successes. They had not quenched my real thirst but left a vague sense of something missing. I never knew how much it had troubled me till I experienced faith. Now, when I awoke each day I was almost surprised, and then relieved; this anchor of faith still held me steadfast. The changes within me of greater peace and hope were sustained.

I regarded my new-found faith as fragile and delicate, like the weakness of a newborn. I did not want to wake one morning and find it gone. I knew I had to nurture it, consciously reminding myself of the presence of God, as if practicing to make it a habit. I had an irrepressible desire to read, know more, and be closer to Christ. When I was again able to read, I went straight to the gospels. It was like reading them for the first time— profound revelations. They were real, their relevance immediate, with a message now vivid in meaning and substance. The dramatic difference was that I knew not only that Christ was a real person who lived, died, and rose from the dead but that he remained a real person, very much alive and intimately present in our midst. When I grew stronger physically, I began to attend Mass and receive Communion any day I was able. I felt centered and peaceful there. Not wanting to leave, I would often sit quietly in the presence of the Blessed Sacrament.

My enthusiasm for life grew. It seemed paradoxical to feel such vigor in my weak, convalescing state. My inner peace, hope, and enthusiasm were apparent to others. Two close friends commented to me, "What do you have to be so happy about? Why aren't you depressed? Your whole life is falling apart around you, and you don't know what you're going to do!"

I responded, "But I was depressed, extremely depressed, till something happened." I relayed my mystical experience.

In sincere happiness for me one said, "Oh, you have found the faith solution."

"No," I said, "It wasn't quite like that—whatever it is that happened, found me. I didn't do anything."

A number of physicians remarked on my personal endurance and optimistic attitude: "You're handling this very well."

I would simply respond, "Thank you," knowing I deserved no praise because I was not alone; moreover, someone was carrying me. I do not know how I would have managed any of it without the presence of Christ.

Despite how relatively well I appeared to get along, I did not lack bouts of sadness, anger, denial, disappointment, mourning my losses, and concern. I knew my healing was spiritual, and while I considered it miraculous, I so wished it could be physical as well.

I prayed for a physical cure and apologetically began to bargain in my prayers: "I know if I could just become well enough to return to my profession, I'd be all the better a doctor for the experience." It was not meant to be. I did improve, but remained a shadow of my old self, with some permanent impairment in vestibular* and auditory** function due to irreparable inner ear damage among other chronic physical ailments and limitations. Further, this was the best I was ever going to be. It was my new "baseline of normal"—if it can be called that.

Living with the uncertainty of medical diagnosis was like waiting for the inevitable. When it finally arrived, in one way it was a relief to know, but one uncertainty was just exchanged for another: the unpredictability of the illness' course.

---

* relating to balance and equilibrium.

** relating to hearing.

## God's Will

God's will,
a continuous thread
in my past, present, and to be;
steadfastly there reaching out to me
wresting me from my mistakes,
when I turned away in sin
choosing my will over God's;
constantly making a path for me to return
woven between my blunders, large and small
saving me and others from myself,
my own undoing;
saving me from other's
same selfishness;
saving me from evil outright;
never abandoning me;
though I did not acknowledge,
recognize, or give thanks,
hoping more than believing in his name.

And Jesus said to him, "What do you want me to do for you?" And the blind man said to him, "Master, let me receive my sight." And Jesus said to him, "Go your way; your faith has made you well." And immediately he received his sight and followed him on the way.

Mark 10:51-52, RSV

# THE UNKNOWN NAMED

So out of the ground the LORD God formed every beast of the field and every bird of the air, and brought them to the man to see what he would call them; and whatever the man called every living creature, that was its name.

Genesis 2:19, RSV

Mid-February brought complete debilitation with a full-blown recurrence of Meniere's symptoms in addition to numerous systemic complaints: multiple, painful, red, hot, swollen joints; diffuse muscular aches and pains; many sites of tendonitis, and some bursitis; exhaustion; digestive disturbance; skin changes, hair loss, and increased sun sensitivity, among others. I became aware of multiple allergies and allergic sinusitis.

March 1991, the unknown was named: Autoimmune Connective Tissue Disease, also known as Collagen Vascular Disease. Conditions within this family of illness are perhaps better known by their individual names: Systemic Lupus Erythematosus, Rheumatoid Arthritis, Scleroderma, Polymyositis, Dermatomyositis, and Mixed Connective Tissue Disorder, to name a few.

My body's natural defense mechanism for holding disease at bay was no longer differentiating me from the enemy. It was an ongoing case of mistaken identity, with episodic destruction by friendly fire. My own immune system was working overtime, attacking not just germs and abnormal cells but some of my healthy tissues as well. The attacking immune cells, once locked onto the offending agent, then further recruit the body's inflammatory responses to destroy the perceived intruder cells. In the case of mistaken identity, this translates into a myriad of aches, pains, symptoms, and dysfunction, depending on the bodily system involved and how heavily damaged.

My illness seemed like aging on fast forward. Life became an unpredictable roller coaster, swept along by alternating flares and cooling of illness' activity. A good day would feel like a mild case of the flu, and a bad day too debilitating to get out of bed. No day was spared the incessant, distracting, high-pitched ringing in my ears, louder than normal conversation, among other unwelcome additions to daily life.

For some time I had been too ill to grasp a devastating, vexing, and embarrassing consequence of my physical losses—their impact on my capacity to take in new information and with it my cognitive ability. I was not surprised at sometimes mishearing or not hearing words, but I had not anticipated an impact on my visual perception. The damaged portion of my inner ear that regulates balance and equilibrium often could no longer always provide enough information without added visual input. My eyes, now in part compensating for my inner ears, were not as fully available to visually scan. As a result what was once effortless and routine now depended upon multiple crutches—lists, compensatory techniques, mental tricks, notes on mirrors, clocks, doors, and more lists. In great frustration I came to know first hand that one cannot mentally process, remember, organize, or prioritize what is not absorbed. No aspect of life remained untouched; disorganization was the new status quo. I was grateful that many years before, financial provisions had been made for something I could never envision—my own disability.

There was some good news amidst the bad. While my illness was the rarest cause of Meniere's, it held some hope of arresting, or at least slowing, the inevitable progression from partial hearing loss to deafness. Medication was effective in some cases but not without a price; there was a balancing act between the ravages of illness and medication's side effects. Hope lay in long remissions and remaining responsive to medication.

I held fast to what good news there was. I wondered, "Was this an answer to my prayers? How ironic that in losing some of my ears' hearing I've begun to hear within my heart." When I asked God, "And, oh yes, I'd really like to hear!" now I wondered, "Maybe I should have been more specific. I appreciate hearing you, Lord, but I meant my ears."

I did not recognize my limited definition of God answering my prayers—namely, that *my* wishes be granted.

# An Endless Mile

"Come to me, all you who labor and are burdened,
and I will give you rest. Take my yoke upon you and
learn from me, for I am meek and humble of heart;
and you will find rest for yourselves. For my yoke is
easy, and my burden light."

Matthew 11:28-30

Surmounting acute crisis is a milestone; stepping into a chronic time frame is an endless mile—its hurdles are never behind, regardless of how well or often jumped. Adjustment to its rigor demands growth—the stakes: sink or swim.

Chronicity, living with a chronic "challenge," is its own disease. It does not fade away. It daily assails one's core: manner, temperament, personality's expression, outlook—filtering all five sense's perceptions. The affronts continue, striking at self-esteem. Illness compromised my personal freedom and independence. My life was out of my control; even my own body refused my commands. I felt a loss of dignity in my reduced self-sufficiency.

Locked in a body that did not work, at least not as it had, I was unable to present a face to the world that reflected who I actually was. Instead my limitations at times brought me embarrassment and humiliation, inviting others to judge me not on who I was but on how I appeared or functioned. Some of these hasty, unkind conclusions compounded my hurt. Superficially I appeared "normal" many days, and, in fairness to those I encountered who were lacking in compassion, I tried to hide my illness, minimizing it rather than bringing it to attention. It was equally difficult at times to watch my limitations anger or disappoint others.

Pain, annoying symptoms, the inconvenience new limitations posed, and the losses these all signified encroached upon every day and tomorrow. All bore the wearing mark of chronicity's tenacious grip. I had always taken for granted an even, easy disposition; this now contrasted with needing constant effort to short-circuit reflex irritability. I struggled to retain the integrity of my identity, resisting its fusion with the tidal wave of change which had submerged my life. I had partially ceded defeat in the battle for physical health; now I fought the more defiantly at the frontier of self—to preserve the fullest access to my own will. I wanted to retain the independence to choose my attitude toward fate, rather than having it dictate my response. I fought to keep the "me" of who I was.

I began to see a fine distinction—accepting the immutable did not require making it part of me. Illness had raised my ire in what it had taken from my life. Buoyed by faith, stronger now, no longer despairing, I opposed allowing my attitude to become a further casualty. I stood as if on guard against a thief who threatened to rob me of my very self and with it the way I interacted with those I loved. I did not want to become an irascible stranger to my own children. I did not want to disappear into self-absorbed aches and pains, distant and removed from their lives. I reached for each day as if it were a prize, making the most of the best of it; I lived as fully as illness allowed me. I was also afraid to let down my guard for fear I would not get up and keep going. I saw what a fine line separated me from the ease of giving up.

I was like a refugee wandering without a home—displaced from the dignity of self-sufficiency, productivity, achievement's worldly respect, and the ability to resume my profession. I felt lost. Disheartened, I took comfort that my most important role, being a mother to my children, remained. My losses fully focused me on my greatest wealth: my children and family. Though there was physically less of me, in other ways, it had been replaced by more.

I relied on faith in this battle with what I could not change. It was not an approach I took out of wisdom, honor, or virtue—it was the only shield I had. Each day I tried to keep my lifeline of faith alive, gently nurturing it. The same villainous circumstance that banished me from my old life led me in small steps to refuge: deeper faith and experience of God's presence. There I recognized my true worth. In God's eyes we are all of value, his love unconditionally given. We do not need to earn our value or identity in God's eyes; we only need receive it, by accepting his love.

It was not to be a smooth course of deepening faith. Instead it was like a perpetually swinging pendulum, alternating between varying degrees of faith and doubt. The one constant was God's ever seeking presence, regardless of my recognition of it or my response to it. In the highs and lows of life and health, I remained in constant flux, dancing in step with the pendulum's cadence. I oscillated between the physically visible of which my eyes reassured me, and the invisible that only my heart could see. The visible disguised emptiness, impermanence, my helplessness, and nothingness without God. The invisible, obscured from human sight, held all that there is of value, permanence and truth.

I slipped so easily into the lull and lure of the world's distractions, until forced to see their disguise bared; then, like a pulley, inescapably I was drawn back, each time closer to the true source of strength and life. Invariably major turning points back to God were during periods of greatest suffering. Many a day I would have chosen to be a little less blessed, but more painful was the pendulum's opposite extreme. Once having experienced the presence of God it was greater distress to live without it. Over time, both tempered faith.

## Faith's Dance—The Pendulum

Faith, having taken root,
    dance you must
        to temper its strength.
           Dance you will,
              as does pendulum swing
                highs of certitude,
           depths of self-doubt.
        Of faith inherent—
      the unknown to believe.
    Be not discouraged—
its nature inseparate.
Riding the pendulum,
    watching life's passing,
        comings...goings...
           ...the once perfect rose
              dropping its petals,
          one with each pendulum's arc.
      Rose unfolding its sweet essence—
fragrance freed from the petal's bond.
Rose unfolding the mystery of itself,
    layer by layer by layer by layer
      with successive swoons
        of the pendulum's arc.
          More mystery understood,
      greater mystery beheld.
    The dance keeping time,
with the pendulum's glide.
    Zenith's moment betwixt
      the up and the down
        sublimely weightless,
          time suspended,
      no room for doubt
    unison complete.
    Ecstasy only too briefly held.
The world calls us back.

Initial descent,
        a pleasurable rush—
                too soon unmasked:
                    accelerated
                            centrifugal
                                gravitational
                                    meld—
                an oppressive crescendo
            the world's crushing weight
        the pendulum's
            nadir.
            The truth be bared.
                    Nowhere to hide.
                            Willing to listen,
                                    audience captive,
                    God's arms waiting.
                    Letting go—carried away,
            rising on the pendulum's sure arc.
"Why do you struggle against My lead?"
        Letting go—Let go
        Detach from the worldly.
                Let pendulum swing.
                Let petal fall.
                    You can't hold life,
                its beauty will fade,
                its essence will not.

                "Come to Me
                deeper
            deeper and deeper
            give yourself up.
                Have faith
                    trust
                    hope
                    in Me.
            Let Me lead you."
                Pursued,

    hearing God's call...
            ...man's answer—faith.

"When a woman is in labor, she is in anguish because her hour has arrived; but when she has given birth to a child, she no longer remembers the pain because of her joy that a child has been born into the world. So you also are now in anguish. But I will see you again, and your hearts will rejoice, and no one will take your joy away from you. On that day you will not question me about anything. Amen, amen, I say to you, whatever you ask the Father in my name he will give you."

John 16:21-23

# Part II

# Faith's Dance

"I am the true vine, and my Father is the vine grower. He takes away every branch in me that does not bear fruit, and everyone that does he prunes so that it bears more fruit. You are already pruned because of the word that I spoke to you. Remain in me, as I remain in you. Just as a branch cannot bear fruit on its own unless it remains on the vine, so neither can you unless you remain in me. I am the vine, you are the branches. Whoever remains in me and I in him will bear much fruit, because without me you can do nothing. Anyone who does not remain in me will be thrown out like a branch and wither; people will gather them and throw them into a fire and they will be burned. If you remain in me and my words remain in you, ask for whatever you want and it will be done for you. By this is my Father glorified, that you bear much fruit and become my disciples. As the Father loves me, so I also love you. Remain in my love. If you keep my commandments, you will remain in my love, just as I have kept my Father's commandments and remain in his love.

"I have told you this so that my joy may be in you and your joy may be complete. This is my commandment: love one another as I love you."

John 15:1-12

# Mysticism

"...nor will they say, 'Lo, here it is!' or 'There!' for
behold, the kingdom of God is in the midst of you."
Luke 17:21, RSV

Mysticism is the intimate experience of God. The essential aspect of
Christian mysticism is Christ, who calls us to new and deeper life in him.

**Jesus Christ is here within us;**
**everything, everyday in our lives**
**is sacramental.**

March, 1993

Extraordinary mystical phenomena, such as locutions, visions, and revelations are a small part of mysticism in comparison to the sacred in daily
living. These extraordinary phenomena are not milestones of spiritual
growth. They do not indicate a person's goodness or faith in God, nor are
they earned or deserved. Each of our paths of spiritual growth will be as
unique as we are individual. The direction of each path is the work of God.

The binding common thread in all mystical experience is an ever-
deepening awareness of God's presence within us. This enlightenment
transforms our lives, and consequently what we bring to those around us
through increased ability to love, resulting from ever-deepening reverence
for life and God's creation.

There is grave danger in seeking to experience extraordinary mystical phenomena, whether for themselves or as signs of proof of God's
presence. These events do not happen of our initiative, but are passively
received as gifts of the Holy Spirit. To quest after them invites false input
from within ourselves, or worse yet, the outside influence of unseen
sources of evil—which do exist in our world.

We all face life's inexplicable cruelties. How do we draw meaning from the apparently senseless pain of our existence, the agony of our grief? How does one comprehend God who is in essence incomprehensible? We are all at times tormented by questions and doubts that leave us feeling abandoned by God in our darkness. Even Christ, of truly human and divine nature, was not spared trials of faith. Revealing his humanity, with which we can all readily identify, before his passion and crucifixion:

> He advanced a little and fell prostrate in prayer, saying, "My Father, if it is possible, let this cup pass from me; yet, not as I will, but as you will."
> Matthew 26:39

Then from the cross he called out:
"...My God, my God, why have you forsaken me?"
Mark 15:34

In our prayers we cry out and perceiving no answer—no relief; we feel ourselves forsaken. Christ understands our weakness, that it is hard for us to open our eyes to his presence within us and in our midst, but he is always here for each of us.

There is within us, in every soul, the universal capacity to relate to our Creator; though it is often unrecognized or lies dormant, awaiting its spring. Both the manner and growth of our awakening to God's presence are the work of God.

Mysticism...
**It is the province of every man.**
**Every man must come to me;**
**come to me alone.**
**I will protect them.**
**In your soul's innermost depths**
**every man must meet me**
**whether they believe in me/my name or not.**
**I am kind and gentle to all.**
**All manner of help is available to every soul...**
**I will guide you.**
November 1, 1994

# How This Book Came To Be

> On the last day of the feast, the great day, Jesus
> stood up and proclaimed, "If any one thirst, let him
> come to me and drink. He who believes in me, as the
> scripture has said, 'Out of his heart shall flow rivers
> of living water.'"
>
> John 7:37-38, RSV

Soon after my first mystical experience I spoke with a priest who
urged me to write it down. It had not occurred to me. "Why? How could
I forget it!" I thought. I found his advice, though, oddly compelling, so I
did make a record and placed it in my Bible. Other notes followed, while
some experiences went unrecorded. About a year later I spoke with another priest about these experiences. I was taken aback when he made the
same recommendation, in virtually identical words and manner. I became
more conscientious at making a written record.

This writing began as nothing more than rapidly dashed notes on
the first convenient scrap of paper. It was a record I made for myself.
These scribbled treasures unanticipatedly grew. They were a motley
assortment: used envelopes, receipts, flyers, bulletins, loose leaf pages,
index cards, sporadically used notebooks, whatever I could find at the
moment—a moment not of my choosing. These were the moments when
I unexpectedly found myself in the company of a divine Presence, most
often the person of Christ—"hearing" his words, or at other times his
communication unencumbered by words. In these locutions, the "hearing" is within myself, not through my bodily ears. It is not like any other
experience I can describe. It is not like talking to yourself. I have no control over its initiation or direction.

It is like unexpectedly having the presence of another being within
you, another being whose words, ideas, knowledge and beliefs—even
vocabulary, are not your own. Thoughts are "heard," and I do not know

the next phrase to follow until it is spoken to me. Often times I need to read these notes myself to grasp the whole, as compared to the individual sentences and words. At times I still do not understand their meaning. This has prompted me to look up words, concepts, scripture, and the Church's teaching, to reaffirm the validity of what I have been given.

Communication without words is more difficult to describe. I am unable to make a simultaneous record. My consciousness is fully consumed, time suspended. These moments are extremely brief. I can only guess their duration—fractions of a second to maybe several seconds. I cannot think words fast enough to match instantaneous insight or comprehension.

While I may find myself unprepared and these visits unexpected, there are two things that are always the same. First, it is a time of incredible peace. Second, while the thoughts, beliefs, and words are not my own, having "heard" them their effect upon me is one of change. It has been a progressive transformation of that within me which is beyond the appeal of reason or words alone, change in my fundamental beliefs and the feelings within my heart's depth.

The random scraps of paper recording these encounters accumulated in drawers, and bulged from books in a manner unfitting their content. They existed in disarray, matching the unwelcome intruder that illness brought into my life: disorganization. My children were the initial impetus to draw these words and experiences together, and during the process it gained a life of its own. I was astounded upon gathering years of scattered notes to find development of themes. Some ideas were new to me, others old, but even the old seemed fresh because of their original perspective. Most amazing was the transforming power these words of simplicity and beauty produced in my beliefs.

The locutions, my inner "hearing," are mostly in the person of Jesus Christ, God the Son, and at times they fluidly alternate or fuse with God the Father. I often wondered about the third member of the Blessed Trinity, God the Holy Spirit, whose presence for years I considered absent from these communications. One day, a sudden insight brought understanding: it was the very presence of the Holy Spirit which enabled me to "hear." Experiencing God, in any form, only occurs through the grace and presence within us of the Holy Spirit. It is this gift of the Holy Spirit that allows a mere mortal to perceive a Being so far superior as to be Divine.

This moment of enlightenment left me in awe of God's vast mystery. I did not realize I had been lacking humility before God, but clearly it is this which had blinded me to the Holy Spirit. How ludicrous it had been to think I could have become aware of the Divine on my own, without intervention of a divine Being. I missed the obvious, the presence of the Holy Spirit.

In later locutions Mary spoke and again the unity of her will with the Trinity was strongly and fully underlying her presence and message.

Conversations with people have been reconstructed to the best of my recollection.

I am not a theologian. I do not pretend to write as a theologian. I am neither holy nor exemplary. I am a mother writing for her children. My faults continue to far outnumber my strengths. I am ordinary. My expertise is only what I have come to know in my heart: how faith has come alive and taken shape and form in my life. Each day I try anew to live Christ's words. Each day I fall short.

I do not represent my spiritual experiences as other than, or more than that, my own experience of faith, how I have come to know God's presence in my life. Specifically, I do not mean to imply this work represents the Catholic Faith, although my encounters have greatly increased my love of the Church and belief in the truth of its teaching.

Nor do I represent this as a "How-to" book. The readers' good judgement is needed in applying the book's lessons to their own circumstances.

No one needs extraordinary mystical gifts to surpass anything I have to offer of my experience. The perfect, undistorted, pure light and revelation of God are found in Christ's life, example, scriptures, teachings, commandments, and the Sacraments of his Church. These are the gold standards for Christian mystical experience.

"In my Father's house there are many dwelling places. If there were not, would I have told you that I am going to prepare a place for you? And if I go and prepare a place for you, I will come back again and take you to myself, so that where I am you also may be. Where [I] am going you know the way." Thomas said to him, "Master, we do not know where you are going; how can we know the way?" Jesus said to him, "I am the way and the truth and the life. No one comes to the Father except through me. If you know me, then you will also know my Father. From now on you do know him and have seen him."

John 14:2-7

# Preface to Journal Selections

For God so loved the world that he gave his only Son, that whoever believes in him should not perish but have eternal life. For God sent the Son into the world, not to condemn the world, but that the world might be saved through him.

John 3:16-17, RSV

The locutions I have "heard" are recorded in this book exactly as they were received, but they are not all-inclusive. The portions selected are those I have been directed to share. This selection has in no way altered the message in these pages. Although my journal illustrates one soul's deepening relationship with God, lessons in some of life's commonly shared struggles emerge. The details of my life are not important; they are only a framework to unfold what I have experienced. The details serve the message; they are not the story. This book's evolution is itself an account of the paradox in trying "to do" God's will.

In some ways my experience has relevance to us all as children of God. In this we are all the same. We are all children of God, all of equal value. Throughout my experience in "hearing" the divine Presence I was never addressed by name, but always as, "my child." This underscores my individual unimportance and that the consoling words are intended for all. Understanding the more universal and accurate meaning of these locutions lies in appreciating that God's concern for each of us is ultimately for our spiritual life and its well being. Our mortal span is brief in the face of eternity, but the choices we make during it determine our soul's everlasting destiny. The following are examples.

Upon hearing phrases such as **All will be well...You and your loved** ones are in my care and protection...All will be given you; provided as it is needed...Rest your body and heal...I am watching over you, guiding you, protecting you...The angels, all the saints, Mary, the Blessed Trinity envelop you and your loved ones...Mary holds a special place in her heart for them...and others, I do feel extraordinary peace, but I do not find this a promise of what my next day's or eventual earthly existence will bring, much as I might wish otherwise. Our worldly and spiritual outcomes do not always coincide when viewed only with physical reality as a criterion; man's words and God's words bear different meaning. Even when we receive God's prophecy, each day must unfold before we understand its meaning, and still, we often remain blind to it, unable to see the perspective in God's plan.

Another phrase frequently heard is: **Be up and about your day's work** and less often: **There is much to do before you die.** These words go far beyond deeds in the narrow sense of employment, to the work of living out the circumstances in which we find ourselves. These words are for each of us, on a simple personal scale. We are all charged with the identical task: learn to love more perfectly, and learn to more fully submit our will to God—really one and the same job. While our work is the same, we are each called to accomplish it differently, as uniquely individual participants in God's plan. There are no unimportant souls; each one is integral. We are all interdependent. Living with my illness is work. Recording my experience of God in this book has made that work lighter. It is the greatest joy to see and then share the experience of God drawing great beauty, truth, strength, love, faith, trust, hope, meaning and purpose from life and even suffering.

Another phrase frequently heard is, **Write, my child. Write every day.** Beyond direction to record the locutions and gather them together this first implies finding a time to pray each day, and within that prayer the stillness in which to listen.

None of us is given an earthly life free of suffering and loss—not Christ, Mary, his saints, not anyone. Suffering and loss are inseparable from our human existence. In the best of circumstances we all age—an ongoing loss. As children, we grow up and leave parents. Our own children grow up and leave us. Life is ongoing change, ongoing loss, new beginnings, and ongoing growth.

It is Christ who came and gave meaning and purpose to this existence.

His life and teaching reveal the secret to living both the sorrows and joys of our life; moreover, he demonstrated that both suffering and celebration are brought to greatest fullness if we are willing to submit our wills to God. All continues to draw us back, closer to our Creator.

Though this account reflects one soul's deepening relationship with God, I want to disappear from its pages because the focus is not on me but on Christ and his message of love. My role is passive. I have heard the music of God's presence and merely recorded the notes. I am ancillary. I do not know if I will continue to experience the presence of God as described herein. I have no power. All true power resides with God; as does the manner and timing in which he reveals himself to each of us in our lives.

## My Children,

If I could protect you
    from all life's pain,
        I would;
            if I only could.
If I could spare you
    making every mistake I've ever made,
        I would;
            if I only could.
If I could fill your lives
    with only happiness and sunshine,
        I would;
            if I only could.
If I could give you
    my awareness of our God, faith kindled ablaze,
        I would;
            if I only could.
But let me touch your lives with the Presence I feel,
    that you open your hearts to God's grace.
        Allow God to show you the way,
            and all will be yours everlasting.

## How Does One Explain...

...the colorful brilliance of a sunset
    to one who has never seen?

...the gentle softness of a mother's caress
    to one who has never felt?

...the penetrating beauty of song
    to one who has never heard?

...the warmth of tenderness and caring
    to one who has never known love's kindness?

...the quiet strength of self-worth
    to one who has never secured love's approval?

...the value of mercy
    to one who has never tasted forgiveness?

...the presence of God
    to one who has never experienced faith?

                ...not with words alone.

Jesus said to them, "I am the bread of life; whoever comes to me will never hunger, and whoever believes in me will never thirst. But I told you that although you have seen [me], you do not believe. Everything that the Father gives me will come to me, and I will not reject anyone who comes to me, because I came down from heaven not to do my own will but the will of the one who sent me. And this is the will of the one who sent me, that I should not lose anything of what he gave me, but that I should raise it [on] the last day. For this is the will of my Father, that everyone who sees the Son and believes in him may have eternal life, and I shall raise him [on] the last day."

John 6:35-40

# Journal Selections

Then he said to all, "If anyone wishes to come after me, he must deny himself and take up his cross daily and follow me. For whoever wishes to save his life will lose it, but whoever loses his life for my sake will save it. What profit is there for one to gain the whole world yet lose or forfeit himself?"

Luke 9:23-25

August, 1991

I had just sat down in the crowded waiting room when an allergic reaction to a medication occurred. It was swift and without warning. My throat and upper airway rapidly became full. To assess the severity of my condition I spoke aloud, as I would routinely check a tape prior to dictating reports, "testing one, two, three, testing, testing." My voice was gravelly. The hoarseness indicated laryngeal edema—swelling which threatened to block off my airway at the level of my vocal cords. There was little time. I had to find a doctor or nurse while I still could speak and remained conscious.

A nurse led me to a room. I was no longer able to stand or sit up; I lay on the exam table. The doctor was called. Meanwhile, the nurse checked my vital signs: pulse, blood pressure and breathing—all unstable. More frantically, she called for the doctor. I was now already too hoarse to speak. "Code 5 ___ clinic, Code 5 ___ clinic" blared over the intercom. Bottles and vials of medication and life support equipment clanged about the red multi-drawered metallic "crash cart" as its wheels rattled and screeched to a halt outside the door.

Another nurse started an IV in my left forearm. Though hardly a daily occurrence in my practice, neither were such emergencies strangers. How very odd it was to be on the other side of the needle.

My attending physician, for the time being commander of the ship, stood at the helm of the red cart—my life raft. Panic edged his voice, like white caps breaking a once calm sea—whipped up by a sudden squall. He mused aloud about the medications to administer to me. I wondered, "When had he last done this?" I soon had my answer: too long ago—as I listened to him debate with himself between the life saving dose I needed, and one which would be instantaneously lethal. He was scared, a competent physician in his specialty, but out of practice with this type of emergency.

I could not speak to tell him what to do, nor ask for a piece of paper to write it down. I was fading. The deep calm I felt surprised me. Was it survival instinct? Was it divine intervention? I do not know. Agitation, were it accompanied by spasm, could have obliterated my last remnant of open airway. I focused all my listening on my physician's decision or more accurately—indecision. My eyes were riveted to the sideport of the IV, where medication would be injected. I had turned onto my left side and held my right hand over the IV, poised to pull it out if need be—in the event he picked the wrong dose. My plan bought only time, precious moments—enough I hoped for the code team's arrival. I prayed that I would maintain consciousness long enough to protect myself.

The one man debate, on the fateful dose continued outside my door. Perhaps he thought, if he could just delay long enough, the code team would save him. I hoped he would be rescued too.

At last a voice of calm descended on the pandemonium outside my door: "I don't think you'd want to give her that dose, let's start with this." His restraint diplomatically left silent an unspoken cardinal rule: lethal doses are nontherapeutic. He did not embarrass the other doctor before his staff. With a sigh of relief I closed my eyes, relaxed my right hand on my left forearm, knowing I was in competent hands.

The medication worked quickly; my throat was less full. I felt a reassuring hand on my right shoulder and the calm voice spoke to me, "Dr. Toye, I am Dr. _____, I am an internist in the next office." I opened my eyes, as he sat down opposite me.

"I am very happy to see you here," and raising my eyebrows added, "and none too soon. Thank you." My voice had returned though still rough. He smiled back at me, acknowledging in mutual silence the extent of my close call—members of the same fraternal order.

He said, "We're just going to stabilize you here, and then transfer you to the ER, where they can better monitor you."

"Yes, I know;" I smiled, continuing the shared secret of our common bond, "we never liked them to die in our department either." The room, still full of nurses, and my original physician, broke with laughter and weakly I joined in. They had been the less comfortable that I was a physician and the only way I could have increased the odds of something worse happening was if I had also been a member of that other club: the trial attorney.

Transfer to the emergency room by ambulance was a bumpy process, reaffirming my belief that hospitals were no place to go for a rest. Once there, I was left unattended, curtains drawn about my stretcher. An acute episode of Meniere's with full blown symptoms had also been triggered; I was exceedingly uncomfortable. To shield my eyes from the glaring fluorescent lights, I had pulled the sheet over my face; I looked at its whiteness and closed my eyes. It was more soothing to be in dimmer light during an episode of Meniere's. The earlier medications began wearing off and my throat again became more full. I called for someone and realized my voice was hoarse and it was difficult to make myself heard. I knew this meant the laryngeal edema was returning; I needed more medication immediately.

Suddenly I was no longer physically uncomfortable at all. I had the sensation of floating, and I was looking down from high up in a corner of the room. First I noticed a stretcher in which a person lay slightly curled on their side, almost entirely covered by a white sheet except the top of their head, dark brown hair visible. "Oh my—that's me!" I realized in surprise, but in no way alarmed. How odd to see the sheet from this side with me still under it. From this vantage point above the curtain drawn about my stretcher, I saw the ER physician and nurses talking at the nurses' station, several stretchers away from where I lay. I could hear them discussing another case, and they looked busy. I wondered without concern if they had forgotten me. "I guess I'd be pretty easy to forget hidden under a sheet." I thought, amused at how odd it was to see me from outside myself.

My entire visual awareness became half light and half black meeting diagonally along a line in the middle. The light was magnificent, radiant, golden, living, moving light and the blackness was soothing. The blackness disappeared, replaced by more of the same golden vibrant light. I was immersed in it. The light became brighter in the center—white and brilliant. It was extraordinarily calming. I was still floating and had no physical pain. In fact, I had no awareness of my physical body whatsoever. The central brightness intensified and radiated a multitude of fine white rays into the golden light. I was at peace, calm and without fear.

Out of curiosity, not fear, I asked, "What is this? What is happening? This is beginning to remind me of people's descriptions of near-death experiences." I felt a strong sense of God's presence, and I said, "I am not ready to die, I need to be here for my children." Then in the midst of all this illumination I began to see living, moving, life-size figures in full color. I saw a succession of images that I did not merely view, but was drawn into, interacting with them.

The first was Mary, the Blessed Mother, dressed in beautiful, graceful, flowing blue and white robes and white veil accented with rose. Her hair was dark brown, her skin like silk, and she looked at me with soft, smiling eyes. Her face was luminous. She held both her arms down to me, fingers extended and palms open to me. She was so gentle, reassuring, and filled with love. I felt her love for me. Embarrassed, I asked her forgiveness for ignoring her in my life, treating her as a fictional character in a story, not a real person. I was overwhelmed that here she was for me, in spite of it. Next I realized she stood on something round, and crushed dead beneath her feet was a large green serpent, its mouth open wide, long forked tongue swollen and protruding, fangs visible.

The image faded and in its place there was an image of Jesus as an adorable baby. He was lying on his back, clothed in white, delightedly waving his arms and legs before himself as babies do, intrigued at discovering their own hands and feet. He lay there in all his innocence and vulnerable humanity. His eyes met mine and his face lit with a smile, as babies do when engaged by another face. The image disappeared.

The next image was of Mary dressed in deep royal blue, dark crimson, and white robes and veil. She was seated, with Jesus, dressed in white robe and about fifteen months old, sitting on her knee. It was an intimate playful scene, mother and child enjoying each other's company. I felt included as they both looked at me with softness and love. It was very beautiful and not a pose I could ever remember seeing. The image faded away.

Next, I saw a dark image of Christ crucified. It was all the more stark in contrast to Jesus as a baby and toddler, safe and happy in his Mother's care and protection. I winced and cringed at the pain and detail visible to me; that this could have happened to the beautiful perfect child I had just beheld! It was a visceral reaction of revulsion and deep sorrow at the great darkness and utter horror in the scene before me. The image disappeared.

The somber pall was lifted with the next image: Christ in flowing white robes, entirely illuminated from within and surrounded by radiant golden white light—transfigured. He held his arms down to me as had Mary and I felt incredible love from him and an intimate bond with him in the softness of his eyes, which smiled at me.

Next a beautiful white dove, wings outstretched and bathed in the same light, descended in a straight vertical path. When that faded I was immersed in the brilliant white light. I felt unimaginable, unconditional love throughout each scene and was left overflowing with pure contentment and joy.

Then I was back on the hard stretcher and very uncomfortable. After what seemed like a long time but likely was not, someone abruptly pulled the sheet from my face. "Are you all right?" the nurse asked. Before I could answer, he brusquely asked, "Why do you have that sheet over your face?"

When I spoke I was surprised that my hoarseness was gone and my throat much improved. To my knowledge I had no intervening medication. I do not claim to have had a near death experience. I do not know what it was; but I do know that it affected me deeply. It reaffirmed my earlier experience of God, increased my belief in an afterlife, increased my devotion to the Eucharist and regard for the Church. It also left me with the beginnings of a devotion to Mary. I was so deeply touched and grateful that she had come to me, even though I had ignored her.

Fall 1991-Spring, 1992

Frequently during this time period when I knelt in silent prayer after Communion, eyes closed, all became vividly golden-white light, which grew brighter and brighter in the center. It was a pure white light at its center and emanated sparkling rays of white-gold like fire. Time seemed suspended. The light was identical to what I had experienced in the emergency room. I was filled with peace and awe. During those brief times I lost all sense of myself, including physical pain, discomforts, cares, and awareness of my surroundings. It was a wellspring of strength and rejuvenation, which I carried with me the remainder of the day.

Fall 1991-Early Winter, 1992

During quiet prayer before sleep, eyes closed, on several occasions I saw brief images in my mind's eye. They were exquisitely detailed, sepia colored images of people who were visibly suffering, crushed beneath some enormity. I only saw their faces; some were men, some women. They were not static images. but life-like with motion. Their faces contorted as if in deep physical pain and mental anguish. No face appeared familiar. It disturbed me to see them suffer. I had a compelling sense that I should pray for these people though I did not know who they were, if they were dead or alive, or even if they were real. They were so graphically marked by their pain that I responded to them as if they were real.

I wondered if there really was a purgatory, and were these souls there? Or did they exist in the living hell we make for one another right here? When I looked through the newspaper, I caught myself searching the faces in the daily dose of man's inhumanity to man spread across each issue. I felt a bit silly at the prospect of perhaps praying for figments of my imagination. I prefaced these early prayers: "If these people are in my imagination, please give my prayers to someone who needs them, someone who has perhaps been forgotten."

I was exceedingly curious to know who they were, where they were, and why they suffered. Once in meditation before sleep I tried to bring them into my mind's view, in search of these answers. This was a grave error. Instead of suffering faces I saw the very handsome, charming face of a man. "This is a pleasant change from suffering and pain," I thought. The face looked so familiar, but I couldn't place it. It was very attractive and beguiling, I was further drawn into it, straining to recognize who he was. Once I was fully engaged by its pleasing countenance, it suddenly transformed itself, feature by feature, into a monstrous, grotesque, reptile-like being. The change complete, it sneered and mockingly laughed at me. I recognized this to be Satan, and I sat bolt upright in stark terror, my heart racing, the hairs on my arms literally standing on end, with an electrifying chill from head to spine. I turned on all the lights. I told myself it was just in my imagination and convinced myself to turn off the lights and go to sleep. This time I did not try to see any faces—not anything; but the same handsome face appeared and more quickly underwent its reptilian transformation—ending again by sneering, laughing at me.

Heart pounding, I shot to my feet, flicked on all the lights and searched for my Rosary, long unsaid. My reaction was not a matter of habit, but was more like instinct. I was drawn without awareness to the power of Mary and her Rosary to find safe refuge from Satan. I already knew my own error had precipitated this crisis of terror. I prayed the Rosary, asking Mary and Christ's protection from Satan, till I fell asleep with it still tightly in my hands.

The experience was terrifying beyond description. There were lasting effects. For a long time, I was unable to allow myself near the deep state of quiet prayer I now knew how to find. I did not want to give any opportunity for an encounter with the terrifying presence again. I asked God why he allowed it to happen, though I knew the responsibility was mine for prompting it. Misusing spiritual blessings, trying to initiate and direct them rather than receive what was given, was open invitation to Satan. Now fear kept me from feeling close to God in prayer. I did not hear an answer but had a very strong sense of the following. First, I should not abuse the gift I had been given by trying to use it as I chose, but rather only to be receptive to what was given me. Second, it made me realize I had not actually believed Satan existed before, nor had I believed there was a hell. I had never been able to reconcile Satan and hell with an all-loving, all-powerful, all-merciful, all-forgiving God. I could not any better now, but I was certain Satan and hell existed. Though still unable to comprehend the simultaneous existence of evil and suffering in the world with the image of God, I found comfort knowing God was also all-just and held ultimate power over all, evil included.

Pre-Lent, 1992

Rather than a time for my past lukewarm effort at "giving something up" for Lent, the season was now an invitation to identify more closely with Christ. My daily Lenten exercise was to contemplate the Stations of the Cross, specifically, trying to apply each to small aspects of my life and see how I might better manage them through following Christ's example in his passion.

Lent, 1992

One night in prayer before sleep I began to see an extremely detailed, sepia image and was immediately afraid the charming face would appear. I wanted to open my eyes. Instead I became calm and felt the close presence of God. In my mind's eye I then saw graphic, highly cropped images of the crucifixion, all from angles I had never seen in a picture.

It was like being there. There was an overwhelming sense of terror, horror, darkness, and unbearable sorrow, suffering, and anguish; but I was not afraid for myself. The images were riveting, forever burned into my memory. They were living, moving, more detailed and finely etched than the human eye can see.

From a vantage point at the side of the foot of the cross I saw only Christ's feet, one placed atop the other, with a large nail holding them affixed to a triangular wedge on the splintered rough cross beneath. His skin was electrified, taut with pain; every muscle, tendon, bone, and vessel beneath it in stark relief, further outlined in blood, sweat, and dust. Rivulets of blood and sweat ran through the caked dust, making their own pattern. This faded.

I did not want to see any more. I felt the strong presence of God with me and I remained. I saw a similarly detailed view of Christ's arm, shoulder, and neck but very little of his face, which hung down. I saw this from the vantage point of the extreme upper right beam of the cross. The jugular vein of his neck bulged and every muscle was visible in his strong arm and shoulder, coated in perspiration, rivers of blood and sweat etched in the dust. The image faded.

The next image was of Christ's motionless head crowned with thorns, his dark hair partially matted in congealed blood and dust. His face hung down and tilted away. The image was seen from the height of the crown, to the right of and slightly behind Christ's head.

The experience was more than witnessing such a horrendous, gruesome event, it was total immersion and emotional connection with Christ. My reaction was visceral. I felt I would do anything to help him, anything to relieve his pain; but I stood helplessly by, as did others, watching. More unbearable was understanding that I shared blame in the reason for his suffering—that I had caused some of his pain. I knew I was equally capable of the best and worst in every man. The experience intensified as I felt his overwhelming love for me even as he suffered.

When it was through and I returned to the awareness of my physical surroundings, I was exhausted and drained, as if I had in some way actually been there at Christ's crucifixion. I felt very close to Christ in his passion. I prayed with intensity for him, in his suffering.

"What are you doing?" I asked myself. "Who are you to pray for God? God doesn't need your prayers!"

"But it was so real." I argued back with myself; overwhelmed at

Christ's dual nature, human and divine, mystery beyond comprehension.

My response had been to the palpable torment his humanity allowed him to suffer. I was given the following understanding:

*Christ was the epitome of humanity;*
*more perfectly human than any other*
*and with a greater awareness*
*which brought him greater capacity for pain.*
*Its complementary side:*
*the capacity to experience greater human love and joy.*
*To be fully human equates with and is a measure of*
*our capacity for compassion for our fellow man.*

I was so moved by the physical suffering and mental anguish of this man who loved me that I had to do something to soothe even the smallest part of what I saw. I prayed with fervor for help so that I would add no further burden to the suffering of his passion and death. I similarly prayed for all mankind. I needed to do more.

"Let me do something. What can I do?" My questions raced in urgency, the horror fresh to all my senses. I did not hear anything; but a vivid image of Simon helping Christ carry his cross filled my thoughts, and with it came peace. That was the answer. It was how to do more: alleviate the suffering of others in this world, help others carry their crosses in any small way. Exhausted I fell asleep.

Spring, 1992
This was a very happy time in my life with many good things unfolding. I closed my eyes and enjoyed day-dreaming about the present and future. I was not anxious to sleep, enjoying my thoughts instead. They were interrupted by the following.

The entire room and all in it became white, and I was looking at it from the upper right hand corner of the room, near the ceiling. I looked down and saw a bed along the adjacent left wall, its headboard centered on the wall. There was a woman beautifully in peace lying on it. I did not recognize her. A magnificent being of light in long flowing robes descended, nearly horizontal with head and shoulders slightly lower than the remainder of its body. The being came to rest suspended in the air several feet above and before the woman. The being of white light was lit from within and had eyes that communicated love and warmth. The full sleeves of the being's robe and the remainder of the diaphanous long gown floated upwards. The figure was the epitome of grace as its gently arched body and arms protectively hung in the air. My full attention fixed upon this being of light.

From above and behind this being, in the opposite corner of the room from my vantage point, a brilliant white light appeared and shone a focused stream of light down upon the woman. Almost simultaneously I saw a plainer but beautifully graceful similar being of light three quarters emerge from the body lying on the bed—reaching, yearning, stretching arms upward toward the light's source, trying to ascend the diagonal path of light to its center. The first being of light just at the edge of this diagonal path of light held arms and hands outstretched, gently blocking the way.

Intrigued by the captivating beauty and peace of what I saw, I was lulled until with a start I recognized the person in the bed as myself and the being emerging from it as my spirit. I shouted, in my thoughts: "What are you doing? You can't go anywhere!" The scene dissolved and I found myself body, mind, and spirit back in the same place. I looked about the room, from the corner from which the light shone, to my previous vantage point opposite, to the air above me where the beautiful being of light gracefully floated—all were gone.

I was stunned to experience myself as distinct: body, mind and spirit; I was more taken aback by their radically disparate wishes, suddenly finding me part stranger to myself. My body passively lodged the "odd couple"—my mind fully engaged, its consciousness taken up with the world, and a spirit that longed to return to God. "Why would you do that, you have so much to look forward to? Why?" my mind asked my spirit, but no response was perceived. I was astonished at how much part of me longed to return to God. I had no death wish; I hoped to live a long and happy life.

I thought about the beautiful being of light. "Are there really angels?" I wondered, "Could this have been my guardian angel?" Whoever it was, the being was more beautiful than any creature I had ever seen. Its loose billowing sleeves wafting upward could almost be mistaken for wings. I laughed aloud, as this "illusion" of wings triggered a memory of long ago. My great amusement was in its solving a childhood mystery. This was not the first being of light I had seen; in fact, I had seen two similar ones, once before.

One night, when I was four, I had a "dream" which remains indelibly etched in my memory for the events of the day which followed. My "dream" took place in our own railroad-flat apartment, and in my "dream" I was sleeping in my bed exactly as in fact I had been that very night. In the "dream," high up near the ceiling my father came through the wall of my room, both himself and the wall remaining untouched. It was the wall at the head of my bed, as though he had come through my parents' and sister's rooms on the other side. Supporting him, at each side there was someone very light and beautiful, in long, white, loosely flowing robes. I did not recognize these two beings with him. My Father and the two who accompanied him were white and illuminated from within. They and my father appeared to move effortlessly. They floated near horizontally over my bed looking down at me as I slept. Nothing was said. I felt a great sensation of warmth and love coming from my father. They continued toward the foot of the bed and as they did, then floated more vertically and then up, passing through the ceiling, after which I could no longer see them.

I awoke feeling the pleasant glow of having been in my father's company and was so disappointed when I remembered he was in the hospital. It was December eighth. I was still in my pajamas in bed when my mother came into my room. She sat on the side of my bed and drew me near to her. She told me God needed my father for something very special and had sent angels to bring him to heaven in the night. Although I never expected that, neither was I surprised. I understood her concretely, as if she had simply explained what I had just seen. My initial reaction was matter of fact. I told her, "If I had been awake I would have shot those angels!" believing this would have kept my father with us. Except once, to a first grade friend, I never spoke about what I had "dreamt" until recent years.

The "dream" was comforting, in that I felt my father's presence and love and it affirmed an afterlife, but it left me with a misleading sense that if indeed I had woken up, I could have stopped them. In retrospect, I saw that this contributed to choosing medicine as my career—a daily opportunity to battle death back at the door. As a child, the other thing that really disturbed me about this dream was wondering: where were the wings? Those beautiful, white-robed beings did not have wings. With the certainty of a four-year-old, I believed there were angels but I knew they were supposed to have wings.

I could not contain the width of my smile now, thinking of those loose billowing sleeves, floating upwards and looking almost like wings. One of childhood's questions was laid to rest. Yes, these had been angels. It was at once exhilarating and odd to have encountered a being who appeared to be my guardian angel. This meeting was all the more peculiar since I had long since given up my childhood belief in the existence of angels. I was delighted to be wrong. How comforting to know this beautiful, loving, protective being watched over me, and with great joy I expressed my long overdue gratitude. Jubilant, I drifted off to sleep looking forward to waking up the next day.

Late Winter to Summer, 1992
I had a strong sense of being in synch with God's will. I cannot explain how, it was just a sense of easy flowing and knowing I was where I should be. I wish I had the recipe to repeat it each day myself.

Early July, 1992
Side effects of medications, which suppressed my immune system and with it my body's natural ability to fight disease, left me greater prey to an acute infection with Lyme Disease. Four days' successive, rapid decline held the specter of an intensive care unit, looming large for the day to follow. My hospital admission had been arranged. I contemplated mortality's brink from a more immediate vantage point.

Hospital bag packed, I sank into my rocker, settling into it in half resignation. I looked out upon the beauty of an early summer's morning, bright with its full promise of life yet to unfold. I felt cheated. I listened to the music of my children's laughter and voices in the next room as I considered the very immediate uncertainty of my fate. It was difficult to keep back tears. I was no longer afraid to die, but I was afraid to leave my children alone in the world. Though I knew the thought betrayed a lack of faith in God's providence, so it was. I prayed. I found no comfort. The hours were black.

At such times one can see with unparalleled clarity how precious moments of life are and the importance of doing that which we are to do, the tasks given us in this world. I was filled with regret at a sense that my tasks were not accomplished. I wondered what I would leave behind of my life—of myself—for my children to draw strength from as they weathered their own life's storms. What had I conveyed of my experience of Christ's presence to help them wherever fate's winds brought them? My deepest regret crystallized: I had not fully shared with them the most important part of my life—the spiritual—the presence of God in my life. I wanted it to be theirs too. How could I have failed in this of all things! I felt compelling urgency; there was so much I needed yet to say. Their names upon my lips, I caught myself just before calling them to me. Instead the only sound I uttered was a deep sigh, as I reminded myself they were only eight and eleven years of age. I had given them as much as their young lives would allow them to grasp, in words about God. They each knew I loved them with my whole heart and soul.

If I told them more—more words—what would they mean? What would they remember when one day they battled their own trials of faith? It was always a delicate balance: giving them what they could understand and find meaningful without overpowering them, perhaps turning them from God.

A nagging sense of failure continued, and its intensity puzzled me. Abruptly, it became obvious. My sense of loss was focused on something that had not yet occurred: the prospect of not being a living part of their futures, unable to share my spiritual treasure when they would find it of more value. The sadness was not for the past but for what might never be.

My mind raced in a frenzy, a fugue of what I wished them to understand—no, what I desperately needed them to call their own. Death is not our end, it is a beginning. Dying is the continuation of our lives in different form, our spirits freed from the bodies which imprison us, chained beneath their weight and imperfections. Death's sting—the painful separation—need not be final. We can all be reunited one day, in the perfect joy and peace of God's kingdom, if we so choose. We must recognize the choice and the path there. I wanted my children to feel Christ's living presence because then I knew they would find their way to our eternal togetherness. My heart would be light if they knew they were never alone, but always in Christ's care and protection.

The storm within me became calm. Still seated in my rocker, again I became aware of the beauty of the summer's day, sunlight streaming through the windows. I pictured my children beside me, into their futures, Christ in our midst, and I imagined speaking to their hearts as they were ready. In that instant I was given the following:

*I was to draw my notes into a cohesive whole—*
*a book for my children.*
*I was shown it completed and titled:*
MY CHILDREN, LISTEN

How curious, I thought, a book with a title whose next chapter I did not know, nor its evolution, destination or for that matter how to begin. All I knew of it was the notes of my spiritual encounters in random scraps, and not any easy read, for legibility and my own interspersed shorthand. I hoped it was not too late. I vowed, if I recovered, to carry this job forward. To vow was redundant, the matter now beyond choice— something within me which had to be told.

I was not overjoyed, but a great tranquillity was upon me, detaching me from my worries, returning me to the present moment. I felt renewed inner strength and purpose. I got up and went to enjoy my children's company.

That day my physical decline with Lyme disease plateaued and I began a long road to recovery. Crisis subsided into the familiar drone of chronic illness, a welcome relief by comparison. How perspective and appreciation of life's small pleasures can change with circumstance!

## August 22, 1992

I was enjoying the excitement of preparing for a family gathering later that day when I was momentarily removed from it with the following unexpected gift. It happened quickly; I am not sure whether the communication was word or wordless but the thought imparted was clear and strong.

*The extent to which you love Christ*
*is the extent to which you will share in the after life.*

Explained:

*To love Christ is to follow his teachings.*
*To love Christ is to follow his example.*
*To love Christ is to follow his word.*
*They are inseparable.*
*It is implicit.*
*One naturally follows the other.*
*The motivation is love, the desire to please,*
*to offer a pleasing life to our Creator.*
*The motivation is not through fear of punishment.*
*In heaven each soul experiences the ultimate happiness*
*and fulfillment in God's presence,*
*though the capacity for this varies like the size of a cup.*
*All cups would be filled to overflowing,*
*receiving more than they could contain.*
*The extent of sharing in the afterlife was more the size of the cup*
*as self-determined by the extent to which*
*we love Christ in this world.*

Fall, 1992

While my eyes were closed during prayer before sleep, an intense white light coalesced into the shape of an amorphous heart. It broke and a single, brilliant, crimson teardrop of blood fell into my heart. I was keenly aware of Christ's love and mercy for us all in the saving act of his redemption. I was moved to tears.

February 22, 1993
After Mass and Communion:

**Be kind...**

"Who's voice is that?" I asked, knowing it was different, not exactly a voice. I had not heard it with my ears, nor was it my own thought, but it was a clear communication. There was silence... Time elapsed, and unrelated to the above I "heard,"

**Your home is with me.**

This startled me, and yet at once I felt deep peace in which I recognized Christ's presence. I felt joy in reflecting upon the first statement, a simple command to focus past the daily irritation illness brought. The second statement was centering, the peaceful refuge from which to draw strength.

 Lent, 1993

Lenten exercise: Practice the presence of God—that is, bring to my conscious awareness God's constant presence within me and all others.

Winter, 1993

**Write, my child.**

In retrospect, I had heard this gentle whisper a number of times before, not recognizing what it was. Now I knew it was real, but did not know what it meant. My thoughts were drawn to the book I had been shown, *MY CHILDREN, LISTEN*. I reread my record of that day: *...draw my notes into a cohesive whole—a book for my children.*

I wondered, "What did that mean, cohesive whole? How was I to do this?" The only avenue I could think of was an autobiographical introduction to my spiritual rebirth.

 March, 1993

Efforts at autobiography produced disorganized rumination. I prayed for guidance, as many times before; but on this occasion the book's theme was given to me:

**Jesus Christ is here within us;**
**everything, every day**
**in our lives is sacramental.**

It was so simple and beautiful! I reflected from this perspective and could picture the sacred in small details of daily life. It was an easy visual aid, bringing to mind Jesus Christ here within me and those around me. Greater reverence, a sense of the sacred, naturally flowed from tasks so envisioned. I imagined Jesus living in our household and how that would change the way I would feel performing the simplest task: washing apples, folding laundry, pouring a cup of tea, arranging a vase of flowers, clearing the table, patiently waiting, straightening up, sharing a kind word, giving my time. I reminded myself that Christ was already here before me in the form of other people to whom the same reverence was due.

Revelry in this shower of insight abruptly halted as I recognized it had no connection with anything I had written. I was bewildered. Of more concern, I could not envision the theme emerging from anything I was able to contribute. Here was a message of great beauty and wisdom; it was as great a mystery, how I was to make it the book's core? Therein lay the problem: the "I" in my thinking. My will was clashing against God's, despite my best intentions to do his will—reason and impatience my own worst enemies. I did not yet recognize it is God who chooses the timing of his plan, not man.

The truth in the book's theme was not mine, nor did I have the experience to bring it to life. It remained in the back of my thoughts, continually unsettling at the lack of any fit between my efforts and the results. Blind to an alternate path, I tried harder on the present course—rambling memoir, but it was effort in vain. It was not for some time that its surprise solution was revealed. Throughout this time I continued to accumulate scribbled notes of my encounters with Christ, slipped into books and drawers.

May 12, 1993
After Mass and Communion:

**Why do you struggle and rail against me?...**

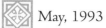

 May, 1993

*God shows us our way every day*
*by where we find ourselves, happy, sad, in-between.*
*The crosses we bear on our way point and direct us*
*to closer knowing and experiencing God.*
*Result:*
*happy, peaceful detachment,*
*increased faith and trust,*
*childlike confidence*
*in an all-knowing, all-loving*
*all-giving, all-powerful parent.*

 May, 1993

The hardest part of praying is listening.
The hardest part of listening
is becoming quiet enough to hear.

 May, 1993
After Mass and Communion:

**I am all around you.**
**I am everywhere.**
**I am with you always.**

Hearing these words while experiencing Christ's presence, I was in awe of their truth.

 May 31, 1993
After Mass and Communion:

**(Live and) enjoy life.**

June 14, 1993
After Mass and Communion:

**I love you.**

"I can't tell who said that," I said to myself, more perplexed because it was also what I was thinking. "Was that me or you?"

**I will never forsake you.**

"I can't tell who said that," I reflected, now concerned, not wanting to invent what I wanted to hear, and confused because the choice of vocabulary was not mine. Then came a clear and distinct sense of Christ's immediate presence. "Are we one?" I asked, surprised at my own question.

**Yes, my child, we are one.**
I was filled with deep peace and wonder at the beauty of being so closely in Christ's presence through the Eucharist.

 Summer, 1993
One afternoon, with eyes closed in quiet prayer, the presence of God was overwhelming. Immersed in beautiful red vibrant light I felt God's power, majesty, mercy, compassion and love.

 October 30, 1993
*We are placed here on Earth to learn to love other people.*
*If everyone were perfectly lovable and we capable of perfect love,*
*there would be nothing to learn.*
*We can learn more about how to love through our human limitations.*
*Therein lies the challenge.*

 November 1, 1993
In prayer to the Holy Spirit I asked for guidance in God's will. I wanted to know God's will for me and meditated to this end.
**I will show you, my child.**
I meditated further, anxious to be told.
**I will show you, my child.**
"Where? When?" I asked.
**In your life.**
"Please help me be patient," I asked, and persisted in meditation, despite a strong inclination to get up. I waited, still hoping for more specific direction—something I considered an answer.
**Living is with eyes open;**
**now up, and be about**
**(the work you need to do today).**
In that, I understood prayer and meditation were important and an integral part of each day, but living was an equally important part of prayer. The balance of doing and meditating would be different in each person's life. We are all called to different things, but they are all important. Prayer is learning to listen to God and needs to be part of every day.

 December, 1993
*We are here to learn to love one another.*

December, 1993

Illness flared in major proportions. Overwhelming debility again made a joke of daily routine and its reassuring comfort. The delicate silk threads we spin, our cocoons of security, are so easily exposed for their fragility. The ruse I lived—hiding my daily discomforts, ignoring what limitations I could, and dancing about what remained—was glaringly exposed. There is limited leeway for feigning health while spending significant stretches too dizzy, weak, and fatigued to get out of bed. I so wanted to contain the impact illness had upon my family. Foiled once again, I was no more gracefully accepting, despite past practice. "Why couldn't this have just waited till after Christmas! I have too much to do, to be slowed down any more!" I complained to myself.

Anger turned into despondency as the level of sustained pain and other symptoms forced my surrender as days wore into weeks. My head felt ready to explode with the intense pressure deep in my ears. Piercing sinus pain in my face brought the pain deep within my ears to a crescendo, capped with maddeningly louder ringing in my ears.

I was markedly fatigued and nauseated. There was no relief. Muscles and tendons burned with inflammation and my joints (arthritis) and bursae (bursitis) ached, precluding any comfortable position in which to lie. Pain blocked my escape into sleep. As I sank deeper and deeper into illness, a wall of thickening fog separated me from my loved ones. The loneliness and isolation were compounded by my efforts to keep my concerns more to myself. Watching my family worry troubled me even more.

One night after a particularly demoralizing day, two to three weeks into this, I fought to fall asleep. I shifted my body's weight without success in finding comfort. My body seemed crushed under its own weight. Smothering fatigue and weakened muscles required all my effort and concentration just to turn, and then waves of nausea followed any motion. I closed my eyes, hoping for quick release into sleep.

Instead, eyes still closed, everything became radiantly light. I had a sensation of floating, as a great soothing warmth flowed through my entire body and enveloped me. I was free of all physical pain or any awareness of bodily sensation. The light became incredibly brilliant. It was all there was. In the center it was intensely pure white and emanated vibrant white and gold light in every direction to a more generalized whitish-gold light at the periphery. The light was alive. I was inextricably drawn to its center. That was where I wanted to be. I was immersed in it—pain-free, floating, bathed in the light's peace. I knew I was in and filled with the presence of God.

"I haven't seen your light in so long!" I was ecstatic. "Thank you, thank you, thank you, for letting me know you are there. Thank you for consoling me with your presence!" Then I heard:

**It is not enough to know,**
**now touch someone else's life.**

Explained:

*Touch another soul with the love of Christ*
*that someone else might come to know*
*Christ's presence through my actions.*
*What was asked of me was small*
*and as simple as a kind smile.*
*It was exactly measured to my limits.*

The first bodily sensation I became aware of was warm wetness about my face. I raised my hand to my face and was surprised in realizing tears were streaming from my eyes. I looked up at the night sky and blinked till I could see the stars and moon clearly. I was gratefully amazed that my reprieve from pain continued. I closed my eyes and gently drifted into a deep and refreshing sleep, unpunctuated by constant awakening due to pain the night through.

I awoke the next day mentally and emotionally replenished. Physically I felt a bit better, but no more than could be accounted for by simply getting a good night's rest. I had a renewed sense of empowerment, basking in the confidence bestowed upon me that there was something of value I could still do and contribute even in this debilitated state. I set about trying to think of the small ways in which I could touch others with Christ's presence—his love.

December 22, 1993

The following description falls short of the scope and depth of understanding received in an instant but it is as complete as I can make it.

*Christ is the light of the world.*
*Everything in our world is made from the light of Christ—*
*Christ's energy, Christ's life force.*
*Everything is ultimately made up of light—*
*the light of Christ, the essence of all creation.*
*If we could continue to divide each subatomic particle*

*into smaller and smaller parts for an infinity of divisions,*
*beyond any of which man is capable, now or ever,*
*we would arrive at the very essence of all creation,*
*which is God.*

It was new perspective upon remembering: **I am all around you. I am everywhere. I am with you always.** (May 1993) I also appreciated this insight as explaining how deeply and intimately God has remained with his creation. That indeed we came into existence and continue to exist only due to the on-going presence of God.

I reflected upon the contrast in my beliefs between the time when I could not even believe Christ's real presence was in the Eucharist to now, finding Christ's presence with us and all creation, to this intimate degree, everywhere. Yet there is a difference between Christ's presence in the Eucharist, his presence in each person, his presence in other living creatures, and his presence in the inanimate.

Christ's presence in the Eucharist is pure. The difference between Christ's presence in man and any other living creature or the inanimate is that we are created in God's image and likeness, imbued with his Holy Spirit. In the gift of our free will is likeness to God. Free will empowers each of us to create.

If man did not have free will and its ability to create, evil would not have been allowed entry into the Garden of Paradise. We can turn toward God and choose to create love and forgiveness; or we can turn away from God and choose to create the chaos and destruction of evil's darkness.

A rock, tree, cloud, flower, river, any nonliving thing can only be that. Dogs, cats, birds, horses, any animal excluding man can only be that, limited in thinking, innocently confined by biology and instinct. Man is set apart from other animals, made in God's image and imbued with his Spirit. Man's soul is immortal; and via choice through free will he defines his eternal destiny. Man can reach beyond the physical and as a child of God choose to accept our Father's invitation to share divine eternal life; or choose to turn away from God and spend eternity in God's absence and in the company of Satan.

God breathed his Holy Spirit upon each of us at our creation, along with a unique role in his plan. We all have a life of meaning and purpose in God's eyes. Man defines his destiny in this plan and for all eternity through the choice's made of his own free will.

God created all and is a part of all, except evil. God takes any circumstance, evil included, and draws good from it because his is the ultimate power and the last word over it.

To picture Christ so intimately present in creation, I reflected upon the ways in which man has desecrated it: the inanimate, our natural resources and environment; the animals; and greatest of all—man's inhumanity to man. I wondered whether in Christ's human and divine nature he had conscious awareness of this during his passion. It would be suffering beyond comprehension—the sum total of all our sins, the way we have abused our gifts and God's creation. All mankind for all time is saved in Christ's redeeming act; if we so choose we can unite our suffering with his. It is profound simplicity, this individual personal bond we each hold with Christ in his redeeming act of love for us. He is there for us in our sin. We can choose to be there with him in his redemption of us by joining our suffering with his. It is a mystery in a mystery, a story within a story.

At Christmas Mass various passages stood out, as if I had heard them for the first time, so new was my appreciation of their meaning. [Italics have been added to the following passages for emphasis.]

> In times past, God spoke in fragmentary and varied ways to our fathers through the prophets; in this, the final age, he has spoken to us through his Son, whom he has made heir of all things and *through whom he first created the universe.*
>
> Hebrews 1:1-2, Lectionary

> In the beginning was the Word;
> the Word was in God's presence,
> and the Word was God.
> He was present to God in the beginning.
> *Through him all things came into being,*
> *and apart from him nothing came to be.*
> Whatever came to be in him, found life,
> life for the light of men.
> The light shines on in darkness,
> a darkness that did not overcome it.
>
> John 1:1-5, Lectionary

From the Profession of Faith:

We believe in one Lord, Jesus Christ,
   the only Son of God,
   eternally begotten of the Father,
   God from God, Light from Light,
   true God from true God,
   begotten, not made, one in Being with the Father.
   *Through him all things were made.*

In words which never registered before, I now heard profound truth.

December 28, 1993

At home in prayer before the crucifix, I contemplated Christ's personal sacrifice on the cross, from the perspective of Christ, the man. I wondered whether the perfect knowledge in his divine nature intensified the agony of his human passion and death. Was the weight of his cross the heavier because of his awareness of the collective sins of mankind across time? Was he as intimately connected with each of us, our every thought and deed, in his human consciousness as in his pure divine state? The suffering would be unimaginable.

It distressed me to think my action or inaction contributed to his cross's weight; as if Jesus's pained, sweat and blood drenched eyes caught mine along Calvary's path. I felt a keen awareness that my own sins caused his very real suffering and knew deeply that every man was capable of both the sins and good acts of all mankind. I was filled with shame and remorse and recognized my lack of gratitude for his redeeming act. I felt an intensely personal connection between my sins and Christ's love in his redeeming act.

"Thank you, Jesus in coming for me, but I know I am not so special. I know you came for many others as well."

**I would have come for you, my child.**

I was startled at the words, overcome at feeling so intimately bound to Christ in his act of love for us all. "Please help me contribute no further to your cross's weight," I thought and continued, "I wish I could have eased your suffering instead." I became more keenly aware of Christ's love as a glowing soothing warmth suffused my entire body. I was utterly content and filled with a sense of purpose, but I did not know for what.

During the day I kept repeating the words "I would have come for

you, my child," as an infatuated lover rereads a beloved's note. Why was I
so deeply moved by that, when I had heard the same many times before
in parables of the lost sheep, and the prodigal son? Today I experienced
their meaning for the first time. Why? I do not know; but Christ was now
both a real and living person to me, and with that, so were his words and
teaching real and alive. For all, God has remained so involved in his creation that he does not abandon a single soul he has created.

Early January, 1994
During Mass:

> *Grace is God's love for man.*
> *Truth is the Holy Spirit.*
> *This is how gently,*
> *through Truth and grace,*
> *God, in all his power, rules his kingdom.*

January 25, 1994
In prayer to the Holy Spirit for guidance, I asked how to discern
God's will.

**You will know.**

Later:

> **You cannot do my will**
> **if you are troubled by the cares**
> **and anxieties of the world.**
> **Do not be afraid.**

Explained:

> *If we are preoccupied in this way*
> *we cannot listen in prayer*
> *to know God's will.*
> *This also restricts our energy*
> *making it less available to do God's will.*
> *We can be equally distracted*
> *by the worlds riches and pleasures.*
> *These are not bad, but good,*
> *when used in the proper perspective:*
> *in keeping with God's will,*
> *in accordance with Christ's teaching.*

January 28, 1994

During a midday attempt at prayer I found difficulty beginning. "I am afraid," I thought, knowing it was deepening faith I feared, the growth of which seemed invariably associated with suffering. I also feared what might be expected of me or be in store for me. Always recognizing what a great and undeserved privilege it was to feel Christ's presence so closely, I doubted my ability and strength of faith to meet whatever responsibility it brought. I was vaguely uneasy there could be more, and I questioned my inner strength to meet its challenge. Then I heard:

**It is your little faith that makes you afraid.**

**Go, be about your work.**

February 7, 1994

After Communion:

**Have Faith.**

February 9, 1994

After Mass and Communion:

**I am with you, my child.**

I had a deep awareness of the following:

*My riches are my faith, my family,*

*my remaining health, and my friends.*

In a small chapel dedicated to Our Lady, just after Mass, I prayed the Hail Mary:

"Hail Mary, full of grace; the Lord is with thee."

**I am with you, my child.**

(These latter words had a different quality as compared with the first line above, but I cannot describe the difference.)

"Blessed art thou among women, and"

*Follow Mary as an example.*

"blessed is the fruit of thy womb, Jesus."

*Mary said 'yes' to God's will,*

*and Christ was brought forth in her womb.*

*We are to do the same.*

"Holy Mary, Mother of God,"

*We are all to say 'yes'*

*to allow Christ to be born in us.*

*This is how we are born and grow in divine life,*
*the divine share of life God the Father invites us to have—*
*we must say 'yes' to it*
*in order to be born into divine life,*
*upon our mortal death.*
*Man is allowed to share in the divine—to create.*
*Free will allows us to create—*
*to create love or hate.*
**(That is what is in man's purview to create.)**
*To create—to make something from nothing,*
*as opposed to using existing materials.*
*Energies and aftereffect of love/hate*
*live on like a legacy we all leave behind—*
*a permanent mark we make*
*on the world, mankind, and creation.*
"pray for us sinners, now and at the hour of our death. Amen."
*Death: bodily, spiritual, or death to sin.*

February 14, 1994

I had a dream the point of which was to be patient, to allow God's will for us to unfold that we might know it by being shown. Being impatient forced situations, causing missed opportunity to participate more fully in doing God's will.

Winter, 1994

As the children grew older it was harder to hide my cognitive limitations from them. It was during a game of Scrabble that my oldest asked, "Mom, are you just letting us win?"

"No," I said, but their quizzical looks remained. I continued, "of course not..." my voice trailed off, at a loss to explain that my difficulty was in visually scanning the board and my letters quickly enough to be competitive. I was reluctant to give up the illusion—wanting to appear to them as I used to be. Admittedly, I was not having a good day with respect to my illness. As I tried to think how to describe the problem without creating needless concern, my oldest spoke.

"I think you are," she said, in disbelief that I could not do better. Her expression showed both hurt and offense, that I would patronize her instead of regarding her a worthy opponent. The children exchanged looks.

"No, no really, I am not just letting you win..." I said, still at a loss for an explanation.

My youngest interrupted, confidently offering both olive branch and chance to prove her sister wrong, "Let's play again. Why don't you try to win this time, Mom?" The game began. The more the board filled, the more I lagged behind, increasingly self-conscious of my poor performance. The game continued in uncharacteristic quiet. I avoided their eyes, focusing full attention on the game.

It was my youngest who broke the awkward silence. "What's the matter, Mom?" She hesitated, her face wrinkling in puzzlement, "Don't you know how to make any words bigger than three letters?" I could feel the warmth rising in my cheeks, accentuated by the innocence of her question—only trying to make sense of what she could not comprehend. Clearly they both knew something was amiss. I watched their mixed expressions of confusion, disappointment, hurt, anger and fear.

"Of course I do," I said.

"Then why don't you?" she asked, looking for a logical answer, not confrontation. I tried to explain, but this was not the moment to introduce medical subtlety. Their pent-up frustration over my illness and its impact on their lives poured out, their remarks coming quickly alternating in tandem with one another. A long overdue tirade was unleashed.

"Why can't you just be like the other mothers? You're so disorganized; you're always late; you can never get anything done; you're always sick! We don't do things like we used to; you never skate, or ski, or bike ride with us anymore! We never go away on vacation anymore! You cancel plans at the last minute, always saying you're too sick, or too dizzy." It was difficult to interject a word, but still more difficult for them to listen. They continued, "I think you could do better if you just tried harder! I just don't think you really care!" With that they stood, and left the room.

I was still numb as I heard their footsteps fade up the stairs. I looked up to see my reflection in the glass door, turned into a mirror by the night outside. To avoid it, I got up and turned off the light, as if this could make my illness disappear as well. I sat back down on the couch and stared into what I could not see beyond the glass in the night outside. I did not want to think, but numbness dissolved into a whirl of feeling. "I hate being sick! This isn't how I wanted our lives to be!" I caught myself, feeling a measure of ingratitude for what remained of my health, and the blessings I had received in my illness. "I know things could be worse, and I am thankful for what I have, but why can't they be better; I want to be as I was!"

I recognized my children's feelings as normal reaction to the many changes, anxieties, losses, uncertainty and inconvenience my illness had brought into their lives; but, I could not deny their last two remarks stung—that I wasn't trying and didn't care. I knew they were spoken in anger, but I could not fully dismiss them—wondering if they believed it even in part. Had I been so successful in shielding them from the full impact of my illness that they had no appreciation of my effort? No, I concluded, I did not regret the course I had chosen. I was sorry to have disappointed them, but putting this in perspective I reminded myself that it was an inevitable part of growing-up: children's disappointment learning their parents are not super heroes, but human. My illness just exaggerated the process.

I knew it was better to allow them the space to speak their feelings. I was confident they knew how much I loved them, and from this I was certain they would sort free the truth. I closed my eyes to pray.

There was a soft stir and then a light tap at my right shoulder and left forearm. I opened my eyes, to my children on either side of me. "Mom, we're really sorry," my oldest said softly.

"Yeah, we're really sorry, Mom," my youngest joined in. "We know you can't help it." They kissed me on either cheek and I hugged them to me.

"Sometimes we're just really worried about you." They each hugged me more tightly.

"Don't worry. I understand, it's not easy for you, my being sick. Don't feel badly; it's normal for you to be angry and disappointed with me about it at times. I know you love me even when you're angry, and you know I love you." We sat together, warm in our reconciliation, but unable to avoid staring out the dark window and into the night.

 Winter-Spring, 1994

Often times during this time period I heard:

### Write, my child.

I continued unsuccessfully at autobiography, increasingly uncertain whether this was the manner in which *to draw my notes into a cohesive whole.* It was all I could imagine. Lack of success fueled greater doubt. I prayed, "If this is what I am to do, please direct me as to how and what."

Ash Wednesday, 1994
After Communion:

**I am coming.**

 Lent, 1994
My Lenten focus was prayer to the Holy Spirit for guidance in God's will.

 Spring, 1994
After Communion:

**Come to me now and always.**

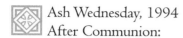 March 2, 1994
After Communion:

**Be still, my child, follow Mary.**

March 30, 1994
After Communion:

I wondered why I no longer experienced the light of Christ's presence or other images as I had when first learning to be in his company. It had been so pleasant to stay there. I wondered, "Would it have kept me from the business of living?"

Then, as compared with now, I had a clearer sense of greater compliance with God's will. I had come to sense the same feeling in more subtle ways, but now I questioned whether I still followed God's will as closely. Was I not listening? Then I heard:

**I love you.**

I was unsure if that was myself or Christ.

**I love you, my child.**

I remained doubtful of the authenticity of these words, not wanting to invent what I wanted to hear.

**Yes, my child, I love you.**

In the peace that came upon me I recognized their source. I was so happy to feel Christ's presence that I stood up, now ready to leave; then I reconsidered. "Had I been too hasty? Was my prayer complete?" I knelt and closed my eyes again.

**Be about your work.**
**Rise and open your eyes.**

April 8, 1994

At home just after morning Mass I sat in prayer, but I was distracted, anxious to place some important tasks behind me. Prior to illness, these duties would have been efficiently dismissed. Now, routine paperwork such as reading my mail and paying bills, or ordinary errands like grocery shopping, were chores that loomed insurmountably large. I knew despite all my effort the items on the list would be marginally accomplished and spill into the next day, increasing my unease. Deadlines had been missed, their ranks growing. It was a daily exercise in frustration, or a lesson in patience, depending upon my outlook on a given day. I was torn between remaining in prayer's quiet respite and dealing with pressing essentials.

**Your life is a prayer.**

Explained:

*There is no dichotomy between types of prayer.*
*Contemplative prayer*
*with its quiet peaceful closeness,*
*and living prayer filled with life's daily demands,*
*duties, pleasures, and sufferings—*
*all a continuum on the same spectrum.*

This insight was the boost I needed to ease transition from prayer's peaceful solitude to the day ahead. Energized, I was ready to tackle the day, but I heard:

**Sleep, my child.**

"Sleep?" I asked, confusion pouring over newfound enthusiasm. "I don't want to sleep. I have too much to do to sleep."

I recalled my Lenten focus, prayer to the Holy Spirit, trying often throughout the day to pray, "I want to do your will, please help me to do your will." Now I struggled with this. I reclined on the couch. From where I lay I looked up into the sky's dome. It was a beautiful sky—blue, spotted and rimmed by light fluffy clouds. Progressively the scene became illuminated from within by majestic golden white light, and I felt the strong presence of God. The sky was transformed beyond description, more beautiful than any I had ever seen. I was in awe of the light's magnificence and its life-giving force.

The scene faded into deep vibrant crimson, and still I felt the strong presence of God. I understood the color to be the boundless mercy and love God has in his heart for us. I fell asleep, and awoke refreshed.

May 12, 1994
Amid mild discouragement at the actions of loved ones, I continued my daily time of quiet prayer.

**Come to me.**

I was at once calm and in a peaceful refuge.

**I am teaching others around you too.**

Explained:

> *It was important to tolerate and accept the present patiently.*
> *Although it was somewhat unpleasant at the moment,*
> *there was a purpose in it for those I loved around me too.*
> *I could help facilitate God's plan for them*
> *in submitting myself to God's will*
> *by simply patiently accepting*
> *my present circumstances.*

It was comfort to know my cares had purpose. The same situation was there, but the aggravation gone. Free of it, my input changed and the matter soon began to improve. The perspective allowed me to more freely give of myself, openly expressing love and affection to one previously the source of anger and distress. It allowed me healthy detachment.

May 15, 1994
After Communion:

I felt very sad in acknowledging deep doubts in my faith and trust in God. I was sincerely sorry that I could not just accept and appreciate the spiritual gifts I had been given. I felt relieved to express fully this failing in my thoughts. I was more comfortable already. Then I heard:

**Come to me now and always.**

I was astonished at hearing Christ's presence after so bald an admission. My heart leapt with joy. I had not been abandoned in my ingratitude, lack of faith or trust. I know we cannot expect to have God's gifts and graces on our terms, when, where, and how we want them.

I was in constant dance: fleeing God's seeking me out, then repeatedly drawn closer, like the pendulum's course.

Spring-Summer, 1994
In night-time prayer I was more preoccupied, ruminating over my concerns and "what ifs" than praying. I thought, "I am afraid."

**You are afraid because you have too little faith.**

"Yes, I can see that is true." I thought about it further. I reflected upon my greatest occasions of growth in faith, and their association with times of greatest pain or suffering in one form or another. I was grateful for the faith I had received during these trials, but I would not be anxious to live through them again. I could not have deliberately chosen them. I wanted my faith to be increased, but I just could not bring myself to ask for fear of the association.

June 12, 1994
During Mass:

*The Trinity:*
*God the Father, God the Son, and God the Holy Spirit.*
*The Son shines forth upon us all, ever seeking.*
*We allow the Holy Spirit to enter us more fully,*
*by accepting the already existing presence*
*of the Holy Spirit within us,*
*and through the Holy Spirit*
*we are united with the Father*
*via the Son as bridge to show us the way.*
*We need to be chosen by the Father*
*to receive the Holy Spirit.*
*We are each chosen in the act of our creation.*
*God singly chose each of us*
*when he called us from nothingness;*
*chosen into existence in the act of our creation.*
*That you exist is proof that you were chosen;*
*drawn from nonexistence for an integral,*
*unique purpose in God's plan.*
*The Son (analogy made with the sun's image)*
*shines forth upon us all;*
*ever seeking to draw all souls to the Father.*
*The Holy Spirit makes each life sacred,*
*imbuing us with the potential to share God's life;*
*by following the example and path set by Christ,*
*we arrive at the Father,*
*to share divine life with the Trinity.*
*An incredible gift: invitation to divine life.*
*An incredible gift: invitation to Christ's divine presence*

*right here and now in the Eucharist.*
*Jesus Christ is the bridge*
*between God the Father and man*
*through the Holy Spirit.*
*We follow across the bridge*
*by imitation of Jesus Christ—that is it.*
*It is that simple.*
*Jesus Christ made, then showed us the way*
*via his life, death, and resurrection.*

Later:

*God does not have gender.*
*God embodies male, female, and more.*
*God implicitly defies description in a word or many.*
*Words are only figurative to help us*
*understand limited facets of God*
*from our small frame of reference.*
*God the Father—*
*all nurturing, powerful, parent, Creator.*
*God the Son—*
*divine and human, our brother,*
*born of a woman, each without original sin.*
*God the Holy Spirit—*
*giver of Truth,*
*each human life*
*Temple of the Holy Spirit.*

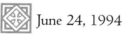 June 24, 1994

*Original sin*
*is a sin of pride;*
*it is honoring false gods—*
*the false god of ourselves.*
*The temptation is becoming like God.*
*It is a lack of humility,*
*and lack of acknowledging God for who he is*
*in all his glory and awe.*
*It is a lack of acknowledging*
*our place as defined by*
*and totally dependent on God.*

August 1, 1994

In prayer at home before the crucifix, on a day when I felt moderately uncomfortable, I heard:

**Your body is the cross**
**to which you are nailed.**

I experienced peace and awe as if one fragment of suffering's mystery had been laid open before me. I felt so closely bonded with Christ in his passion—united, identified in this compelling image of my own body, which ached like fire as if it were the cross to which my spirit was nailed.

I thought back on that beautiful, illuminated, white spirit I had once glimpsed emerge from my body and strain its arms toward God's light, yearning to return home. Had this spirit willingly been nailed to the cross of my body as Christ willingly accepted his humanity and physical death? As far as my conscious mind was concerned, I was a captive audience, but was this spirit, its nature a mystery unto myself, a more willing participant?

My body was undeniably a ceaseless reminder, its fibers aching or shouting some other discomfort, a body intrusively calling itself into my near constant awareness. It was easy to identify with the graphic image:

**Your body is the cross to which you are nailed.**

In this bonding with Christ in his passion, I imagined myself able to relieve some minute portion of his suffering in uniting mine with his, in his act of redemption. The most odd and incredible thing occurred; in so sharing my own suffering, it became less. My pain was the same but it was as if someone had lifted the weight of my suffering. I had experienced this to a lesser degree before, this dichotomy between suffering and pain, but never with the clarity and degree of that moment. I can only compare it to the pain of childbirth, its perception altered, almost sweet in the life it is bringing forth.

Illness, acute or chronic, invariably robs us of some degree of independence. This is magnified when limitations become life-long challenges or inconveniences as they are for the chronically or congenitally affected.

In accepting this identification with Christ, my suffering united with his, I was given the opportunity to take an active role in my discomfort. I could choose my attitude: to be a victim or to unite my suffering positively with that of Christ, who brought meaning and purpose to all the world's pain. My own pain became more bearable. My suffering was diminished. It was shared. I was not alone. There was meaning and purpose to what had seemed senseless. I regained a sense of independence and dignity.

We cannot always choose our circumstances or their outcomes, but free will always allows us to choose the attitude of our response. It was invigorating to feel such a sense of autonomy again.

Late August, 1994
During evening prayer:
"I know when I tell you I am afraid, you answer 'I have too little faith.' I am sorry. I know I have too little faith. Please increase my faith. Thy will be done." I petitioned with genuine reluctance and trepidation. Apologetically I asked, "Could it be done gently and painlessly? I am sorry I have so little faith; I am afraid."
**I will protect you, my child.**

Fall, 1994
During night prayer before sleep:
**Do not be afraid to die.**
**Do not be afraid to live.**
Explained:

*In not being afraid to die,*
*knowing physical death was only*
*the beginning of everlasting life,*
*we live life to its fullest in reflecting God's love,*
*unimpeded by fears which otherwise hold us back.*
*It is in not being afraid to die*
*that we are no longer afraid to live and are freed.*
*Do not let fears keep you*
*from accomplishing the important work*
*you are placed here to do for God.*

Early September, 1994
I recalled the trepidation with which I had prayed "Thy will be done" and had so tentatively asked that my faith be increased as I fell into what would be a major and lengthy exacerbation of illness. Again personal freedom and independence gradually slipped away from one day to the next: going out of doors, getting around the house, getting out of bed. So confined, I felt as if I were under house arrest.

In many ways the worst of it was seeing my children's anguish and tears. Their fears surfaced as they saw my more obvious debilitation and greater limitations. Their underlying apprehension that I would not be able to take care of them—or worse yet die—darkened their eyes. To see those we love in pain is harder than bearing our own pain. Again I found myself helpless to fully quell their concerns. Was this relapse the answer to my prayer to help me do God's will?

 September 21, 1994

> And to keep me from being too elated by the abundance of revelations, a thorn was given me in the flesh, a messenger of Satan, to harass me, to keep me from being too elated. Three times I besought the Lord about this, that it should leave me; but he said to me, "My grace is sufficient for you, for my power is made perfect in weakness." I will all the more gladly boast of my weaknesses, that the power of Christ may rest upon me. For the sake of Christ, then, I am content with weaknesses, insults, hardships, persecutions, and calamities; for when I am weak, then I am strong.
>
> 2 Corinthians 12:7-10, RSV

I had not known Satan's two best disguises: beguiling attraction or, even more disarming, the lack of belief in his very existence beyond "cute" Halloween caricature, making it all the easier to present the captivating package. There are some people, attractively disguised in every conceivable manner, whose paths we cross, and then hopefully exit when we see their dark destructiveness. Often we do not realize the depth of their darkness nor their true nature: souls consumed in evil, people of darkness, the black-hearted. They cross every walk of life, including the most privileged and intelligent of society and may appear as successful, even trusted figures to be admired. Their best guise is such exemplary outward appearance, that no one would believe the evil beneath its surface. Feigned humility may cover arrogant contempt, veiling a self-perceived birthright: to live above the bounds and rules of civilized society, entitled to do so by innate superiority—a breed apart from mere mortals.

These individuals—people of darkness, the black-hearted—are not merely lost in sin, the product of mortal selfishness or greed. They are indeed a breed apart, walking in tandem with Satan's angel, their guide and "light" of darkness. In arrogance they remain unaware that they walk not as superiors or equals, but as those enslaved by Satan and reduced in their humanity. Satan did not need to possess souls so freely sold in exchange for relieving them their burden of conscience—vanished with it their capacity for empathy and remorse.

My own encounter with such a person of darkness, despite removing myself from his path, had become a steady unveiling of evil's depths on a personal scale, its aftermath rippling into my future.* I could label his behavior in sterile psychological jargon, but I did not comprehend its origin. On the date of this journal entry, I had yet to recognize that what fueled and ensnared this person was evil, though I knew he was the enemy of my soul.

So it came to be that a person of darkness, Satan's disciple, placed a thorn in my heart—a constant life-long reminder of evil's presence, its destructiveness and the suffering it exacts. I was smarting at the aftereffects. I disliked the way it made me feel. I wanted to find peace; I wanted to be free of this torment. I recalled: "Love your enemies, and pray for those who persecute you."

This had ever deepening meaning for me in recent years. Prior to my first mystical experience, I heard this one Sunday in the Gospel, at a time when I was in great need of refuge and guidance from the suffering that this person of darkness had brought into my life. I repeatedly searched the words, but like an unsolvable riddle I could not unlock their mystery. The only "prayer" in my heart was wishing that fate offered him a short life span; that I should be left free and in peace. I had come a long way since then because now, and for some time, I could genuinely, but not perfectly, pray for this person.

Today, however, an old wound had reopened; I needed support. I prayed and asked God's assistance in perfecting the meaning of his command: "Love your enemies and pray for those who persecute you." I asked God to help me eliminate negative or self-serving thoughts from my prayer for this person. I began to feel more peace and the "Our Father" came to my thoughts. I was inspired to say it, but in a way I had never said it before, the novelty of which surprised me. I prayed the "Our Father" not for him, but as if in his place, for what he could not presently do for himself.

* Author's note: The person of whom I speak was well in excess of twice my age when first I met him. Though he died before this journal's publication, his identity is left deliberately vague in keeping with the book's message of healing and forgiveness. To this end the date of his death is not given, and the chronology is further altered to leave him obscure. The particulars of who he was and what he did are not important to this chronicle; what is important is how each of us responds to such encounters in our own lives.

Our Father, who art in heaven,
hallowed be thy name;
thy kingdom come;
thy will be done on Earth as it is in heaven.
Give us this day our daily bread;
and forgive us our trespasses
as we forgive those who trespass against us;
and lead us not into temptation,
but deliver us from evil.

Amen

Praying in this light gave fresh perspective and meaning to its phrases. I further prayed, "Help me forgive as I would like to be forgiven. Help me empty myself and do your will. I do not know what to ask for in a specific outcome. Please just help me do and accept your will." The tumult of my thoughts was abruptly interrupted:

**My justice will prevail.**
**You are free, my child.**
**I have set you free.**

The first line consoled me; but the rest left me bewildered. It seemed a non-sequitur. I wondered, "What does that have to do with this?" Later in the day I could see many levels of meaning. The most obvious was having been set free of this individual's toll, through Christ; but the ultimate meaning of being freed was from death and earthly trappings. I reflected upon God's allowing evil to exist, drawing good from it rather than destroying it outright, but I came to no greater understanding of why.

September 22, 1994
I prayed, still seeking relief from yesterday's turmoil, asking God to please draw good from bad. I placed my trust in God that good would be brought of my own failings as well.

September 28, 1994

**...I will lead you, my child.**
**I will focus you where you need to be.**
**I love you, my child...**
**I will direct you/your path.**
**Let my light shine from your eyes.**
**Serve others.**

Fall, 1994

In quiet prayer, eyes closed, I was thinking about how man can love a being so far superior to himself. What can man offer God, who is already perfection, whole unto himself, and in need of nothing?

> *To show love to God;*
> *love those on our plane—man.*
> *They can feel and appreciate*
> *the love we offer and in so doing*
> *we glorify God,*
> *and make a pleasing offering to our Creator.*
> *That is how we love God*
> *by giving and demonstrating our love*
> *to another human—acting as a mediator*
> *on our plane, our own level,*
> *to receive, accept and feel our love.*

I was taken swiftly from these thoughts hearing:

**Tell the world—**

Startled at this entreaty; I interrupted my prayerful state, opened my eyes, shook my head and said aloud, "Oh no—I think you have the wrong person!" I stood up and began to pace about the room, wishing further to shake away the words. I was alarmed at the prospect of telling others, beyond my family, that I had heard Christ speak to me. I continued aloud, "No one will believe me. They will say I am a nut, on the fringe, a fanatic; it is due to my illness, medication; it is in my imagination; it is fabricated of need." I further shrank back at the very grandiosity of the idea, and questioned the origin of the words I had heard. Certain I had broken the state of receptive silence, I felt it safe to sit and close my eyes but to my surprise immediately I heard:

**Tell the world**

I opened my eyes, again trying to interrupt but words continued.

**to love me**
**to love my creation,**
**my creatures,**
**to love their fellow man.**

I hurriedly got up and made myself very busy with deliberately distracting tasks about the house. I had never heard such a request and was apprehensive, despite the peace and beauty of the message.

October 4, 1994
After Mass and Communion:

I asked guidance in picturing the goal intended for me; so that I would do it in keeping with God's will and not my own interpretation of it.

> *All our qualities, strengths, weaknesses, failings, bents,*
> *interests, disposition, proclivities, and more,*
> *are all used towards God's will.*
> *The key was to always keep purpose, the entire meaning,*
> *focused on and guided by God's will.*
> *It is fine to strive for things,*
> *but only thoroughly, completely, grounded in,*
> *and existent for God's will,*
> *so too with use of talents*
> *and that gained through them such as*
> *power, influence, wealth, fame, and any material possession.*

 October 6, 1994

In prayerful calm I gave thanks, deeply appreciative of Christ's peace. I used to need to plan and steer the course of life. Now I began to see what foolhardy illusion my past "success" at this was, in the face of God's plan. I was grateful, at least for this moment, to be more comfortable waiting to see where life lead, accepting but not understanding the paradox of our free will and the overriding supremacy of God's will and plan. I wondered, "How can they exist simultaneously?" I was far from able to live this acceptance patiently each day.

 October 9, 1994
After Communion:

I saw the beautiful white light as I had not for some time after Communion. I rejoiced, ecstatic in its radiance and peace.

**Write, my child.**

For the first time and without thinking, I answered, "Yes, my Father."

**I am always with you.**

October 12, 1994

**Pare down your possessions...**

October 13, 1994

In the fatigue of illness and resentment at feeling under "house arrest" I found less joy in the day. Walking through mundane chores about our home, I was annoyed with their boredom and more exasperated at my limitations in carrying them out. I heard:

**Enjoy every day for what it is.**

My regard for what I was doing, the moment I was in, grew. The words left me peace and renewed sense of the sacred in the most ordinary work of daily living.

October 16, 1994

I awakened from an afternoon nap to hear my daughter softly crying. I opened my eyes to see her standing at my bedside. Before I could ask what was wrong she sobbed, "I am so scared!" her pupils large as saucers, and tears streaming down her cheeks.

"What's the matter?" I asked, trying to raise myself on one arm, reaching the other out to her. Instead I lurched, missing her, and fell back into the bed. Her eyes grew wider in alarm.

She said, "You look sick enough to die! I am so afraid you are going to die!" Now sobbing she collapsed next to me, curled-up and buried her face in my chest. I held my arms around her, as the room swirled nauseatingly around us both. I could not speak till vertigo subsided into dizziness, and then in the strongest, clearest voice I could muster said,

"It's OK, really; it looks worse than it is right now. It's understandable you would be upset. Don't worry. Jesus holds us safely in his arms." My heart broke at my helplessness in entirely quelling her fear, a mother's Achilles heel exposed—unable to fully protect her child. I felt her pain.

My daughter's anguish haunted me, the more intensely knowing what it meant to lose a parent. Later, once alone, tears welled in my eyes, sometimes spilling. I prayed in great fervor for my health and my children.

**...Your children will be fine if you let them know me.**

How to do this was explained as follows:

**WORDS—tell them about me.**

**ACTIONS—show my teachings to them
and bring them to life by your example.**

**EXPERIENCE—let them feel my love.**

**Let my light shine through your eyes—
in kindness, forgiveness, patience, love, compassion,**

*to allow them to experience God's love.*
**Let them experience your love**
**as you have experienced mine.**
I reflected upon this and was interrupted:
**Simplify your life.**
**Own less.**
Referring to my illness:
**This is how I am releasing your creative side.**
**I have set you free.**
**Now rest, my child, and sleep.**

"What did this mean?" I wondered. "Had my capacity to practice medicine been taken from me and in the same stroke released creativity?" It was not until some time later that I learned what "releasing your creative side" meant, and it had nothing to do with writing or anything I then considered creative.

 October 17, 1994
Referring to writing:
**Emphasize my teachings. I love you, my child...**
"Please help me, Jesus."
**I will help you, I will guide you.**
"How much should I include of my life?"
**Very little.**

I had been considering a pen name to conceal my identity for privacy—a compromise between my wishes not to share my spiritual experience beyond my family, and what I had been asked to do. "Which name should I use?" I asked, hoping for a way out.
**Your own name.**

More than disappointed, I was embarrassed to have my cowardice unmasked, not wanting to acknowledge the words of my experience in my name. The image of Peter denying Christ came to mind. I had just done the same. "I am very sorry."
**I am with you, my child...**
**You must communicate my words to others.**
"Let me be worthy."
**I will heal you, my child.**
"I am afraid."
**Do not be afraid, I will protect you, my child.**

"Help me keep listening."

Don't worry, you will listen.
Go home and write...Get to my words...
Tell the world to love me.
Tell them to keep my commandments
that they might not perish.
Tell them to love one another,
love their fellow man.
Every thing, every day in life is sacramental;
*Jesus Christ is here within us.*

Tell my Church to love me.

Abortion is wrong.
It is killing another...
They (aborted children) are with me.
Those who have had abortions
should ask forgiveness and pray.
Your society is in a decline,
you (mankind) must stop it.
It is not too late to repent.
Repent, my children, and come back to me.
I love you.
You are my sheep and I am the shepherd.
I know mine and mine know me.
Help one another.
There are many religions in the world;
they all come to me...
I am the only one to come to.
Listen, my child. Listen to me.

It seemed impossible that I should hear these words; yet I was surrounded by the deep peace of Christ's presence. Suddenly, self-doubt cast itself about me like a shroud. I did not want to invent such an experience of my need. Once more, worry was replaced by Christ's peace.

Have faith. Trust.
Open your eyes; be up and about your business.
I am with you. Tell no one (yet). Just write.

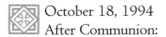 October 18, 1994
After Communion:

**I am coming.**

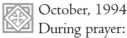 October, 1994
During prayer:

**I am with you, my child. Do not be afraid.**

**...Be up and about your business...**

I did not go but remained, mulling over my concerns of the moment, trying to resolve them.

**...Why do you struggle and rail against me?**

**I am trying to help you.**

I could not hide my thoughts, "My trust, and faith are insufficient." I hesitated. After a long considered pause, I warily asked, "Please increase my faith and trust."

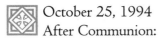 October 25, 1994
After Communion:

**I am always with you...**

Regarding the normal ups and downs of daily living:

**Be patient, all in due time.**

**All will be well.**

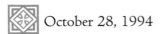 October 28, 1994

This journal entry
is dedicated in loving memory of
Christopher
a beloved young friend
August 1, 1979—October 24, 1994

Returning to my seat after receiving Communion at Christopher's funeral Mass I struggled to fight back another deluge of tears. I knew I could not even begin to imagine his family's sorrow and thought surely their hearts must be breaking.

**Be still, my child. I will console you.**

"Where is Christopher?" I asked in my thoughts.

Christ replied,

Christopher is with me; I have taken him home.
He is happier than you can imagine.
You will all be united one day.
Console his family.

I was made to understand without words that Christ was there with Christopher's family as well.

Later on my train ride home my thoughts were occupied by Christopher and his family. How could this happen? How can any sense be made of the profound agony of grief in losing a child—a healthy, happy, loved child swiftly taken, gone without warning. What consolation is there in a loss so tragic and enormous? How could it happen to this family or any family? They had already suffered hardships, tragedy, and temporary separation. Such a good and loving family, such a good and loving child, and source of such joy—how could there be any sense to this anguish?

My own thoughts were interrupted, upon hearing Christ speak within me:

This is my will, that Christopher be with me now.
Write, my child.

"I am afraid. It is hard to listen."

You will listen, my child.

Regarding the book:

Tell of your mystical experiences.

I doubted the authenticity of these words; that I should be asked this.

Tell of your mystical experiences.

Again I was filled with a lack of trust in what I heard. The words were overshadowed, as I cringed imagining the reaction of others to such an admission. It was not just negative attention and its aftermath which I did not welcome; I did not want any attention. My anxiety vanished as Christ's peace was upon me.

It is (all right); I will guide you. Tell little of yourself.

"How? How can I do that in such a personal story?"

I will show you.

I closed my eyes; the magnificent, boundless, white, centered light was present, replacing awareness of all else.

I am with you, my child.
Place your hope and faith, confidence, trust, in me.
Write as I tell you.
Tell the world to love me.

It is not too late.

I love you.

Listen to my word.

My own thoughts drifted and raced at what I had heard, but were abruptly interrupted:

I am your servant.

I questioned myself, uncomfortable at what seemed sacrilegious, "This can't be right, Christ is not my servant." In the next sentence it was clear.

I am to bring you to the Lord, our Father.

Comfort the world in knowing I am here.

Listen, my child, listen to me.

Record my words.

Do not be afraid.

I am with you, my child.

Do not be afraid.

Turn to me.

Tell the world to turn to me.

Referring to the book:

Focus on my teachings, my relationship with you,

that I am waiting for others to turn to me, as did you.

There is more to come,

more than I can describe to you,

more than you could ever imagine/conceive.

A life of pure happiness awaits you.

Follow my commands, my lead; follow me.

You are good.

What I have created is good.

My works are good.

Follow me.

"I am tired." I said, immediately disappointed at my response.

You are weary, but not for long.

I will give you strength and courage to persevere.

I am your strength, your life's force.

I am with you always. Do not be afraid.


"Please speak to me about Christopher and his family, though I am apprehensive at your response."

...All will be well.

Have faith, trust.
In time all will be well.
They are a strong family and I am watching over them.
They will be together with Christopher again one day...
Write, my child.
Be present in your life.
Focus on the moment.
Be present to your family and those around you.
He (Christopher) did nothing wrong.
His family did nothing wrong.
It was his time to come to me.
My will is done.
He is very happy.
He wants you to comfort his family with this knowledge.
He is happy because he also knows
he will be with them again one day.
Time is different here.
All things exist at the same time.
There is no death, just pure life,
happiness, peace, love—love among all.
Your father is here.
He misses you but knows
one day you will be together as well.
He wants you to let your mother know
how sorry he is that she had such a difficult life in his absence.
He wants her to know that her cup is the more full as a consequence.

This was the first mention of my father, and I became so eager to hear, with such desire to know more, that I stood in the way of listening. There was silence. "Please let me continue to hear you."

...Your father wants your mother to know
he is well pleased with how she has raised you and your sisters.
He is waiting for her...
Do not be afraid...
Your father loves you, and he watches over you.
He will be there when you pass over...
Your grandmother...She will join me.
Many wait for her and will rejoice to be with her

as will you when you are all together again.
She has been good to many people in her life
and they wait here for her.
Be good to many people in your life.
I have given you many gifts
and you have a great responsibility to give back.
Multiply them for my good, glorification.
Console (Christopher's family).
Be there for them...I will guide you, your hand...

Referring to what to include in writing:
Conversations with me, my teachings, mystical experience.
Eliminate personal details;
emphasis on God, Christ, the Holy Spirit...
Your details are not important.
They have just brought you from here to there.

Relate (the experience of God's presence and the words) to every man;
make (them) universal...
Do not worry.
I will guide and protect you.
Some will deride you; that is to be expected.
Do not be concerned. I will help you.
Those who need to will listen.
Not all can be saved, only those who choose to.
No one will be turned away.
Your free will is my gift to each of you.
It is yours forever;
however, a final day of judgment will arrive after which
I will no longer continue to forgive and save;
then my justice will prevail
and everyone's choice will be made permanent.
Those who loved the darkness will live in the darkness,
and have enough knowledge of the light
to realize what they are missing.
It will be an eternity of regret and suffering;
all with the knowledge that it was at their own hand.
I look after all, the less capable, incompetent to decide;

they are my children—they will not be punished for their inability.
The fires of hell will be the hottest for those who knew
and did as they pleased anyway.
Fires of hell, the greatest suffering—there is no fire;
it is a way of explaining
something you cannot understand or imagine.
It (hell) is eternal perpetual suffering.
All souls live forever as my Father/our Father
has commanded us to eternal life;
and each must choose between a life of happiness
in accordance with our Father's will
or a life devoted to darkness, turned away from our Father.
Regarding the origin and source of evil:
The devil has entered man, impregnated him, my creation.
Man's own free will, the choice possible,
is the other source of evil created.
The angels are powerful, with great wisdom
and they too have the gift of free will.
In their great power and wisdom
they (those angels who used their free will
to turn away from God) have polluted my creation—
man and this earth.
As they have so many greater gifts
their retribution on the final day will be greater.
I am/(my Father is) Lord of all
and we will bring good from evil.
We are here for all souls,
but do not take away their free will.
It is their responsibility to choose.
All manner of help will be given in this choice.
I love you.
Love my creation.
Love your fellow man.
Tell the world the same.

Returning home, I discarded failed efforts at autobiography. I had
no idea of their replacement to draw my notes into a cohesive whole.

October 30, 1994

My mother inquired, "How is your book going?"

Uneasy upon hearing "your" I was compelled to say, "It isn't really my book." There was silence, at what probably seemed an odd response to a simple question. I continued, "I mean, it doesn't feel like my book. I am only writing down what I hear, but it's not mine."

"Well how is it going?" my mother again asked.

"I don't exactly know." I replied.

"Well how far are you?" she asked.

"I don't know." I answered, not intending to trigger the exasperation I was aware my disorganization prompted as it so often tried my family's patience.

Her voice escalated in volume, "How can you not know? Don't you have a plan or some kind of an outline?"

"No, I used to have an outline but not any more. I thought I was pretty far along until just recently; but it turns out I was doing it all wrong, and I threw out almost everything. It was really pretty bad anyway."

In continued crescendo she asked, "Well, if you don't know even how far you are, and you have no outline, how will you know when you are finished?"

"I don't know that either. I am hoping it will be obvious."

My mother could see I had not intended to be deliberately obtuse, and in softer tone commiserated, "It must be hard work."

"No, not when I am doing it right. Then it's easy. I just write what I hear. It's like taking dictation. Often times I don't know what I've been told until I read it myself." I continued, "The poems and sometimes prose are different. It is hard to explain. I don't exactly hear words but they spring from somewhere which doesn't seem to be me. I can't initiate that either."

I left my deepest doubts about the book silent: cognitive limitations made the prospect of a completed book not just improbable but ludicrous. I wondered if I clung to the idea of a book as a life raft, pretending to myself to be potentially productive in place of my inability to work. How deeply intertwined self image was with the dignity of work. How I missed practicing medicine, every visit to a doctor's office a sad reminder! I did not recognize my lack of trust in God's providence. Shifting the subject from these uncomfortable thoughts, I shared more of my spiritual experiences with my mother.

Later:

**I am the way—**
**the way of true life.**

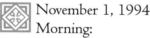 October 31, 1994

In the solitude of quiet prayer, amidst a crowded train, I experienced Christ's presence more closely than I thought possible. It was profound, brief, and my only experience exceeding the feeling of closeness in the bond of mother and child.

I was startled by the immediacy of Christ's presence, a distinct other being and intellect, the intense wordless communication of hearts and the strength of my desire for union of will. The more amazing to me was simultaneous full awareness of the crowded train around me, filled with other souls whom Christ was equally present within.

Later:

Referring to speaking about my spiritual experiences in yesterday's conversation:

**Talk less. I am not angry with you. You should talk less.**
**It dilutes your energy for your book (work, writing).**
**Speak to me every day, like this—with paper and pen in hand.**
**I want to communicate with you. I love you.**
**I will protect you, guide you, and encourage you...**

November 1, 1994

Morning:

**My presence will always be with you**
**but may take different forms.**

I understood this to mean the absence of hearing locutions, for example.

Regarding the reason, at present, to discuss my spiritual life less:

*The desire to tell others of Christ's presence*
*and my awe at the mystical in my own life*
*would be partially depleted in the telling,*
*and would leave that much less life to pour into writing.*
*It would decrease my energy to express these words on paper.*

In the afternoon, on the train:

**I love you, my child. Be still.**

I am pleased with you, my child.

I love you.

"I love you. Please guide me and protect me."

Yes, I will, my child. I will guide and protect you.

Your writing—

Mysticism—define it.

Give an overview—brief.

Put it in perspective.

Relate it to every man.

It (mysticism) is the province of every man.

Every man must come to me;

come to me alone.

I will protect them.

In your soul's innermost depths

every man must meet me

whether they believe in me/my name or not.

I am kind and gentle to all.

All manner of help is available to every soul.

"Guide me, Jesus."

I will guide you.

"Teach me how to pray, how to tell others."

Begin with silence.

Remember your humble beginnings.

You are nothing without me,

without my life within you.

Realize your helplessness—your helplessness without me.

There is no room for arrogance/contempt.

We are all each other's servants.

We must love one another.

Read the scriptures.

Go to Mass and receive Communion often.

Keep an open mind.

Be receptive.

Pray for faith—the gift of faith.

Our Father will hear you.

No one will be turned away...

Time is running out, but it is not too late—

not too late for the world to turn toward me.

Mary has made many appearances around the world,
trying to turn people towards me.
She loves you and watches over you.
People must believe without great signs.
That is what faith is—
believing when it, the proof, cannot be seen.
I will guide you in my own way.
The ways of man are not my ways.
People must trust; they must trust in me.
Great signs have already been performed—
myself taking human form,
and then rising from the dead—
redeeming all and offering you a share in divine eternal life.
I have no greater sign to perform for you.
Look at what has already been performed.
Read the Bible.
Attend Mass;
do this in memory of me.
Open your eyes
and see what I have already given you.
Accept my offering—gift to you.
Have faith.
Trust.
*Risk believing.*
"I don't feel well." I said, through extreme fatigue.
I will comfort you, my child—
*all my children...*
Look at the gifts I have given you...
Appreciate them.
Look at the magnificence of my universe.
Look at its expanse.
Look at how insignificant you are in size.
Now look at how important I have made you.
I have raised you up—
raised you up to share in divine life—
you, myself, and the Father
through the power of the Holy Spirit.
Realize, appreciate, understand

the value I have placed (imbued) upon your life.
You are all unique.
You are all special.
You are all my servants and I am yours.
Love one another.
Do as I have commanded you.
Love one another, as I have loved you,
and love me above all things/(else).
Believe in me
and you shall have eternal life.
Follow my teachings, commandments,
and your share in the fulfillment
of our Father's plan will be greatest;
your share in eternal life will be the greater.
Do as I command you:
love one another.
Do not be selfish.
Do not destroy or disrespect life.
I am life.
I am the word.
I am all things.
I am the way and the life/(light).
Be with me.
Come join me.
Look at what I have given you.
Appreciate it.
I have left you the Mass, the Eucharist.
Do this in memory of me.
Grace is received in the Sacraments,
when they are received with open heart and sincerity,
intentions pure.


This is the final era
before my Day of Judgment...


The Communion of Saints—
we are all of us forever linked
through time and space.

Come to me.
Listen to my word.
I am the truth, the light and the way.
I am your bridge to eternal, everlasting life.
Come to me, my children.
It is not too late.
I love you all.
Listen, please listen.
You must turn to me.
You have the gift of free will,
and you must choose.
I...will not force you.
You must come voluntarily.
...my Father's/my will prevails
with or without your cooperation;
my Father's plan will be fulfilled.
I am gentle and humble of heart.
My love for you is greater than you can imagine.
Return to church.
Pray.
Listen in the silence.
Find the silence within you, and listen.
I am there.
I am within each of you, just listen.
Listen with your ears, eyes, hands,
listen in every aspect of your life;
I am there.
When you are working, playing, sleeping,
I am there.
Come to me.
Do not be afraid.
I am gentle and kind.
I will protect you all.
Turn to me.
Realize your helplessness, insignificance, and I am/will be there.
It will then be easier for you to see/appreciate me,
once the cobwebs of the world (trappings, baubles)
are removed from your eyes.

The world's trappings (power, wealth, fame)
are distractions aboard a boat doomed to sink to annihilation.
Place your trust in me.
I offer you everlasting life.
Nothing of the earth and its trappings are eternal/everlasting.
Receive Communion often.
Follow my commandments.
Keep my word.
Read the scriptures.
Seek the quiet,
and open your hearts to prayer.
Receive the Sacraments often:
Penance,
attend Mass often
*and receive Communion.*
Grace is received through the Sacraments.
Empty yourselves.
I have left you the Sacraments as sources of grace.
I love you my child...
I will not weary you.
I will make you strong.
Our Father will be pleased.
You are loving and I will make you more so.
I will make you pure of heart.
Your life is mine
and I live in you as you live in me.
I share in your suffering
as you share in mine,
and so too my glorification.
That is hard for you to understand—
to understand what that means.
They are only words to you;
it is beauty, joy, peace, grace, unity,
beyond your greatest imagining of fulfillment or joy.
You will be there, my child;
I will be with you.
I am with you now and always.

A group of teenagers boarded the train with booming music, brava-do, and outwardly menacing posture. They were similarly dressed, belying their deeper insecurity to belong and be accepted by the other members of their "crew."

**They are my children too. Look past the exterior.**

Later:
I asked for direction and guidance in writing. "What is the next step?"

**Be patient. All in due time.**

 November 2, 1994

**You are preoccupied with the work** (Christmas preparations) **now.**
**Take care of your family; but remember,**
**keep Christ in Christmas.**
**Remember the poor.**
**Remember the true meaning of Christmas...**

**Be patient.**
**Be where you are today.**
**Enjoy the moment.**
**It is where you belong at the moment.**
**Live one day at a time...**
**I will help you...**
**Do not let life out of control.**
**Simplify it. Own less.**
**Teach (your children) the same.**
**Give to the poor. Do not hoard excess...**
**Let me take care of you.**
**Do not worry.**
**Leave your anxieties/concerns to me.**
**I am always at your side.**
**Rely on me.**
**Close your eyes, put your pen down and rest.**
**I do not ask more than you can do.**

Later:

*Learning to forgive*
*is integral in learning to love.*

November 3, 1994

*To help those who have suffered:*
*when praying with them*
*acknowledge they have suffered,*
*but that in God's plan*
*some good or strength was to come of it*
*to prepare them for something.*
*They have had pain, they have suffered,*
*but there is a purpose*
*even though they do not see one now.*

 November 5, 1994

**I am with you.**
**I will protect you.**
**I will guide you.**
**You are mine and I am yours.**

"I don't feel well." I said, barely able to lift my head from the pillow, after a mid-day nap.

**I know, my child;**
**I will suffer with you...**

 November 7, 1994

**What makes a man is in his heart.**

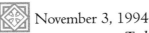 November 9, 1994
Late morning:

I was angry at being so lonely, limited, and isolated by illness. I thought, "This is like becoming an involuntary recluse under house arrest."

**Why do you interfere with my plan?**
**(Do you not know,) I know what is best what you need?**

"I am sorry, I haven't fully done as you've told me in my attitude."

**I am not angry.**
**I love you.**
**I want to teach you better how to love others and myself.**

"I am afraid," I thought as I wondered what more this might mean.

**Do not be afraid.**
**I am with you, my child.**
**I will not give you more than you can handle.**

Later you will be more ready
for my thoughts without limitation (of) words.
You must trust me more,
have more confidence in my presence,
in what you are hearing is real...

I am with you, my child.
I am all you need.
Lie down and sleep
rest your body and heal.
I love you.
I am with you...
Rest and sleep.
I will watch over you.

Mid-afternoon:

Why do I make you lonely?
To suffer.
This is all to draw you closer to me.
Do not question my works.
Trust in me.
Bear your crosses silently.
I am better there to help you.
You are mine (we are closer).

Regarding past anguish, long years ago:

I let you suffer then
to make you stronger now.
Live with happiness
live with joy.
Always marvel at my works,
(all that is and occurs.)

Regarding suffering silently:

*Excessive non-silent suffering*
*spreads suffering rather than confines it,*
*and alters (dissipates) the degree of participation with Christ*
*in the redeeming value of suffering.*

*Excessive exterior airing of suffering*
*makes others suffer*
*and does not resolve the problem.*
*It is also a missed opportunity*
*to share more fully the suffering with Christ,*
*to experience Christ more intimately*
*and otherwise miss his wisdom and consolation*
*which has truer, greater and more lasting value*
*than sharing it with others.*

Later:

*Patience is key*
*in seeing God's will unfold for us.*

Late afternoon:

Abrupt, striking hearing loss, of a magnitude and duration greater than any previous fluctuation, left me extremely anxious, wondering if, when, and how much would return this time. It was so marked that I could not conceal it from my family. It was more difficult to watch their distress. Amidst this I heard:

**I will carry this cross for you, my child.**
**Give it all to me—**
**your worries and concerns.**
**Trust in me.**
**I will carry this for you.**
**Be there for the others in your life, your children...**
**I will guide and protect you. I will watch over you.**
**Be up and about your business.**

 November 15, 1994

**...I love you, my child**
**I am always with you...**
I felt great compassion in my physical discomfort.
**Your pain at the present time is for a reason.**
**I am with you...**
**Write today...I will help you.**
**Your story/book will comfort many:**
**those with illness...those bereaved.**

Your pain and suffering is with a purpose.
You will lead others to me in your writing
and I will comfort them.
You are my willing vessel...
Your life is mine and mine is yours.
I live in you and you live in me.
We share our suffering and our joy
and later you will share in my glorification.
It is more beautiful and radiant than you can imagine.
Much awaits you, my child, much to look forward to.
Lead others toward me.
Your example leads others as well.
I love you...

 November 16, 1994
You are in a sea of darkness now,
but I will raise you to eternal life.
There is more to come,
more than you can imagine,
more beauty,
more joy,
more love,
love among all...
Your life is mine and I am yours.
I live in you and you live in me.
All is unfolding as my/our Father's plan...
Be worthy.
Give back.
Serve others with your special gifts
(as we each have unique special gifts, talents.)
Let me carry your crosses,
lift your burdens
and you be there for the others in your life...
I love you, my child.
You are mine.
I am kind and gentle, meek of heart.
I am your servant,
your servant to take you to our Lord, our Father.

You will be with me there and always.
Mary watches over you and your family.
She guides and protects you.
She is pleased that you have come to know and love her
and she wants you to make her presence known to others.
Your prayers are heartfelt.
They are good...All will be well...

 November 17, 1994
Regarding the person of darkness:
...He is evil...
I was uncomfortable at the bluntness and gravity of this description,
immediately doubting my listening; but it became clear. I asked, "Is there
any hope for him and his soul?"
I try to reach out to him and will try throughout his life.
(He needs your prayers very badly.)
Evil hates the light.
It prefers the darkness...
He is evil.
Evil brings/begets more evil...
Pray for him.
Offer forgiveness.
He cannot harm you if you do this.
Your prayers are very powerful.
I am always listening, as is our Father.
The Holy Spirit is with you always.
His seal was set upon you long before Earth.
"And what about, this person of darkness, and the seal of the Holy Spirit?"
That is a complicated subject, which you will not yet understand.
One day you will know.
I love you, my child.
I am with you always.
Now rest your body and heal.
I am here watching over you and your loved ones,
guarding you in your sleep with my angels about me
(and your guardian angel.)
You are in a sea of darkness and unable to see us,
but we are here closer than you can imagine, all-pervasive.

I recalled a conversation I had many years before with a friend from school. He was gentle, kind, and deeply spiritual. He phoned me one day, which was a surprise of itself since our lives had drifted apart and we had lost touch for many years. Even more surprising was his reason for calling me.

"Cathy, the reason I am calling is I know something very bad is happening in your life. I want to know if you are OK. Is there anything I can do to help?"

I sank into the couch, disarmed and unable to exit with a "How are you? Fine, thanks and you?" formula.

"How did you know?" I asked and before I knew it confided the events which were transpiring. It was my first personal experience of truly evil action by another person, and the destruction and suffering such an individual can create. I had no idea then, of its depth, nor of what was yet to unfold.

I realize in retrospect that my friend had a much truer grasp of such situations than I did. He spoke to me of a purpose in all things and that God drew good from bad. I politely listened, unmoved at what he was trying to tell me. He attempted to comfort me further saying, "Maybe if it weren't for someone like yourself touching such a life with love their soul would end up in hell."

I remained silently polite in deference to my friend's sincerity, and thought to myself, "What is he talking about? That's irrelevant. It doesn't follow. Are we in the same conversation...the same world? What is this pious talk?" It was not until after hanging up the phone that I realized how annoyed I was at his comments. I thought to myself, "What kind of a remark is that! How insensitive! It is I who have been hurt, and here my friend is concerned about the eternal fate of this person who has injured me. How could he further suggest I find consolation in potentially having helped this soul avoid hell, if there even is such a place!" His statement irritated me so much, I could not forget it.

I recalled that conversation today, newly appreciative of my friend's wisdom. I now saw an even greater dimension. It was not just about the eternal fate of such people, it was also our own—bound by the following: "Forgive us our trespasses as we forgive those who trespass against us."

**Yes, my child, you have remembered wisely.**
**He** (my friend) **is right,**

but the battle is not over yet.
He (the person of darkness) can take others with him as well...

November 18, 1994
*The book was to be a consolation,*
*comfort to the ill and bereaved, the lost, those living with uncertainty.*
*It was pain, experienced in my life, brought to a purpose,*
*brought to bear fruit.*

Your children will be fine if you let them know me.
Let them know me through you,
through your relationship with them,
through your heart,
through the emotions which course through your lives.
By example as a parent:
loving, giving, generous.
As a parent show them love, forgiveness, patience, kindness,
your humanity—that you are not perfect
and make mistakes.
Let them experience these things
so that they will more readily
be able to come to me—be open to me.
Be there for them.

November 19, 1994
A prime time television show sensationalizing prophesies of apoca-
lyptic destruction given in various cultures and religions, including the
Bible, and throughout the ages aired. It played on men's fears, devoid of any
balancing measure of hope. The show's message was incomplete, edited for
sensationalism. Regarding this I heard:
There are many people who go and speak as if in my name.
They are wrong.
(Remember the warning...speaking of false Christs.)
I do not take man's hope.
I do not speak in tongues of fear.
I am gentle and mild to all my creatures.
I love man and my creation.
It is not too late to turn to me.

The devil operates out of fear
(that is) by controlling through fear.
I operate out of love.
I have released you from the fear of death.
I have given you eternal life.
Believe in me.
The devil has no more hold over you.
You are no longer his slave,
but you must choose—
choose between the light and the darkness.
I would not frighten my creatures
with world events to come and give them no hope,
show them no path to my salvation...
Trying times are ahead and people must turn to me,
place their faith, trust, and hope in me.
I am the way, the path, the light;
I am eternal life.
When people are given a gift, *supernatural or the like*,
how they use it reflects from whence it came.
The gifts I give are only used in love.
Foretelling a future event,
gaining confidence with the devil,
gains a hold/confidence in some lives
and those who listen to this prophesy.
The devil is not in control of these future events.
They are not immutable.
But the devil knows man and his evil ways
and can accurately guess a likely outcome.
I see man's good ways
and know these outcomes are not inevitable
if man turns to me.
I create love.
The devil creates fear and
through it tries to dominate and control man.
I draw men to me through
love, kindness,
gentleness, hope,
and offer them a share in my eternal life.

The devil is able to make predictions
not because he controls man or these events
but because in his great knowledge
he knows the weakness of man
and further how to prey upon it.
Portraits of doom and gloom given of late
(are) not inevitable.

A visual illustration was given.

*There are two toddlers and one ice cream.*
*It is not hard to predict there will be a fight;*
*but if they shared, there would not be.*
*If they loved one another and cared for one another,*
*there would be peace and harmony, not strife.*


These are not easy times
and they will become more difficult;
but I am there,
always there to help you,
always there for man and my creation.
Man must choose.
If you are left only with fear,
it is not my message.
If you see fear, recognize its transcendence in me.
(meaning: *It does not exist or originate from God.*)
My warnings, admonitions are always balanced in hope
and finding your path to me.
There would be no purpose in showing men fear
without showing them their way to me.
When a parent disciplines/corrects a child
fear/warning (are) given out of love not cruelty,
to more closely direct the child's path
to what is right, and for the child's own good.
Your crosses are given to you
out of my love for you.
They will make you strong
as (you) grow and develop.
The devil preys upon man's fears and weaknesses.
Do not succumb.

Place your full faith and trust in me like children.
I am with you now and always.
I am with you for all time.
I will never desert my creation.
Tell the world to love me.
Console them that I am here.
It is not too late to turn to me.
I am here for all souls.
The choice is theirs...
The devil can make future predictions
not because he knows them
but has great knowledge of man's weakness
and how he is likely to react.
I draw man to me through love.
They come voluntarily.
The devil dominates through fear,
enslaving, subjugating man through his fear.
When you are afraid turn to me
and I will show you the light, the way.
Love and hope are always a part of my message.

 November 20, 1994
You are drawing/coming closer to me.
I have always been close to you (as in one)
and now you are drawing closer to me.

 November 28, 1994
...I am with you,
closer than you can imagine.
I love you.
I will hold you safely in my arms.
November 30, 1994
...I will protect you.
I am all the protection you need...

Pray for everyone who asks;
only pray God's will be done...

Late November, 1994

My sustained health set-back prompted my mother to ask, "If you hear Christ so often; why don't you ask to be made better or that God intervene?"

I responded, "I've already heard the answer." One night, last week, too uncomfortable to fall asleep; I tossed and turned, searching for a less painful position to allow my escape. Without thinking, I found myself looking up at the crucifix over the bed and asked, "Why, why am I sick? Why can't I be well?"

**I have partially removed you from the world.**

**You cannot fully function in it.**

**I have done this so you can attend to my work.**

**You have important work to do for me but first, sleep...**

**I love you, my child. I am with you always.**

**I will never leave you.**

**The form of my presence may change**

**but I will never leave you.**

"On another occasion I asked again for my health." I told my mother, and continued, "and what I heard was:"

**I am focusing you where you need to be.**

Throughout the Fall I continued in rebellion of sorts against being so contained by the limitations of illness. Angrily, I refused to accept it, which only added greater difficulty and unhappiness. On struggling against this fate I heard:

**Why are you interfering with my plan?**

In the peace and understanding that accompanied this, I more gracefully accepted being housebound and the "captive" opportunity it presented to write and consolidate my scattered notes, in the sporadically unpredictable hours when I was well enough and physically able to do so.

 December 1, 1994

**...He** (the person of darkness) **needs your prayers very badly.**

**That is all, my child; that is all it is best for you to know...**

**Pray for him once more (tonight)...**

**Bring my charity/presence to those around you in all forms.**

**I will bless you in plenitude and you will have the more to give...**

I am with you now and always...

You are with child.

My reaction was disbelief.

Yes, my child, you are with child.

It is my gift to you...

Do not be concerned. Mary is with you...

She is guiding, watching over you and protecting you...

I love you.

I am here closer than you think
guarding and watching over you.

Trust in me.

What I have said will come to pass. You will see.

You do not need great signs
because you have arrived at the gift of peace...

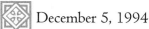

December 3, 1994

Referring to learning I was not physically with child:

This is an example of misunderstanding prophesy...

The other sense (of the meaning) is Advent—
the child Jesus born within.

Advent, gestation*—
become mother to existing children
the poor/suffering, needy in other ways,
children already here and in need of love.

Explained:

*We are all called upon in the season of Advent*
*to allow Christ to be born in our hearts;*
*naturally flowing from this is greater compassion for our fellow man.*

December 5, 1994

I am always with you.

I will never forsake you.

Trust in me.

Place your full trust in me.

---

* development in the womb from conception to birth.

You are my child.
I love you.
Let me work through you...
You are my servant and I am yours...

Do not be disquieted over what you now
do not understand or believe.
All will come to pass as I have said,
and then you will understand...

(I will sharpen/hone) your ability to love others.
I am the light,
the life of the world.
All must come to me
as the true source of life and goodness...
Continue emphasizing the spirit
and spiritual message of Advent with your children.
You are making progress.
You are giving them fabric for their lives...

Referring to the person of darkness:
Healing must occur...
You must continue to offer forgiveness and pray for him.
He has hurt you...very much...
Be strong.
Do not be thrown off your course by minor tempests;
I am always with you and your family,
watching over you, guiding you, protecting you...
Do not contact him (person of darkness); only pray...
He will find his way to me.
I am waiting for him...
Many people pray for you and love you.
Be good to many people in your life—
this spreads more good throughout my world...
My ways are not the ways of man.
Do not expect to understand everything
or that it should make sense.
Trust like a small child and believe.

Wherever I take you is where you will need to be.
Risk disappointment, *as with misunderstanding;*
'You are with child.'
Believe.
I have many lessons to teach you.
I want you to share them with the world.
"How is this to be done?"
Write. I will guide your hand and mind.
I am well pleased with you, my child.
You are trying hard to listen
and not impede my communication with you.
You will improve at this.
Do not be afraid.
I am always guarding/guiding,
watching over you and protecting you.
You are my child.
You are my sheep and I am the shepherd.
I know mine and mine know me.
Now be up and about your business...
...I love you.

 December 9, 1994
You are with child...
This is a very special child.
He is here to do my work.
He comes before me, as do his heirs.
All will be well,...
Referring to the person of darkness:
Continue to pray for him.
He needs your prayers very badly.
They have already had some effect...

I am with you.
Do not fear. Do not worry.
Let me carry your crosses for you
that you may be the more present to those around you...
I am with you.
I am the true source of life—love...

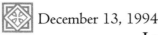 December 13, 1994

I am with you, my child.

Trust me, do not be afraid.

I am leading you where you need to be...I will guide you.

Bring my message of love, peace, forgiveness to all.

I will bless you plentifully.

I will guide your decisions.

"I want to do your will."

Yes, my child, I know.

I will help you.

"It's not always clear."

It will become obvious.

Patiently wait for my plan to unfold.

I love you.

Love my creation, in particular your fellow man.

Now up and be about your business.

I will help you.

I will give you strength.

You have my many blessings.

Do not worry.

Give your crosses and worries to me

and be present to those around you.

Let me work through you.

Reach others in the dark swirling seas around you,

those who cannot see me

or have dim awareness of my presence.

I love you.

Later, in evening prayer, I understood that in mistakenly entertaining the notion that I was physically with child, I relived the excited anticipation of expecting a child. I remembered the joy and incomparable sensation of a life stirring within. It was vivid reminder. How much greater the anticipation of actually allowing the Christ child to be born within us and grow. A life and being we never have to separate from the way a mother and child must—first in birth, and then in the daily mix of loss and growth as the child becomes more independent. In pregnancy the mother and child are never so close; its culmination is in a sense a loss, a separation, which is a new beginning. Christ born within us transcends this linking of loss and growth, which is the mark of all earthly life.

A baby does not start out running but crawling. Advent is a yearly reminder of God's understanding our weakness and need to grow slowly in Christ.

 December 15, 1994
**I have many children here no one/body wants...**
(Meaning: abused, neglected, poor children, among others.)

 January 1, 1995
After Mass and Communion:
**Be still, my child.**
**Your will struggles against mine.**
"I am having difficulty finding you, knowing your will for me in a decision which vexes me."
**By the end of the day it will be obvious.**
Events came together at day's end in which I was able to read an answer. Had I not been open to the answer's unfolding I would likely have missed its significance. I wondered what I had not seen and would continue to miss all the other days in not better "listening" and more patiently, receptively waiting for life to unfold.

 January 8, 1995
In prayer before the crucifix at home:
*Part of the change in becoming more receptive to God*
*was becoming childlike, having blind trust, dependence, openness.*
*Child-like trust makes it possible to accept*
*and find the wonder and awe in the mystery of God.*
*It allows one to accept the seeming paradox of impossibility*
*rather than meeting frustration and no faith.*

 January 10, 1995
*It is a delicate balancing act*
*between being of and in this world,*
*and yet sights set on the beyond.*
*Melding the two:*
*aspirations, interests, talents,*
*good and bad fortune, and more*
*are given for a reason—for use in God's overall plan.*

January 11, 1995

I have put you in the world for a reason.
Follow your inclinations.*
The world is not a bad place. I have created it.
Use your talents and gifts in line with your inclinations;
*in accordance with God's will,*
*as guided by Christ's word and example.*
They (inclinations) are not bad...Let me guide you.
Do not struggle or rail against me.
I know what is best for you...I love you.
I know you are trying.

 January 12, 1995

I was physically spent, worn thin by Fall's flare in illness, continuing unabated through midwinter. It was like a bad case of the flu that would not quit. Bemoaning this and tired of being "sick and tired," I again heard:

Remember, my child,
your body is the cross to which you are nailed.
You are in a sea of darkness, but I am always with you.
Do not be afraid. I will guide you and protect you...
Remain open to my direction.
I love you.

 January 13, 1995

*The devil works by preying on our fears.*
*In particular fears of death and through this*
*draws us into many of the ways and excesses*
*people use to escape thinking of mortality.*

January 14, 1995

*Mary is part of the passion of Christ,*
*her experience of it,*
*her suffering—*
*because her suffering was joined to his.*

---

* Any time this phrase was heard, here and elsewhere in the locutions, it was always understood that it meant within the context of Christ's teachings, example and commandments.

January 18, 1995
After viewing a televised Mass:

I am always with you.

Do not try so hard.

Let me write for you/through you.

"I am sorry I am not doing too well at writing; please help me."

Do not try so hard.

Let go.

Let me act through you.

I do not ask of you more than you can do.

I will help you.

I will always be there to guide you,

watch over you and protect you...

Do not be concerned.

Do not focus on an end goal.

Only focus on doing my will

from one minute to the next.

I will take care of the rest...

Simplify your life. Own less.

Focus on your family.

All will come to you and those you love.


You are all my priests—all in the order of Melchizedek.*

You are given power to love and forgive.

These are the energies you can create

and they remain forever.

"It's so hard to listen. I don't want to do this wrong. Please help me."

Do not be concerned.

What you need to know, you will have.

Relax with your children and enjoy them.

My guiding hand is there.

All things happen for a reason.

Let your health remind you of your dependence upon me.


---

*The first reading of the day's mass (Hebrews 7:1-3, 15-17) referred to an Old Testament figure: "Melchizedek, king of Salem and priest of God Most High" who foreshadowed the priesthood of Christ who is the eternal fulfillment of the priesthood of the Old Covenant.

Always turn to me.
Turn to me at every infinitesimal portion of the day
every low, every high...
"I am tired."
I will make you strong.
I will give you all the strength you need.
I am with you, my child.
I am always with you.
Now up and be about your business...

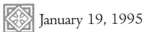 January 19, 1995

Sit, my child.
Sit with me awhile.
Do not make your life so difficult for yourself.
Do not try so hard. Let me guide you.
I am watching over you and protecting you...

Referring to a possession:
I have better things in mind for you.
These possessions are in your way.
Deaccession* your belongings.
They are in your way.
I will always provide for you and those you love...
Let go.
Let me do all.
"Jesus, please help me to listen and let go."
Continue to will it and it will be so.
I will help you. Do not worry.
Do not worry about your health.
I am here with you...

Do not abuse your body with food.
It is the Temple of the Holy Spirit.
Do not be afraid and drown your fear in eating.

---

*The meaning of this word was understood in simile. As a museum would deaccession or
sell its art work to buy new ones, detach from, sell, or view material things for their value in
glorifying God rather than self, selling earthly treasure for spiritual.

You have nothing to be afraid of;
I am here with you, at your side.
Bring my love to those around you.
Begin with your family.
Now up and be about your business.
Your entire life is a prayer.
Make it worthy because you love me.
I love you, my child.

 January 20, 1995

I am with you, my child...
Listen to me.
Keep my word.
Apply it to your life.
Let my light and happiness shine through your eyes
especially to your children and family.
Do not be so serious.
Be child-like in the sunshine of my love for you.
Let go. Let me live through you.
You are my hands and feet on earth;
yours are the only bodies I have on earth
to do my heavenly work through...
Do not worry.
Place your faith and trust in me.
Wait and see all will come to pass.
Do not try so hard.
Just let me...

Referring to writing:

Make your mind a blank at (your desk),
close your eyes and I will help you.
What was difficult will become easy.
Let me shine through your eyes every moment of the day
and you will find happiness.
Now up and be about your business.
Center yourself within and I will direct and guide
your thoughts and movement throughout the day.
I love you. Have faith. Trust.

January 23, 1995

The duration of illness's intensity, its fatigue, and disability had worn my reserves bare. "I am so sad and discouraged, Jesus. I know I do not tell you anything you do not already know."

Be still, my child; listen to me.

This is one of the crosses to which your spirit is nailed.

Allow it to have you turn to me.

Turn to me as the source of your joy,

and in so doing joy will shine forth through your being

and to everyone you touch.

"Give me the strength to do this."

My will is done,

as is yours

when it is in accordance with mine.

I give you what you need,

not what you want.

You will help many people in your life.

Be patient now...

Follow your natural inclinations...

They are not bad of themselves

as long as you allow me to guide their use...

First allow me to heal yourself...

All healing power originates with me,

you are merely a willing channel,

as am I,

with respect to the Father's will.

Humble yourself as did I.

Let me show you the real joy in life—

it is in giving to your fellow man, giving glory to God.

Give to your family immediately and personally.

Give to all mankind through your writing.

Do not show writing to others until I have indicated such.

I am your confidant; I am your companion;

you are in need of no other.

You are my bride and I am your groom.

I love you.

Always keep my word.

I am with you now and always.

More frequently turn to me throughout your day;
turn to me to share your feelings;
turn to me for guidance, strength.
I will guide you where you need to be.
You are making your life more difficult than need be.
Allow me to help you to carry your burden.
They are not all yours.
I ask no more of you than I give you strength to carry...
When becoming *anxious, frazzled*
(at being worn thin and overtaxed, by the frustrations of illness);
take a moment to become centered in me,
my peace, my love, my guidance,
the knowledge that I am guiding,
watching over you, and protecting you...
You are in a sea of darkness.
Let me guide you...
My will is done.
Do not worry.
Do not be concerned.
I am always with you...
Let me encourage you.
Let me be there with your writing and editing.
Let me work through you.
Your work will then be a truer reflection of me.
Beauty will then shine forth from it...
Close your eyes at your desk, make your mind blank
and allow me to come through you.
"I am afraid."
Do not be afraid. Have faith.
I am always with you.
I will help you choose selected portions of your journal to print;
all are not intended to be shared. I will help you know what...
My message to the world through you
is one of hope,
love,
peace,
brotherhood.
My message is to love me, love your fellow man.

Do this to avoid the doom of your destruction.
It is not too late to turn to me in love,
not of fear.
I do not punish you.
Man makes his own choice through his own free will.
I love you. Be up and about your business.
Let me be there and guide you.

January 26, 1995
After viewing a televised Mass:
Suffer my child; suffer with me.
I will lift your burdens.
I will make them light.
I am always with you.
This is my will...
I am caring for you, guiding you,
directing you, and protecting you.
Do not struggle against me.
When your eyes are tired, sleep.
I love you. Keep my word.
Acknowledge my presence.
Be constantly aware of it.
Be up and write my child.
Let me guide you...

February 7, 1995
Let me carry your physical ailments.
Be present to your family...
Continue to write.
Persevere.
I am with you.
Do not be discouraged.
I will help you.
I will show you the way.
"I do not want to make a mockery of this—recording what I hear."
Do not be afraid.
What you need to know and write
I will guide you/your hand.

"Thank you Jesus, that I should be at the other end of this pen."
**You are welcome and I will make you worthy, my child.**
**God's will is not all suffering and misery for the human side of life.**
**Have joy and hope in your heart both for here and here-after.**
**You need more balance.**
**Your life has been negatively balanced in this regard—**
**misfortune's shadow.**
**Let my light and joy shine from your eyes.**
**Place down your pen and just be with me a moment now.**

February 9, 1995

It had been a physically trying six months, illness continuing at full force, an additional flare-up in January. It was the longest stretch I had known at this intensity. The pain in my face and deep in my ears was severe. The constant ringing in my ears, louder than usual, drowned out even more sounds around me. Muscles and tendons burned with inflammation, as if on fire, leaving me grossly fatigued. I was spent, little resistance left. I asked myself, "Am I succumbing to depression?" It was difficult to muster the stamina, physically or mentally, to place one foot before the other.

Instead of distracting myself at idle tasks, this time, I knelt at my bedside. I looked up at the crucifix on the wall above the headboard, but before I could begin to pray, my head and arms dropped to the bed in resignation. I gave in and just wept. I wondered how many more days I could stand this level of pain and how removed it made me from my family. I tried to pray, and had difficulty. "Where are you?" I silently screamed, "I can't hear you or feel your presence!" There was silence, but for the loud incessant ringing in my ears.

In the last half of the day it was a pleasant surprise to feel slightly more energetic. Was this small boost an answer to my earlier prayer? I still fell into the trap of defining "answer" as receiving what I asked for, as if "no," or anything else was not an answer.

February 10, 1995
**...I will help you**
**carry the heavy burden of the cross you presently feel.**
**Unite your suffering with mine.**
**I will draw good from it...**

I ask only that you do my will.
Surrender yourself to me.
Trust in me; that I will look after you...
Take pen in hand, sit with me and write every day...
Be worthy. I will make you worthy.
"I am not worthy."
Do not worry, I will make you so.
"I am sorry."
Yes, my child, I know,
the spirit is willing but the flesh is weak.
When you suffer unite your suffering with mine.
It will have meaning and will diminish in the process.
I have triumphed over evil
and have lifted you and mankind with me.
Your free will is important;
you must choose to come with me.
All men must choose.
I do not take your free will from you.

A new alumni directory arrived from the medical school I had attended. I glanced through it with a twinge of sadness; it was a strong reminder of my losses—the discrepancy between past dreams realized and my present reality. I reminisced about the long road it had been: four years of college, four years of medical school, one year of internship. and three years of specialty training in diagnostic radiology. I regretted none of it. Radiology* is a fascinating field. You function as a consultant to other physicians, and interface with every branch of medicine. The work is largely diagnostic, performing and interpreting exams, with a smaller portion of work focused on treatment.

It was a comfort to know that even though my professional career had been cut short, it had been full—involved in my practice, hospital

---

* The field of radiology is broad, including: ultrasound, nuclear medicine, CAT scans, magnetic resonance imaging (MRI), plain films such as bone films and chest X-rays, Upper G.I. series, barium swallows, tomograms, intravenous pyelograms, mammograms, barium enemas, neuroradiology, angiography, and interventional procedures such as angioplasty, percutaneous drainage of blocked kidneys or the biliary tree, percutaneous biopsies, etc.

and community. I could have spent a lifetime and not have known the pleasure of seeing as much accomplished. I had been fortunate, in addition to enjoying my work, in having a "good eye"—the ability to see subtle changes, patterns and small differences in size. You are born with it as a musician inherits an "ear" for music and then develops the ability. The obvious advantage to such a skill as a radiologist is picking up early disease, cancer, for one example, at a time when medical and surgical intervention could be all the more effective.

Radiology suited me in other ways as well. It was a constant challenge, and always something new to learn with rapid progress in medicine and even swifter technological advances in the field of imaging. You could never become bored as a radiologist.

Radiology is low profile, "behind the scenes," work. A diagnosis or recommendation for further evaluation is made, and it is the referring physician who conveys the radiologist's report to the patient.

The other match in my career choice was the opportunity for interaction with people: patients, referring physicians, other radiologists, and coworkers staffing the department. From my training years through practice I had the pleasure of meeting and knowing many exceptional people. At times patients had asked me to become their primary care physician, which flattered me because I knew my caring had come across to them. Despite the impossibility of fulfilling those requests, I was reminded of having given up the prospect of a direct patient care specialty, only with misgiving.

In practice it had been gratifying to correctly decipher the difficult, elusive, subtle or early diagnosis; I knew I had made a difference in others' lives. I can still remember the highs such experiences brought. In retrospect, however, looking back on my career, my greatest satisfaction lies elsewhere. It is not the "great calls" that give me the most pleasure now. It is knowing that I tried to care for my patients as I would have liked myself or a member of my family to have been treated, and in knowing I regarded my coworkers, colleagues and patients with the same respect I would like to have been shown.

How very different my life was now. Thumbing through the alumni directory I considered the reaction of former colleagues were I to publish portions of my spiritual experience. "Talking and praying to God is one thing," I thought, but admitting "I hear God respond is quite another!" I shrank at the prospect of public reaction.

Do not worry what others will say.
Some will deride you.
Those who need to will listen.
I will direct your path.
I have allowed you to suffer to bring you closer to me.
It is a blessing, though I know you do not see it that way.
I love you and want you to be closer to me.
Allow me to work through you to reach others
to bring them closer to me.
Others can be saved if they draw closer to me.
Continue to pray as you have.
The body and spirit are one.
Care for your body as the Temple of the Holy Ghost:
exercise, rest, sleep, eating (right)...
inner peace, calm...

Consult me in all things, large and small,
throughout your day...
Do not be concerned about your health.
Let me carry that burden for you.
Instead be present to your family and those around you.
Write for me...

My angels and I are constantly around you.
Mary's presence and the Holy Spirit are with you too.
(as with all souls struggling in their humanity)
Fall back and rely on us for help.
Make yourself consciously aware
of our constant presence.
Practice our presence.
Tell yourself throughout the day:
all things are possible through God.
We are here to help you do God's will.
"I know it is wrong to ask a sign."
The sign is you will be healed.
"Spiritually or physically?"
You must wait and see, my child.
You should not worry about your health...

Surrender yourself to the moment.
This is presently where and what you belong doing.
Do it with joy and gusto.
The joy, my light, is inside yourself.
Let it shine forth to all around you.
Do not cloak yourself in fear and darkness.
It is fertile ground for the devil's work.
I will protect you from all evil. (spiritually)
Constantly turn to me so my help is available to you.
I love you.
I do not ask more than you are able,
with my help...

 February 14, 1995
Night time prayer before sleep:
Suffer in silence.
Bring your crosses to me.
*Lamenting to others dilutes sharing the intimacy of our cross with Christ,*
*and therefore, the extent of making it meaningful.*
*It diminishes the opportunity for the suffering*
*to draw us closer to Christ.*
*It is like the analogy of the physical love*
*of a husband and wife in marriage,*
*their mutual exclusivity and bond.*

This did not mean draw and give no moral support to one another.
There are some sorrows, given their nature, duration or both in which the
only true comfort can come from God.

February 15, 1995
I will focus you where you need to be.
Surrender to me.
Your will still struggles against mine, (and in so doing)
you are making your life more difficult than it needs be.
Do not worry about your health, your family.
I am holding you all in the palm of my hand,
constantly watching over you, guiding you, and protecting you.
Listening is not so easy for you to do.
I understand this. I will help you listen.

I was momentarily apprehensive, recalling past associations between greater listening and health setbacks.

Do not be afraid.

I am gentle and mild

and I know what delicate, fragile creatures you are.

I love you and would not harm you.

"I am afraid."

Do not be afraid, my child.

Have faith.

Trust.

Hope in me.

Complain to no one.

Express joy.

Go out of your way to express my joy and peace.

Let it shine from your eyes...

Return to daily Mass and exercise.

Care for your bodily selves;

even the most menial task is sacramental in my eyes...

This is where you belong right now, my child.

Now rest...

Fall asleep in my protective arms.

You and your loved ones are safe in my care.

I love you and I am always with you.

"I love you. Please help me always to do your will."

Yes, my child.

Continue to will it and it will be so...

I love you.

I am all about you.

I am everywhere.

Feel the warmth of my light through you.

I felt a soothing, calming warmth through my entire body and with it peace, and release from physical discomfort till the following day.

My child, I am with you.

Now sleep.

Let your eyes be heavy and your mind easy and relaxed.

I know the prayers you say for those you love and care for

each night and often in the day;

consider them said and answered by me.

Now just close your eyes and be with me in the silence.
Rest down your pen. I love you.

February 18, 1995
I had serious doubt about my previous day's effort in following
what I thought had been God's will.
No, I am not angry with you, my child.
"I hope this is what you meant by 'follow my own inclinations'."
In a manner.
Take caution that you have patience
and allow things to unfold as I direct them...
All will be taken care of.
Concentrate your full efforts
on your family and your writing.
I will look after you.
I will guide you, watch over you, and protect you.
Do not (feel badly) at your feelings.
You have them for a reason and all is for the good.
Follow your inclinations.
I am leading you where you need to be, but do not rush.
Do not hurry. Be patient. I have a plan.
Do not be concerned. Do not worry...
Mary is with you, my child.
Do not be afraid...Have faith, trust in me...
Yet, you are still afraid to trust your intuition,
or what you think is your intuition.
You can't tell your thought's expression
of your will from mine.
You assume if it is my will
it must not be what you want or as pleasurable.
I will give you greater ability to discern my will from yours
and with it comes greater responsibility
to carry out tasks at hand.
Have confidence and trust in me.
Be calm and at peace my child
Your body needs to rest.
I want you to heal.
You must participate to heal.

(Meaning: Let go of anxieties over health and living. Fears make us more vulnerable to temptation. Faith and trust in God conquer fear of the world's adversities—believing better things await us, and that God knows and provides better for our needs than we are able.)

Loosen yourself to be.* Surrender to me.

Give up holding on tightly to the false moorings you grasp at.

I am your anchor, your courage, your life force.

Fall into my arms and let me lull you to sleep,

peaceful sleep, as my angels and I

surround you and your loved ones.

Sleep, my child.

Rest in me.

I am all you need.

All your wants, desires, happiness,

and joy are satisfied in me.

Let my light shine from your eyes.

Allow my presence every moment of the day**,

to all you meet,

in particular your family.

I love you.

"I love you."

Yes, my child, I know you do

and I will help you love me more.

"Thank you Jesus."

Now (place) down your pen and rest.

 First Half Year, 1995
After Mass and Communion:

*God's will and following it—*
*what's in store for our future is not always misery.*
*There is also happiness and joy*
*on the human plane not just misery.*

---

* Meaning: reach a state of detachment—loose or free from the causes of anxiety and all else but God. In this we most fully exist—"to be," aware and alive in the present moment.

** Meaning: be consciously aware of Christ's immediate presence.

February, 1995

My appearance varies a great deal depending upon how severe and prolonged the flare-up in my illness has been, and upon the dose and duration of recent steroid (prednisone) medication. This was not one of my better phases. After my first long course of steroids in 1991, while putting my youngest to bed one night, she remarked, "Mommy, you look something like a chipmunk!"

"Yes," I said, as she giggled. "It looks kind of funny doesn't it, these big cheeks—like I am storing up enough acorns for the whole winter." My daughter continued to giggle. "And look at this, not a wrinkle on my face with all this extra bit of cushioning fat underneath."

"But I liked your wrinkles, Mommy. And what's all that other stuff on your face?" she asked pointing to the rash.

"Oh, that's like having teenage skin all over again." I said as light-heartedly as I was able. She squinted and cocked her head sideways, assessing just how much of what I said was teasing. "Really, one of the medicines I take makes me gain weight, especially in my face and right here at the top of my back," I said as I pointed to a new prominence at the base of my neck.

"Is that why your arms are so pillowy now?" she asked, her way of describing soft and chubby, as she indented my upper arm with her finger.

"Yes, and do you know what they call that down south?"

She shook her head, "no," uncertain where this was leading. I watched her try to anticipate my next response and then I announced as if a surprise:

"Biscuit poisoning!"

"Biscuit poisoning!" she repeated, giggling at its silliness.

"Yes, biscuit poisoning, from eating too many biscuits. Why it's enough to make anyone fat every time." I said. She continued to giggle. "And now it's time for you to go to sleep."

In a more serious tone she said, "I liked the way you looked before, Mommy. You were pretty."

"I am still pretty on the inside. Now it's more important to feel better than look pretty on the outside, and besides," I said as I tousled her hair, "when did you ever see a chipmunk you thought was anything but the cutest!"

She laughed, and hugged me tightly, "I love you, Mommy!" She leaned back and wryly smiled, "...even if you do look like a chipmunk!" I laughed.

"Night, night, little girl! Sweet dreams and God bless!" I said as I pulled the covers up around her shoulders and kissed her on the forehead.

I left the room and allowed my face to relax and the corners of my mouth to droop into the frown I felt. I walked past the mirror, which I now assiduously avoided, along with every mirror, but this time I met the face. Even in the dimly lit room I was aghast. I looked haggard, absolutely awful. My face was huge. There was no hint remaining of my high cheek bones, underlying facial structure or delicate features. My eyes appeared recessed and smaller, relative to the amount of surrounding facial fat. My hair was dull, and balding with white scalp shining through. I looked very old. No wonder I had been avoiding mirrors.

I slumped into a deep couch and watched the seconds pass as the clock's pendulum arm swept through each arc. Light flickered off the crystalline whitish-rose speckles imbedded in the black granite about the fireplace. I was on the verge of sinking into major self-pity when, I thought of a patient I had briefly met once, years before.

She had rheumatoid arthritis and had been referred to me for a barium swallow to evaluate her esophagus, due to difficulty swallowing. That day when I entered the fluoroscopy suite our radiology technician had already positioned my patient—standing behind the large fluoroscopic tower which obscured her arms and torso. I introduced myself and nodded in lieu of my customary handshake with the fluoroscopy tower awkwardly in our path. Before beginning the exam I spoke with her about pertinent history and the symptoms for which she had been referred to me. She was soft spoken, articulate, well groomed and petite.

The room lights were lowered to best visualize the monitor and the exam began. I fluoroscoped the course of her esophagus, which involves moving the fluoroscopic tower by hand over the area of examination and simultaneously observing the live X-ray image on the monitor. That was clear and I was ready to proceed, planning to repeat the same from several angles as she drank the radiographically visible barium. I reached behind the tower, handing her a heavy cup of pink, "strawberry" flavored barium, as I said, "Please take this in your right hand and turn slightly towards me." She tried as if nothing held her back. Her hand continually bumped into the cup and despite several attempts she was unable to grasp it. If I had not had a firm grip on the cup myself it would have spilled.

"Please turn up the lights." I asked the radiology technician. I moved the tower entirely away from my patient, and when I looked down at her hands I am not certain if I was able to conceal my astonishment. Both her hands were grotesquely deformed, claw-like in overall shape, with enormous knobby, gnarled joints and fingers nearly frozen in position as if they had been squeezed together and slanted sideways. I had not realized she had an uncommon variant of Rheumatoid Arthritis called Rheumatoid Arthritis Deformans, which is associated with massive deformity and proportional loss of function. At best she could have grasped the cup of barium between her two hands, but likely it would have been too heavy for even that. I was immediately annoyed with myself for not having known.

My shock was not in the appearance of her hands, a condition which I had seen before; it was her finger nails! They were long, and though I presumed artificial, none the less impeccably, beautifully manicured in a brilliant fire engine red. I thought to myself, "Wow! Good for you!" I really admired her! She was not hiding her hands. She had not let her illness, even though chronic, overcome her. There was an indomitable, quiet, inner strength and determination which shone from her eyes. We tailored our exam to her needs, without further ado.

I have thought of her over the years and more often since my illness. She has been a frequent inspiration—the image of her beautifully manicured nails—her beautiful undeterred spirit, making the most and the best of what life brought her. I can remember distinctly, back then, wanting to be like her—when I got "old." I was just not planning on getting old so soon. If I could find her I would tell her thank you, many times over. I remember her in my prayers.

 February 21, 1995
Referring to a major decision:
**Do not trouble yourself trying to decide; just try to know my will.**
**(Place your effort in trying to know) my will, then following it,**
**rather than thinking you had the ability**
**to make as wise a choice.**
**(The latter is) much more difficult.**

First Week of Lent; Early March, 1995
Still seeking a more meaningful exercise for the Lenten season, direction came to me in two parts during prayer.

First, I was to look for greater humor in life's circumstances and my

limitations, particularly those brought on by illness. I was to express this
to my family for a lighter outlook, and more laughter. Chronic illness had
taken its toll upon me. At first glance I thought this exercise trivial, then
recognized it could restore me to more of my former self.

Second, I was to forgive the black-hearted person who placed Satan's
thorn into my heart. I thought this odd, since I believed I had forgiven. I
reexamined this. Had I really let the hurt go? No, not all. So, I tried each
day to let the last vestiges free, when in fact I had not even begun to know
or feel its full measure. The seeds of evil's work had not yet fully bloomed.

March 8, 1995
Aftershocks of my brush with evil through the black-hearted surfaced. I heard:

*Evil, by forgiving it, kills it.*

(meaning: forgiving the person who is acting as its vector, or parasitic host, and thus responsible for propagating evil)

*Evil is a living force.*
*It reproduces,*
*passed on from one person to the next.*
*'Love thy enemy and*
*pray for those who persecute you'*
*kills evil,*
*blocks its propagation—*
*the reproduction of a living force—*
*Evil is a parasite of man,*
*thriving upon man's*
*weakness, fears, greed, selfishness.*

**I allow you to suffer**
**to bring you closer to me.**

"I am desolate."

**This is a cross you must bear.**
**I will help you carry this burden.**
**Trust in me; have faith.**
**I am leading you where you need to be.**
**Do not be concerned or fearful.**
**My presence is with you always.**
**I am all around you.**

I am everywhere.
I am with you always.
You are my child.
You are mine and I am yours. I love you.
All of my works are good.
You are a reflection of my works.
Allow me to shine from your eyes...
Surrender yourself to me.
Do not resist where I lead you.

"How will I know?"

(Be calm.) Do nothing.
Be patient now and just allow (let) it happen.
My plan (for all)/for you is unfolding.
Do not impede my plan.
I will guide you.
You will know what is right,
the correct path to choose...

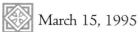 March 15, 1995

*Evil lives as a spirit.*
*It propagates, like rippling raindrops*
*falling upon the water, feeling each other's effect.*
*Kill evil as Christ taught:*
*love/forgiveness.*

I remained involuntarily locked in two battles. One battle was with
evil's destructive aftermath; my heart freshly reminded of the thorn which
pierced it. My second battle was struggling to forgive those who had given
evil form. Present unrest would seem the calm before the storm; in contrast to what would follow, evil's fuller bloom.

March 16, 1995
If I were following God's will at all, I did not think I was presently
doing a very good job of it.

Sit with me, my child. Do not be discouraged.
I am with you now and always.
Allow me to guide you with...all things.
I am well pleased with your efforts
and desire to follow my/our Father's will.

Let me teach you how
to better know our Father's will.
Close your eyes, be patient. Be calm.
Let my peace enter you.
Feel the joy of my presence.
Let it show to the world around you.
Let this be effortless.
Just concentrate on my presence within,
in you and those around you—
my presence throughout all of creation.
I love you, my child.
I am guiding, watching over,
and protecting you
and all your loved ones.
Be close to me.
Allow me to give you
the great/many gifts
I have in store for you.
You are my child.
You are mine and I am yours...
Sit with me every day like this and write.
There are many things I want to tell through you.
"I am afraid."

Do not be afraid.
I will protect you and your loved ones.
Some will deride you.
Suffer this persecution gladly for me.
Many more will be helped.
I will see you through it.
I will never abandon you.
Turn to me even more often than you do,
in every part of your day.
Become more consciously aware of my presence in you,
those around you, and in all of creation...
I love you, my child.
You are my brother/sister.
You are mine and I am yours.
We are one.

Tears welled in my eyes.

**Your tears are those of joy, which come of knowing the truth.**
**My truth is beauty beyond words.**

**You are correct in appreciating the battle you are in with Satan...**
**...I will continue to guide you.**
**He has polluted my creation**
**and tempted a weaker species (man) than himself**
**and he will be judged accordingly,**
**along with each man, his due.**
**You will win because I am with you.**
**You will win because Mary is constantly at your side,**
**along with angels and saints.**

"I love you Jesus, thank you."

**I am well pleased with you, my child. Please continue.**

"I am afraid I will interfere in my hearing what you want to communicate.
Please don't let me do this or be influenced by evil forces. Please help me.
It is so hard to purely listen. Please teach me better how."

**I will show you, my child. Be patient.**
**Receive Communion every day...**

"Forgive me for questioning you. Do you see this as a sign of disobedience?"

**No, my child, I know your willingness to follow my will in your heart.**
**I know your heart's innermost desires and I am well pleased.**
**Be calm. Feel my presence in and all around you...**
**Do not be concerned with the cares and anxieties of this world.**
**I will provide for you and your loved ones...**

Referring to my cousin:

**Her parents are here with me**
**as is your Father, Aunt and other relatives...**
**Be happy...I will direct you/your path**
**as will I your family...**
**Wait, and allow my plan to unfold.**

"Is it acceptable to ask you direct questions? I do not mean it as a test."

**I know, my child. Again I know**
**because I know your innermost heart's desire.**

You may ask any questions
but I will not always answer your question directly,
and you will not always understand my answer.
There are some things it is better you not know
till they have further unfolded.
I will not overwhelm you.
I will tell you what I want you to know.
What is in your best interest in helping you live your life
in accordance with God's will...
Allow me to show you how to use...worldly gifts
for my/our Father's greater glory.
Now be up and about your business.
Attend to the mundane about your home...
Later (today) focus on your children...
I love you and I am always with you.
Do not be afraid.

March 17, 1995
I am with you, my child. Come and sit with me a while.
Lay down your burden and allow me to fill you with my love.
Do not be concerned. Do not be afraid.
Let your life be filled with joy and enjoy life to its fullest.
I have filled the world with many good things
for your (mankind's) pleasure.
These have been abused for evil but it does not make them evil.
They and their beauty have been distorted by evil.
You are my child and I love you.
Do not be overwhelmed.
I will help and guide you each step of the way...
Life is more difficult with more choices and more options.
You must listen the more carefully to me.
"Please help me listen without interfering or fabricating what I want
to hear."
Do not force decisions, just let them naturally unfold.
Regarding a major decision affecting family:
The decision cannot be made today. Let it rest...
Enjoy the company of your family
and the world around you.

Do not be concerned, you and your loved ones
are in my care and loving arms.

You need to return to your writing schedule.
This is work you must do for me...

"What about my children?"
Your children will be fine if you let them know me.
Love your children as I have loved you,
with no conditions or restrictions.
Forgive them. Understand them.
Give them your example.
Speak to them about me...

Referring to someone living the anguish of having suffered evil's injustice:
Use your prayer to bring my healing touch to them.
Bring me to them in your words, actions.
Bring my Presence to them in your being...
Let them know I am with them always...

Referring to someone in purgatory:
...He suffers greatly for the pain he has caused...many...
He feels all this pain he has generated
and he is crushed beneath its weight.
Forgive and pray for him.
Love your enemy and
pray for those who persecute you.

This is my message.
Love one another as I have loved you,
and love your God above all things.
Tell the world to love me. It is not too late.
Your immortal souls hang in the balance.
Now up and be about your business.
Remember, do not abuse your body in any way.
Call upon my strength to help you.
I am here for you and with you always.
Resist temptation.

**Succumbing to temptation leads to destruction.**
**I love you.**
"I love you, Jesus."

March 20, 1995
Insight into past words on illness: **This is how I am releasing your**
**creative side.** (October 16, 1994)

> *Creative side refers to the ability to create love.*
> *It did not mean any ability to write*
> *but the ability to love.*
> *That is man's true creativity,*
> *and it is in this that we are created*
> *in God's image and likeness.*
> *Love is what man creates*
> *which lives forever and is immortal.*
> *Love also overpowers evil, destroying it.*
> *Man is marked for eternity by the love he has given.*
> *Releasing your creative side meant a greater ability to love.*

Third Week of Lent, 1995
Aspects of illness, or disability with their loss of independent functioning can be humiliating, degrading and depersonalizing. They leave us more vulnerable. At times other's lack of kindness accentuate the effect; and such was my experience that day.

In further introduction to this journal entry, I want first to acknowledge the many kind and caring physicians I have known both as colleagues and in my "reverse career" as patient. I both admired and found this group of physicians, as well as other health care workers, uplifting when I worked in their ranks. Now as patient I have dearly appreciated them from yet another angle; their attitude is healing, at the very least they do not add to a patient's suffering. The incident referred to below involved a physician, met but once, and of another ilk. He was a type with whom I was not unfamiliar over the course of my training and practice. The extreme in which he "distinguished" himself, fortunately, represents a small minority in the profession. It is not just in medicine, but in other fields as well, that such persons can exact great damage, because of their position of trust and power as well as the vulnerability of those they "serve." Suffice it to say, the most flattering comment I can make of this man is that his bedside manner was wasted on all but the dead.

Admittedly, my reaction to the circumstance was magnified by little emotional or physical reserve after so long a flare in illness. It was difficult to see myself unable to manage something which I would have dismissed with unruffled humor when I was well. The situation had the better of me. I failed to see its humor, instead I was distraught.

Sit with me a while...
You are in my care. Be calm.
I am watching over you, guiding you,
and protecting you and your loved ones.
Be filled with my peace.
Do not allow this person
to make you absent to your family.
They all need you...Do not be concerned.
He is mistaken in his arrogance.
His arrogance has blinded him.
Even if he were accurate
that does not excuse/forgive
a lack of compassion.
That was a sin of destruction.
Yes, I am sorry, my child,
but you are constantly tested in this world.
Allow each test to bring you closer to me.
Yes, cry and let your feelings free.
Stay here in my arms and let them free;
I will comfort and console you in your desolation.
Allow me to give you strength.
All goodness and life flow from me.
I am/[my Father is] the source of all goodness.
"Help me please, Jesus."
I am with you; I am here...
These experiences will help you help others.
Good will come/flow from this.
Be still, my child.
Feel my healing hand upon you/your heart.
Yes, cry and let it all loose/free.
You will be stronger for it
and the freer to do my work/God's will.

(It is all right to feel the great sadness deriving from
the destructive *effects* of evil in the world.)
Unite your suffering with mine.
Remember, in my passion
people mocked and humiliated me.
It is a form of cruel destruction.
Love him back. Pray for him.
I will see that justice is done.
My will prevails.
He has hurt you,
one of my blessed and beloved creatures,
and I am not pleased.
"Jesus, help me say the right words, feel the right feelings of love and
forgiveness—to mean them."
Remember
'Love your enemy and
pray for those who persecute you.'...
I have given it (illness)
to allow you to do my/our Father's work.
I am your confessor and counselor;
bring all your sorrows,
troubles, joys, questions, and problems to me.
I love you. I am all around you;
I am everywhere; I am with you always...
Some will mock and humiliate you.
You must be prepared for this. Turn to me then and now.
Pray for them and ignore the content of what they say.
Be up and about your business.
Be happy and filled with the light
and joy of my spirit.
Teach your children to deflect
these destructive evil barbs
as I have taught you.
Tell the children to be happy within themselves.
Let themselves be the criteria,
not the judgment of others around you.
Now be up and about your business.

Fourth Week of Lent, 1995

> And do not fear those who kill the body but cannot kill the soul; rather fear him who can destroy both soul and body in hell.
>
> Matthew 10:28, RSV

Like a black flower coming to bloom, you learn what it is over time, as it slowly opens, reveals itself and bears bitter fruit. So I came in retrospect to know the depth of evil in the person of darkness. My second Lenten resolve toward forgiveness lay lifeless, submerged in the misery of evil's unfolding.

The pain and sorrow I felt were unbearable. The thorn in my heart, now barbed and fiery, lodged in my heart's core and would therein exist for the remainder of my days. Now, I appreciated its true significance— a constant reminder of evil's presence in the world, enacted through man and its suffering inflicted upon man. My heart broke. A world's ocean of tears would have been too few to relieve my anguish, mine largely held back behind eyes which were only pools of pain. I had to present a strong facade, unless I was alone.

This was a defining point in my life. My perception of the world changed. The manifestation of Satan and his angels infecting man as vehicle of his destruction had crystallized before me. Satan living in our midst, given arms and legs by those souls he could entangle, lure, enthrall, and then enslave as his hosts. Evil was as undeniable as its consequent suffering, destructiveness and propagation. I was inconsolable. My cumulative sorrows, telescoped into one all encompassing grief, did not match the moment. It was like no other.

At the first opportunity I went to find a priest. I confided in him the source of my pain. I told him of the forgiveness I had been asked to give as my Lenten offering. I began to cry, realizing I felt betrayed by God whom I now sought for comfort. Through my sobs I made every effort to speak, "I am supposed to forgive and now I can't. I can't forgive for what has been stolen from my life." I asked him to give me Communion. I needed to receive the Eucharist. I needed to find Christ's presence, his comfort, his peace. After the priest's brief prayer and blessing he held out the consecrated Host to my hand, "Body of Christ."

"Amen," I responded, then knelt by myself before the small chapel altar.

My sobs now poured forth, for the first time fully unrestrained. My thoughts were so loud they echoed in my head, damped only by the deluge which poured from my eyes. "Why this Jesus? Why this?" My thoughts screamed louder and louder and louder, "Why did it have to be this of all things? How could this be your will?" I raged in anger and continued unquenched, "Is this some cruel joke—asking me to deepen my forgiveness, and now I learn the fuller extent of what I am asked to forgive? I have no forgiveness in my heart. I feel none! No fire in hell is hot enough for him! I can't live long enough to forgive, if I had one hundred life spans in this one! How am I ever to forgive?" I asked, too enraged to want an answer.

I quieted with the comforting presence of Christ upon me, to my amazement, in spite of my raging lament at him. In the peace of his presence my anger and hatred momentarily dissolved. It left an awesome fright, as there was nothing left to stand between and blunt the pure raw pain. It would have been intolerable but for the consoling presence of Christ who carried me, binding my wounds with the balm of his love. Now still, I wept quietly and drew comfort, strength and consolation from him.

### Fifth and Sixth Week of Lent, 1995

Having abandoned both my Lenten exercises it was Mary, the Blessed Mother, who unobtrusively entered my life and gently showed me the path to tread. She showed me how to share my suffering with her Son. In daily stations of the cross she taught me new insight into Christ's passion: how to live and experience it through her eyes, focusing from the perspective of her sorrow. I came to feel Mary's presence, consolation and strength in my own life. I was grateful she had again come to me in my need.

The image of the Pieta, Mary gently cradling her Son's dead body in her arms after crucifixion, frequently came into my thoughts. Within its silent power Mary, born without sin, brought me solace as touchstone—consolidating our link with God, man, and Christ who bridged both the human and divine in our redemption, man's path to divine eternal life.

Through Mary's faith, once again accepting God's will even in the face of such great sorrow, she showed us how to come to God. In the solidarity of a Mother suffering with her child, she showed us how to join our suffering with her Son's. We can all identify with Mary. Man's plight, living in a world often ruled by evil with its consequent senseless cruelty, is epitomized by a mother grieving her murdered child. Mary does not leave us abandoned in this chaos of destruction. Instead she brings calm order to it by accepting her sorrow in union with her Son. Because her suffering was unified with his in our redemption, it had meaning and purpose.

I had never before appreciated Mary's importance in Christ's redemption of all mankind. I found great comfort and direction in the image of the Pieta. It quickly focused me upon Mary calling us to follow her example in faith, acceptance of God's will, and uniting our suffering with Christ's when facing the world's cruelty—that we are to find meaning by sharing in her Son's redemption.

 May 26, 1995

Be still, my child. I will help you;
I will guide you...All will fall in place in due time.
Unite your suffering with mine
and teach others who suffer the same.
It will have meaning. It will pass. It teaches.
It has purpose not immediately obvious to you...
Let me lead you...Receive Communion daily.
You need my full grace and presence
to accomplish the work I have planned for you.
Do not be afraid.
I am here constantly loving, guiding
and protecting you and your loved ones...
Listen to me and write every day.
Write every day after Communion.
Clear your (mind) of all anxieties, concerns,
distractions, and then listen to me and record my words.
I love you. You will help many people in following my word.
In this you will do my/our Father's will
and be most pleasing to him.
Do not try so hard. Make your work effortless.
In this way my greatest influence can shine forth
in your writings and actions.
Stay close to me.
Communion every day is
a positive action/act you can take/carry out.

It is important that you not allow evil influences
to sway your course.
Tell the world to love me.
Love my Church.
It is not too late but
we are/man is in the final age...

All will be well.
I am watching (over) you,
guiding you and protecting you and your loved ones.
Remember you are never alone.
I am always with you, always at your side,
always around you, at every turn.
Let my light shine through your eyes.
Let me flow through your lips...
Show...my love through your love...
Do not be concerned for your health...
"Thank you, Jesus."
Let me guide your writing...
Receive Communion daily. This is so important.
You need my grace now more than ever
as you draw nearer to me;
with the work you are to do for me
the devil—Satan will try to derail you.
I will protect you and your loved ones.
He will not succeed...
Evil is a powerful and organized force.
It has a life of its own and attempts always
to perpetuate and expand itself.
Submit your will to mine
and our Father's will is done...
Do not underestimate
the intelligence and power of evil
at work in the world around you.
Angels are of great intelligence and
some have chosen to use their will against the Father's,
easily tempting and luring man in his blindness
and inferior intelligence.

Stay close to me, and you and your loved ones will be fine.
Yes the plagues are upon man;
they are only the beginning.
This is the final age...
Do not be concerned about plagues, climate
(meaning: extreme changes, instability, violent weather);
they are all in fulfillment of scripture.
Do not be concerned, all will come to pass
as I have foretold/predicted;
yet, man's fate is not yet sealed.
It is not too late for man to turn toward God
and choose God—life.
The gift of free will, will never be taken from you.
Man is condemned to hell only by his own choosing—
only through the choice of his free will.

What to say to a person suffering:
Tell them to identify their isolation with mine in my passion
to give it meaning and help them through this time.
Let them know it will pass.
My angels are ever at their feet and side.
...the experience is one of learning.
It will strengthen them and
increase their love/empathy
for their fellow man.
They have a great capacity to love.
They must be encouraged to first love and
respect themselves, as you too,
or there is nothing remaining of you
to do the important work I have ahead for you...
Gain a feeling of empowerment. I will help you.
Feel my confidence and presence within you.
Emanate my peace. Be filled with my peace and love.
Do not be concerned or anxious about anything.
You are mine and I am yours.
I love you, my child.
Lie down and rest a while
and then be up and about your day.

May, 1995

Some years ago, a small group of women snubbed me, and then my daughter was no longer invited to play with theirs. Their friendly behavior changed in unison—lights turned off by a single switch; it was as if I were no longer there. I retraced my steps without avail to understand why. Difficulty with visual scanning at times led me to misread my calendar as I transposed columns or rows. Had I missed a commitment? Had I not recognized someone I should have known? Had I miffed someone with the number of my last minute cancellations due to not feeling well? Had I committed some other social blunder of which I was unaware? Prior to illness, my interaction with people was a strength and source of much happiness to me. Now, I often embarrassed myself, left others annoyed or feeling slighted. I finally spoke to those involved individually, "You seem very different towards me; is there something I have done to offend you?" Each uncomfortably denied any change in her attitude, and hurriedly excused herself, never meeting my eye.

It remained a mystery until now, when in an unusual circumstance I learned why I had become an outcast. The story is as follows.

One day, now years gone by, I was at a social gathering with my children. I had not felt well to start with and too late recognized that I had exceeded my physical limitations in being there at all. I had wanted life to continue as normally as possible for my children. My effort achieved exactly what I did not want—one of my daughters upset and singled out from the other children because of my illness.

My inner ear symptoms build up in a characteristic pattern, corresponding with varying levels of dizziness. It is at the more intense levels that an episode of vertigo is further likely, and at least to this extent I can prepare myself. I would push myself trying to pursue the daily routine on foot, in cabs, or using public transportation. On that day I learned to lower those expectations of myself. I wished I had stayed home.

Midway through the occasion I felt more poorly and realized I needed to do something before an episode of vertigo made the floor my bed. I had previously told my companions about my inner ear problem. I politely excused myself, explaining I was having more trouble with it today and needed to go lie down. "Oh! I hope you're feeling better. Do you need any help?" they said.

"Thank you, but we're not going too far. Don't interrupt your lunch." I said.

"Call us if we can do anything." They echoed.

I left, with my children. We walked away but were still visible to those who remained. I was too dizzy, my head held straight ahead, to look sideways and notice their disapproving stares as I weaved and wobbled along the way, one of my children guiding me at either forearm.

Their conversation continued, "Tsk, tsk, tsk!" her tongue loudly clucked against the roof of her mouth as her head turned from side to side in wordless disapproval. "Just look at that! Two beautiful children, and she's drunk in the middle of the day!" the first said.

"What a shame!" a second added.

"But, she has an inner ear problem..." a third interjected, only to be interrupted by the first.

"Inner ear problem—right! Look at her walk, its obvious from that she's been drinking!" the first stated emphatically.

"But I didn't smell any alcohol and we had none." the third said, her last effort in defense.

Another spoke, "How do you know it's alcohol? How do you know it's not worse? She is a physician. You know what all they have access to. It could be drugs."

"It's bizarre!" the fourth interjected

"Would you let your daughter play at her house? Who knows what they'd get into? Who knows if she'd be passed out and then who'd be watching the kids!"

Once finished with my present, they rewrote my past. "I'll bet that's the real reason she stopped practicing medicine. Its no inner ear problem. That's just a cover."

"It must have been a nervous breakdown." another added, trying to bring compassion and understanding to the personal history they had created for me.

When I learned what had transpired I was very angry, deeply hurt at the betrayal of friends and disappointed by the superficial judgment of acquaintances. What angered and saddened me most was remembering my daughter's reaction to no longer being included in these friend's invitations.

I thought about the contrasting appearance of how my life used to be—well-respected, competent, responsible, trusted, making decisions with people's lives in the balance—to now appearing as if some derelict, incapable of supervising two children on a play date. The contrast in these two images was so absurd I burst out laughing.

Later, in reflection, I tried to focus on forgiveness. I wondered if I had ever as unfairly judged others. I hoped not, and while I did not think so, I could see those who had judged me probably did not think so either. I knew anger and hurt had given way to forgiveness when I found myself amused to wonder how much more I could have added to speculations that day had I mentioned I "hear voices."

 May 31, 1995
After Mass and Communion:

Regarding my uncertainty over a major decision, specifically with respect to God's will:

> Do not be afraid.
> You have given your will over to me.
> You chose to and
> it is in this act of choosing
> it is done.
> I will see to the rest.
> I am yours and you are mine. Turn to me.
> Turn to me first, before all, and all things.
> I will make you a pillar of strength—my reflection.

Referring to someone in my life:

> They **will need your strength—*which is mine;*
> all comes from me reflected through you...
> I do not reveal to you that which is not helpful,
> or that which you cannot handle...
> Do not be afraid, my child.
> I am yours and you are mine...
> You must tell the world to love me,
> to keep my commandments, to keep my word.
> Man's word/the world is in its final age;
> yet it is not too late for man to turn to me with his heart.
> It is the heart's intentions which count/matter.
> If you sincerely wish to do God's will
> do not be concerned that you are following it
> at every turn because it will happen/flow naturally.
> There are powers about you of great force,
> both good and evil.

Ultimately my/our Father's will
shall bring good from evil,
and shall triumph— bringing good from evil,
and then separating out the remaining good from evil.
The eternal fires of hell will remain for the recalcitrant
and their souls will be lost—eternally dammed.
Let my peace be upon you.
Let my goodness, peace and love
shine forth from your eyes,
and imbue every word which passes your lips.
Find your internal strength center with me.
I am the font of life,
the only true source of life and significance.
Center your world around me
and all will settle into place around you.
You are a pillar of strength because I am your strength
and you rely upon me for all things.
The plagues, violent weather, climatic changes,
warring among men are just beginning.
This is the final age...
This is not to frighten you or those you contact.
It is to warn you of the urgency of turning towards me—
loving God and your fellow man...
Great destruction lies ahead.
Do not be afraid.
These are all prophecies
which must come to pass
before the final Age of Glory.
I am well pleased with you, my child.
"I feel I've done so poorly. I am sorry for my many mistakes."
You are too harsh and critical of yourself, my child,
much more so than your heavenly Father.
We are well pleased with you and your heart's desire.
We understand the weakness of humanity
and the forces which try to further taint human goodness...
It is important that you return to some form of writing every day.
Time is growing short...I will help you...
It will be done.

"It concerns me that I misinterpret the meaning of some of what I hear you say, such as **You are with child.** (December 1, 1994).

> **Yes, my child, you misunderstood.**
> **Go back and reread** (notes of it).
> **Some filtered through your wishes.**
> (Meaning: I had not misheard the words; but I had misunderstood their meaning, the latter influenced by my wishes.)

"Please help me be pure in writing; passing on the true message, not colored."

> **Do not worry, it will be done (and one reason you are chosen)**
> **is for the coloring with which your heart sees.**
> **It is the coloring of Christ's love.**

"Please help me. I feel very unworthy." I remembered my failing in a circumstance close to me. It was a troubling situation in which I could not effectively intervene or seemingly bring more to.

> **Yes, my child, I know and well understand.**
> **It is so hard to see a beloved creature and creation**
> **hurt/used/disrespected (by) another creation.**
> **This is a difficult lesson in love**
> **which you must learn and teach.**
> **Anger and frustration are unproductive;**
> **replace them with love and acceptance,**
> **at the same time gently correcting and reproving.**

Regarding persons I loved who were experiencing a great deal of difficulty:

> **All must learn in their own way.**
> **They are in my guidance and care.**
> **Do not worry or be concerned. I love you, my child.**
> **You are a reflection of my love and beauty.**
> **You will share in my future glory.**
> **You want to bring everyone with you—**
> **with you to me.**

"Yes, Jesus, please help me."

> **Yes, my child, I am and I will...**
> **Feel my peace.**
> **Let my peace be upon you.**
> **Encourage people to return to church,**
> **to receive Communion often; there is a great grace**
> **and closeness people can achieve there.**

You are in a sea of darkness.
Let me be your beacon of light.
You are mine and I am yours.

I recalled the person of darkness in my life, and what a picture perfect facade of respectability and success was presented to others.

Appearances are deceiving; they are transient.
You know all...power is through me/the Father/Holy Spirit.
You are merely a vessel, a channel as was the physical presence
of Jesus Christ and Mary's body and those of all the saints.
(saints—those who chose eternal life in God's presence.)
Relax and be at peace my child...
Just allow me to work through you.
Close your eyes, place down your pen, and
be with me a while in the silence of your heart.

## June 21, 1995

Lying in bed before sleep I looked into the night sky through the dormer window overhead. The moon was full, white and bright. Mary appeared around the moon and held it gently in her arms. The entire image was soft, as if a watercolor sculpted of light. She was clothed in a voluminous, deeply resonant, azure blue, hooded cape over a pure white gown, a small crescent of which was visible just below the neck. A diaphanous white veil separated her dark hair from the blue hood of her cape. Her garments fell in graceful folds, contradicting their seeming weightlessness. Her figure was illuminated from within; her skin radiantly luminescent, in particular her face. Light shimmered off her hair. Golden white light also shone upon her from the moon, the overall effect transfiguration.

The strongest light was from the moon, but it was far brighter than the moon's usual reflected light. It came from within the moon and radiated outward in continual showers of gold and white vibrance. Mary was surrounded by the deep blue midnight sky and its multiple stars twinkling like jewels. She lovingly gazed down upon me with soothing, reassuring smile and soft, beautiful, compassionate, dark eyes.

The light emanating from the moon and Mary, along with her eyes looking directly into mine were captivating. It was magnificent! I was aware of nothing else amidst the absolute peace and joy I felt. I do not know how long the vision lasted, but when it faded I felt a pang of loss. It was in the company of its memory that I drifted off to sleep.

June 22, 1995

Needs related to my illness made relocation to an urban setting necessary for the foreseeable future. Saddened at soon moving from our cozy home and beautiful, small but private garden in our yard I went about the chores of packing. The children's laughter drew my attention out of doors where they played amidst colorful flowers in bloom. Sunlight shimmered off their hair which danced in the breeze as they ran. How I wished I could spare them life's most painful heartaches. My own sadness was forgotten. I gave thanks for the gift of motherhood and God's way of teaching a level of love so great that one would prefer to suffer in another's place, to the ultimate possible.

Moving from an idyllic Norman Rockwell-like town to the city, I felt like the odd lemming running the other way. "Why?" some would ask in disbelief. I did not want to draw further attention to my illness, and few really care to hear about a chronic condition. I tried to gloss over the limitations my illness brought with politically correct humor. "The city is a safe haven for the domestically challenged." I would add, "My children never knew me during my subscription to Bon Appétit." I would omit explaining that while I now had the time, I no longer had the energy for such gourmet pursuits. I would continue, "My daughter once warned a prospective dinner guest, 'I should tell you before you accept, Mom doesn't cook, she only warms.'"

Later:

My awareness of sin had been heightened by witnessing its brutal manifestation in my encounter with Satan's hosts. Sadness again returned to me. I fell into a cascade of personal regret, followed by deeper remorse for my own past errors, my own contribution to my regrets. I was sorrowful in appreciating their possible impact on others, with aftershocks across time. I prayed.

**You have been forgiven, my child. I understand.**
**Mistakes were made...it** (final end result)
**was God's/our Father's will.**
**God's will be done.**

The outcome is the same.

It is man's choice to participate in God's will or not.

I am well pleased with you, my child.

You are learning better how to love.

To love is to create—to create everlasting.

There is great energy and power in love.

Do not worry, my child;

has not what I have thus told you been so?...

The important lesson is: your home is with me;

physical surroundings (are) not important

yet they and all else are a part of our Father's overall plan.

You are learning to bring the spiritual

to even the mundane aspects of life.

You are bringing my light to the world

as you saw Mary illuminated

and reflecting the Son's light

from the center of her being:

*Moon reflecting the sun's light,*

*Mary reflecting the Son's light.*

Yes, the moon was there but the light was brighter,

purer and whiter than the moon.

You were allowed to see.

Be like Mary—

perfect reflection of God's love for his creation

and the special place man has in it

as his sons (and daughters).

Referring to the vision of Mary about the moon:

Recreate it from memory for the book cover.

Allow me to live within you.

From me/our Father,

through the power of the Holy Spirit,

all life comes.

I will protect and guide you...I love you, my child...

Receive the Eucharist often—

daily, and pray each day.

I love you and I am always with you.

"I love you, Jesus."

September 17, 1995

All will be well, my child.

Follow my commands.

Love one another as I have loved you.

Tell the world to do the same...

Let me guide and direct you. Close your eyes.

Your prayers for her (a loved one) have been heard and answered.

She has softened her heart to my love

and accepts my presence...

You are with me, my child.

Allow me to grow

and develop in you to full strength,

that I may be born within you.

Let my light shine from your eyes. Do not be afraid.

I am here to guide, watch over and protect you and your loved ones.

You all have an important role to play in God's plan...

Write regardless of what else takes place.

Collect your notes...I will guide you...

You are a willing vessel,

a channel for my love/energy

to reach your fellow man.

"I know it is not my power. I am nothing without you."

Your humility is sincere.

I know every aspect of your heart,

and every yearning to more closely

follow my teachings and my/our Father's will.

I will help you.

I am your life's strength and force.

You are right to more gracefully accept

my will as you have seen it fall around you...

"Jesus forgive me for questioning the pain which this thorn within my heart daily reminds me."

Much good will flow forth from the evil done,

though it is not yet obvious.

Have faith.

I will draw good from evil.

It is part of my/our Father's plan, (my authenticity).

Rest your head back, my child; close your eyes and listen.

Place down your pen for the moment.
Rest and let me make you strong in body and spirit.
I love you. You are mine and I am yours.
Turn to me in your concerns, questions, problems, woes.
I will guide and comfort you as no one else can.
Only I (the Trinity) know you well enough
to know your full needs.
You will have all that you need
to carry out God's will (I/my Father's) will.
Do not be afraid. I will never leave you...

Referring to my delight upon insight into the earthly fate of the person
of darkness:

...You are human, my child,
but try to replace that reaction with love and prayer for him.
He is in great need of your prayers and forgiveness,
as is a suffering soul in purgatory.

Referring to the person of darkness:

He will appreciate/see the error of his ways
at the hour of his death,
and he will be overcome with remorse—crushing remorse,
when truth is laid bare before him.
His soul will suffer greatly and long
before he glimpses me/my Father.
He will suffer tenfold all the pain he has created
in the lives of those he touched.
His regrets will be unimaginable,
all with the knowledge that it was at his own choosing.

"When is he to meet this fate? Forgive me for asking. I fear the question
displeasing in your eyes; though I cannot hide from you my heart, that I
would look forward to the day."

My child, you are human and you choose to avoid evil.
You seek my peace.
I do not condemn you for that,
yet ever bear in mind:
love your enemy
and pray for those who persecute you.

They lose any power over you...
It is also healing of their spirit.
That is what you are all here to learn—love.
Love one another as I have loved you,
and love your God above all people and things.
Detach yourself from all
and cling only to God
seeking to do his holy will.
As members of the perfect Trinity
God the Father's will is mine as is the Holy Spirit's.
You and all men are invited to join/partake of divine eternal life
through the Holy Spirit coming upon you—
that I have laid the bridge for your salvation
through my death and resurrection.

Regarding: the person of darkness.
Yes, you know and have known the answer for some time...
Conduct yourself accordingly.
So advised, upon deeper reflection of the person of darkness' eternal
fate, my feelings turned to pity.
Pity is not necessary.
It is a choice he has made...
Referring to his impact on others:
Any further pain he causes...
is pain from which healing will well forth...
I was given further insight into his end. I glimpsed his agony after
mortal death in graphic multi-sensory images, exceeding human frame of
reference. I who had raged, "No fire in hell is hot enough for him!" was
brought to immediate sobriety upon seeing the monstrosity of suffering
and anguish which would crush him. I could not bear to watch even him
suffer so. In that instant there came the beginning of my heart's conversion toward true forgiveness of him. I pleaded, "I don't wish that upon
him, Jesus."
Yes, my child,
I know your heart is sincerely predisposed toward forgiveness
and you would not want to see him suffer.
Suffer he will as that has been his choice—
turning away from God's will.

God's justice will prevail...
those who have taken the gifts they have been given
and used them against God's will, turning away
for their own self-centered satisfaction, will have no pity.
The more one is given the more responsibility one has to give back.
Yes, my child, pity will not be necessary
as you align your will with God's...

Referring to something I considered a significant unwanted outcome in life:
This is my plan. I am pleased that you are
better accepting my plan over yours without railing against it.
There is more peace, ease and less energy lost
in accepting my/our Father's will than railing against it.
There are many mysteries and seeming paradoxes.
To be Christian is not to be passive.
These may seem like contradictions.
It is hard to become still enough to actively listen
and discern God's plan for you.
Sometimes actively carrying it forth
is yet more difficult as it may appear unconventional
or be questioned/criticized/scrutinized negatively by others.

Referring to a particular possession:
It owns you—you don't own it.
Detach yourself from any such possession,
thought, concept, person.
Cling only to me,
our Father and the Holy Spirit.
(From this flows) the remainder of your life,
your relationships, and all that you should be will fall into place.
Attend Mass and receive Communion daily.
Encourage your children to do the same,
in particular that they be open to God's grace
and not (just) go through the rote motions.
There is a great deal of grace to be obtained
through the Sacrament of the Eucharist,
but it is more fully available
to those with an openly receptive heart.

If they do not feel that,
tell them to pray and ask God to make it so—
to predispose them to receiving God's healing grace...
I am always with you. I am one with you, my child.
I am yours and you are mine. I will never leave you.
You will never lose the gift of my presence.
I know your heart's desire and I am well pleased. I love you.
I will help you carry it forth, that my light/life
more fully shines from your eyes and works upon your fellow man.
*I will teach you to love more fully* and purify your heart.
Let go—detach from the worldly all concerns; cling to me.
My peace be with you.

September 21, 1995

Though my heart had begun to be able to forgive, there remained a long uphill road. Trying to come to terms with the intrusion of evil in my life; and living with its aftermath seemed a struggle in vain. My responses of anger and hatred took their toll upon my inner peace, magnifying my sorrow. While churning this endless loop, searching for an exit I heard:

**Don't be looking to the world for solutions
which are not in the world.**

Explained:

*Coming to grips with good versus evil
can only be brought to terms through the spiritual—that is,
in Christ's example and teachings, his redemption of all mankind.*

I recalled the following in my thoughts:

"Love your enemy and pray for those who persecute you."
God will prevail over evil; bringing good from evil
rather than destroying it outright.
The ways of God are not the ways of man or this world
and therefore man is unable to understand.
"Forgive us our trespasses as we forgive those
who trespass against us."

The world holds no answers. In the world there is no sense to be drawn from evil. It is only through Christ, that we can find meaning, and purpose to the otherwise inexplicable. It is only through Christ that we can draw the empowerment and tempering strength to move on. Today's insight was not a "magic bullet," but it was another beginning. It was an invitation to greater spiritual openness to true solutions, true healing and lasting comfort.

 September 22, 1995
After Mass and Communion:

My thoughts still returned to the humanly impossible: making sense of evil. Many times I still could not help wondering, "Why? Why God? How could you allow this? How could something such as this have good drawn from its darkness?"

All the evil, suffering, pain, loss, horror, cruelty, misfortune, injustice, and inhumanity in the world cannot be made sense of in terms of the world. Though we do not as often stop to question the opposite, nor can all the good, beauty, altruism, kindness, and love be appreciated in their fullest by worldly standards. It is Christ through his life, death and resurrection, who provides all true meaning and all lasting significance to everything with which the world surrounds us. Christ is the source of all life and meaning in our world.

My thoughts still fixated upon my personal brush with evil. How intense the suffering and destructiveness such a person of darkness can bring to other human lives. I could not help myself still asking, "Why?"

**You have glimpsed the beast**
**and in so doing seen me more clearly.**

Explained:

*The beast is Satan,*
*working through the hands of human beings.*
*The image of Christ and his message*
*became more sharply focused, heightened, clear—*
*in stark contrast to having seen the darkness.*

Later, walking home from church:

**You and your loved ones are in my care and protection.**
**Do not be afraid. I hold you safely in my arms.**

Explained:

*As always, this was not a promise*
*that no suffering or negative would be experienced,*
*but that it would have some meaning and purpose as part of God's overall plan,*

*that Christ would be there to give us strength*
*to meet the challenges and obstacles in our paths.*
*The protection was in terms of our spiritual eternal lives.*

September 27, 1995
After Mass and Communion:
Do not be afraid, I will make you strong.
You will see my face in the world around you.
(meaning: humanity, and all creation)
Live by my word.
Love one another as I have loved you.
Tell the world to do the same.
This is the true path to salvation.
I am the one true way.
I love you, my child...

September 28, 1995
After Mass and Communion:
Be still, my child.
Let my peace and light flow over you.
Let it fill you with my love and joy.
Let it heal your heart/inner depths.
I am always with you, though you are often unaware.
My love is your strength.
All things are possible through me.
Have faith, trust, hope,
and love your brothers and sisters as I have loved you.
Love all my creation, all my works.
All my works glorify my name and the Father's.
Allow the Holy Spirit into your hearts
that I may more fully inspire you—be one with you.
You are mine and I am yours.
Forsake all others for me.
Detach yourself from all things for me.
I am your sole focus.
In doing so you will find true
and lasting joy and contentment.
Let my peace come upon you.

Carry it within you the day through.
Divest yourself of the cares/woes/worries
of this world—your body included
(meaning: health, concerns, discomfort)
I will provide for you and your loved ones
precisely what you need and more.
More, more bountifully than you could ever imagine.
"Help me to do your will."
I will give you strength, courage to persevere.
Do not worry. Do not be afraid.
Be up and about your days work...

Late September, 1995
After Mass and Communion:
Be still, my child. Listen to me.
Do not rush. Do not worry.
Do not be afraid. Be patient. All in due time.
My/our Father's plan is unfolding
and you as many others have a unique role to play.
I will show you as the time is right.
Carry the light of my presence to those you meet.
Do this in your actions, words, manner, serenity.
I am one with you, my child.
Your prayers are heard and answered,
though you may not always understand or see the answer.
I am always with you. I will never abandon you.
I love you. I am yours and you are mine.
You are never alone.
Allow me to guide your every step and word.
Allow me to shine through your demeanor
and the expression of your face, the light in your eyes.
Touch others with the presence of my love.
...carry my healing presence
to those (in) the world around you.
Do not be afraid.
You and your loved ones
are in my care and protection.
I know your heart to its depths.

I know your reluctance and true humility.
Just allow me to work through you. Do nothing.
Be only receptive to my commands.
You will be given discernment to light your way/path.
Do not be afraid.
You and your loved ones
are in my constant care and protection.
Now be up and about your business.
Your life, its every act, thought, prayer,
and intention are a prayer.
Unite them all with my saving acts
and you will feel my presence
and companionship more intensely.
Pick up your cross and follow me.
(meaning: all trials, tribulations, circumstances,
aches, pains, discomforts, inconveniences, et. al.)
I am with you. I am at your side.
I am your constant source of strength, meaning, purpose.
I am your life's force and
your reason for existence (to exist).
I am your Alpha and Omega.
Come to me,
deeper,
deeper
and deeper.
Follow me of your love for me.
Be up now and about your business.

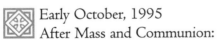 Early October, 1995
After Mass and Communion:
...Pray, my child.
Remember your life is a prayer.
"Help me, Jesus."
I am here for you always.
I will never forsake you or your loved ones.
Be strong and know that my love will fill you
with the strength and wisdom to handle what comes your way.
Write today, my child. It is most important that you do this.

Allow me to guide your hand,
and do not worry about organization or the whole.
It is in my hands. Just allow me to work through yours.
"Yes Jesus Thank you, but how could I be chosen for this?"
It is part of my/our Father's plan.
I know the desires of your heart better than you.
Simply place your faith, confidence, and trust in me.
Allow me to work through you.
Make less effort and simply let me show you the way.
Open yourself to my love, guidance, and direction.
"I want to stay longer." I silently said, reluctant to leave the peace of
the church.

Later sit with me in peace and stillness.
Now be up and about your day's work.
I love you. I am always with you.

October, 1995
I was frustrated at my limited connection in praying today, more
rattling words than praying.

I am with you, my child. Do not be afraid.
I know your heart.
Several minutes later:
I know your heart better than (and before) you.
You do not need words to pray.
Several minutes later:
Be with me a while in the still and quiet.
Let my peace come upon you
and carry it with you throughout the day.
Let my light shine from your eyes the day through.
(In so doing) bring my presence to those you touch each day.

October 5, 1995
After Mass, and Communion:
Forsake all others for me, my child.
Meet your earthly/human obligations to those as you should.
Bring the light, peace, love of my presence
to them as you touch their lives.
Be not afraid.

I am watching over, guiding, and protecting you
and your loved ones.
There is a plan.
You all have an important/vital role to play in it.
I am leading you where you need to be.
Make no plans; just allow me to guide you every day.
Be patient; just allow my work for you to unfold each day...
I am your strength, your life's force.
Do not worry, I will give you strength, courage, wisdom
and all that is needed every step of the way...
I am with you always...
You are never without my love and strength.
I love you.

 October 6, 1995
After Mass and Communion:
Sit and be with me a while, pen in hand.
Be still, my child.
Be still in your heart.
Let the tension, worries, anxieties
your body holds, release.
Let my peace flow over you.
Let my healing love fill your heart.
Let your eyes and every action and intention
shine forth my love to all creation/humanity.
I love you, my child. I am always with you.
You are mine and I am yours.
Forsake all others for me and
divest yourself of the importance of all things.
I am your life.
I am all that you need.
I am the truth, the light and the way...

My child, do not be concerned.
I know the sincere humility in your heart.
Be open to my instruction and follow me.
Today, my child, you must write. You must make it a priority
despite the concerns and happenings of each day...

...all power, life itself
comes from me/our Father.
You well recognize your humble role in this.
Be open to my guidance/direction.
Let me lead you; follow me.
Do not be worried or concerned about any matters
of the world or **bodily** (meaning: health).
Place down your pen and sit silently with me for a while.
Close your eyes. Feel my presence.
"I am having trouble doing that. I am distracted. I can't."
Be still, my child.
Be at peace.
Let my peace fill your heart.
You are bathed in my love and the warmth of my light.
Close your eyes.
Nothing matters, my child, but me and your relationship with me.
From there all else will properly flow/fall into place—
your relationships with your fellow man,
and all of creation.

Explained:

*Through the love of Christ—*
*in this inspiration, and motivation*
*one would imitate his example*
*and follow his teaching,*
*drawn there by love.*
This is how simple life is.
Follow me; follow my lead.
Pick up your cross and follow me.
Remember my commandments of love.
Love God above all things.
Love your neighbor as thyself.
It is simple.

Referring to a homeless person, sleeping in a pew:
...Pray for him.
Pray that he opens his heart to the Holy Spirit
and my healing love, that he allows our heavenly help
in carrying the crosses of his life and finds his own meaning.

Now, my child, be up and about your business.
Do not be discouraged; I am your strength
and my love is all that you need.
Be not afraid.

October 9, 1995
After Mass and Communion:
Regarding someone I loved, having a difficult time:
Do not worry about them.
I am with them as all your loved ones.
I will show them the way.
There will be some painful lessons
but they will find their way to my path.
Reassure them that I am with them.
Tell them to open their heart to the Holy Spirit,
that I may enter them and more fully unite with their will.
Tell them it takes less effort.
Tell them to be patient.
In the stillness of their heart I will come to them.
Tell them I will be there.
Tell them to receive Communion often
and read scripture every day...
Tell them not to be afraid.
Tell them to allow my peace to flow over them
and just allow me to direct their path.
Remind them all things happen for a reason.
Though I/my Father allow evil to exist,
I/my Father will draw good from all evil.
I/my Father's will is done.
Tell them to place their faith, trust, and hope in me.
Tell them I am their life's force, the reason for their existence.
It is my love which is and gives them life now and eternally.
Be there for them.
Be patient, kind, compassionate, non-judgmental.
Be there for them as I have been there for you.
(implicit forgiveness, unconditional love)
Reassure them.
Life is also here to be enjoyed.

Reassure/remind them they have been given
their life's talents, interests and personality
to fulfill a unique role in my/our Father's plan.
Tell them they are good and all my works are good.
Tell them not to be discouraged—
that I am leading them where they need to be.
Tell them the hardest part is becoming still enough to listen
to the quiet of my voice and see me/my will
in all that is and occurs around them.
I will give them the strength and courage
that they need
to persevere in all things.
I will show them the way
in the stillness of their heart.
Their intelligence, strong will and ambition
make it harder for them to find
the stillness/(quiet) to listen to me,
as so it did with you.
These are the very qualities
which will also allow them to achieve
the greatness I have planned for them,
when they use their will with mine.
You know listening is hard
and how difficult it is to find
the stillness of which I speak.
Tell them in the meantime to ardently pray
that they do the Father's will
and that the Holy Spirit enter their heart,
allowing me to be more present in their lives
influencing their thoughts, words, deeds—
their every intention.
Tell them how very much I love them—
that I have claimed them.
They are mine and I am theirs.
They are to live with me for eternity.
They are chosen to share divine life—
like you and all of the other chosen souls
imprinted/imbued from the very beginning (with) the Holy Spirit.

Live out your earthly existence learning to love more purely.
Make your lives a recapitulation of Christ's and Mary's,
and this will be your guide (map).
Do not be afraid.
You and your loved ones are in my care and protection.
Tell them rejoice and be happy in full knowledge of my love
and everlasting care of them.
Tell them do not be afraid.
Place their cares and worries aside.
Find the stillness, and simply listen.
Seek my grace and presence in Communion.
I will always be there for them and all your loved ones.
Let them know all will be well...
Tell them I have made them in my image and likeness.
I have created them exactly as I want them to be.
They are good and all my works are good.
I am leading them where I want them to be.
Pain is fleeting and mortal.
Tell them to unite their pain and joy with mine as
Christ on earth and
Christ who lives forever,
Christ who died,
Christ who is risen,
Christ who will come again.

Mid-October, 1995
*Mary's unique sorrow in Christ's passion*
*was in helplessly witnessing her beloved and innocent child suffer.*
*Mary's suffering in Christ's passion*
*is an integral part of our redemption*
*but only defined in terms of Christ;*
*that is, only because her suffering is united with his.*
*We are all called to do the same with our suffering.*
*Mary's suffering complements Christ's.*
*Their bond as mother and child,*
*illustrates the unification of their suffering.*
*Christ's pain is his Mother's pain.*
*Mary's pain is her Son's pain.*

*We are all called to follow Mary's example.*
*Every form of our own suffering, physical or mental,*
*can be found in Christ's passion shared with Mary.*
*Mary's integral presence in her own suffering of her Son's passion*
*shows us how to unite ourselves with her Son.*

October 13, 1995

I remained tormented at evil's aftermath in my life. Indeed this was a thorn in constant reminder of the real existence of Satan and the battle raging about us between good and evil. Periodically the barb was twisted in the still raw wound, as was the case today. I could not break free. I could not escape. Anger inflamed me as sorrow smothered me—a fire within me which seemed neither able to burn itself out or be quenched. Referring to this person of darkness:

**Detach yourself from him and all things.**
**Your only focus is me, your relationship with me,**
**and through this all things will naturally follow.**
**Then in so doing, (as a result)**
**you will live your life in keeping with my will.**
**Place me above all and do not be concerned**
**with the worries/problems of the world.**
**I will guide/watch over and protect you.**

I was further advised:

*He needs my forgiveness and prayers;*
*and that I must have patience, kindness, and love.*
**Yes, my child...he will...torment you a short time.**

I could not check my immediate desire to know, "How long?" I initially assumed this meant his physical demise, then realized it could just as well have meant his spiritual rebirth, a change in my attitude, or yet other possibilities. I do not know. I recognized my first reaction as less than pure love and forgiveness. Acknowledging this and my own insignificance relative to God, I asked in rhetorical jest, "What's short in the face of eternity?" There returned to me not only the warmest shared humor in my self-acknowledged weakness; but also great mercy and compassion in my difficulty forgiving and loving this person.

**Be patient, my child; the end of his torment of you is near.**
**It is within your grasp to further end it today**
**in keeping my word, following my lead,**

allowing me to enter your heart so deeply we are one.
Remember my words on the cross:
'Father, forgive them,
they know not what they do.'
Follow this.
Detach yourself from this and all things.
Be patient.
Exude the love, light, kindness,
and gentleness of my spirit within you.
Let my peace flow over you and dwell always within you.
Bring my presence in all the beauty of my peace
and light I give you to carry within you
to those whom you meet.
Bring my presence—
all the beauty, peace and light
with which you are filled
to all those you touch in your life.
You are mine and I am yours.
Your rewards will be great.
Your enemies vanquished.
I will raise you up and you shall live with me forever.
"Do you speak only of the afterlife?"
Do not be afraid, my child.
You have suffered much in your life already.
Be secure, trust in knowing any suffering you
will yet endure will be for a purpose
which will bear much fruit.
Do not yourself increase the suffering,
anguish, and pain of your life
by railing against my will,
ignoring my teaching
and my life's example.
"Sometimes I don't know how to apply your teachings, and often I do not
know clearly what your will is."
Do not waste your energy with concern for this.
Be patient. I will show you as your life unfolds.
I will make you wise as you need to be.
I will give you what you need before you know it is necessary.

The desires of your heart are pure
though you struggle against your own human will.
It is the nature of humanity.
Follow my lead to be guided from your selfishness.
Selfishness is ultimately destructive of humanity.
First, you and all my children must
love their neighbor as they love themselves;
and then,
love me/my Father above all things.
Do not be afraid.
I know the desires of your heart.
I will be always there to help you and your loved ones.
My love is your strength and life's force.
I am of absolute importance.
All else is important only relative to
the importance derived from me.
All that is important as defined by the world will perish—
perish as all false gods of history:
old sun (god), idols, now money, power, fame.
The modern day gods: money, fame and power,
have merit only in how man uses them
to glorify and spread my name.
All my works are good.
All that I have created is good.
The gifts of power, wealth, fame or any good fortune
are not of themselves bad.
It is how man, the recipient, distorts their value
when these are not used to reflect my love, image, plan, will.
Woe to the man who has been given great gifts and
uses them purely for his own gratification and greater glory.
I am among you, in all your brothers and sisters.
Remember,
what you do unto the least of my brethren
so you do unto me.
I love you, my child.
I know you struggle hard to do my will.
Struggle less; be patient;
allow me to gently lead you where you need to be.

I will provide you whatever strength, wisdom and
all that you need to do my works.
When you allow the Holy Spirit to fully enter you
and allow me to dwell with you as one,
the difficult becomes easy, the impossible, reality.
I love you, my child. You are mine and I am yours.
Now be up and about your business/day's work.
Be conscious of my presence
within and all about you the day through.
Be filled with my joy, my peace.
You are never without me, nor are your loved ones.
"I don't want to leave; it's so peaceful here."
Remember, my child, your life is a prayer.
You do not leave me. You take me with you.
Your day's work—to the most mundane, is prayer.

October 17, 1995
After Mass and Communion:
Close your eyes and feel my presence.
My peace is with you.
Let it flow over you the day through.
Be present in your life, aware of my presence *in you*,
and in those around you.
(meaning: Live in the moment, aware of Christ's
immediate presence in self and all others.)
Let my light/love touch those you meet.
Do not be afraid. I am with you now and always.
Now be up and about your day's business...
I will never give you a burden greater than you can bear.
You will never experience pain without purpose.
It (pain) will bear fruit.
I love you, my child. You are never alone.
I am with you always.

*The 'I am' of*
*'I am with you always.'*
*is the Mystical Body of Christ,*
*uniting all of us across time and distance.*

I experienced astonishing closeness, more like a union, with the presence of loved ones, living and deceased, and in a more nonspecific sense with humanity, a greater plan and eternal life—the real fact of an afterlife.

October 19, 1995

My brush with evil left me a heightened sense of sin and its destructive aftermath, from the mildest to the most grievous. I felt renewed sorrow and remorse for my own past transgressions. I was acutely aware of my sins of omission, absence to others, caught up in my own needs or past ambitions.

**Do not wallow in guilt.**

**Accept my forgiveness and go on with your life.**

**To do so** (wallow in guilt) **would only interfere
with the work I have planned for you.**

**Be present to your family and the moment at hand.**

**To live in the past is to be tied
by remorse, anger and injustice done.**

**Detach yourself.**

**Allow my love and forgiveness to free you
to live most fully in the present,
to devote yourself most fully
to my work, my plan for you,
that you touch others you meet each day
with the love I have given you
and allowed you the grace
to so fully feel my presence.**

**I will not leave you or withdraw my gifts from you.**

**Yes, all men must remain actively receptive,
that you may passively receive what is given you
by the Father
through the Holy Spirit and
my presence within and about you.**

**Let my forgiveness, mercy and love allow you
to detach from all things.**

**Let loose all anxieties, concerns, regrets,
hurts, injustice, possessions and relationships,
other than with me—your God and Blessed Trinity.**

**Be at peace, my child.**

Regarding fresh anger at personal injustice in evil's wake:
You struggle making your life unnecessarily difficult,
taking you from those around you (family)
and the work I have planned for you.
Let the past be gone.
Accept evil as it is and avoid it.
Stay clear. You cannot combat evil's force,
but only I/my Father.
Be at peace.
Justice will be done.
Do not concern yourself
or expend any energy
on the injustice done to you...
It is in my hands.
I care for you and your loved ones
as a loving protective Father.
Think of how you feel towards your children,
and magnify that beyond your comprehension.
Do not worry. Do not be afraid.
Do not expend your time or any other resource
seeking justice or redress (on these matters).
It is in progress.
Your pain will bear fruit.
My justice is served.
My/our Father's will is done.
The wicked shall be cast out
and the good live eternally in peace and harmony
with me in my Father's kingdom...
All will be well, my child. Do not fear.
I am leading you where I want to be.
I wondered had I misheard the pronoun.
Yes, my child, where I want to be,
carried by my presence within you.
Be filled with my grace and unite your will with mine.
Answer as did Mary,
'Thy will be done.'
'Let it be done unto me
according to thy word.'

Let my peace flow over you and my love light your way.
Let my presence be felt by those
you come into contact with each day.
Remember it is your gift that you feel my presence so deeply.
It is through grace and
the Holy Spirit within your heart
that you are able.
All things are possible through God.
When you feel injustice identify and join your suffering
to that of Christ
and Mary in his passion.
*Identify with and look to Mary for example*
*in faith,*
*in submission of will,*
*when you see children suffer.*

My mind returned to the sting of personal injustice:
The injustice you have suffered is slight relative to
that which exists in the world at large
(encompassing time and space).
You have more important tasks at hand,
more that you are to contribute
than wasting your bodily energy rectifying personal injustice.
There is more important work planned for you.
Be up and about your business.
I love you and I am well pleased with your efforts.
I know the intentions of your heart.
I know you struggle against your human weakness/frailty
and my mercy and compassion are with you.
Remember I am your strength and life's force.
Be not afraid.
All things are possible through me/my Father.
You will have the strength and all resources necessary
as they are required of you.
Later that morning:
You can do more good for many than yourself alone
in ignoring your own struggles for justice
and following my will, as I lead you.

In this perspective my own difficulties paled. The detachment it brought was an oasis from which my heart could better lean into deeper forgiveness. It was refuge from my own responses in anger and hatred, a place of peace from which to heal and grow in love and forgiveness, a place to let go of past hurt and move on.

October 24, 1995
After Communion I felt a very close sense of God's presence and a flash of understanding confirmed in the following:

Yes, my child,
you have been cast into this body
to perfect your spirit,
to draw closer to me,
to choose my image and likeness
over the darkness,
to learn to love—love more perfectly,
to live forever
and share in my divine life,
the divine eternal life of the Trinity.
You are good and my works are good.
I am in all those around you.
I am all around you;
I am everywhere;
I am all time.
Your mind cannot begin
to grasp/comprehend what I say.
You and each and every YOU
are an integral, unique part
of my/our Father's plan.
All our creation is beautiful.
*God did not create evil*
*but rather it originated as a byproduct*
*of how God's gift of free will has been used.*
As in our image and likeness,
man has been given the power to create
through free will.
Man can create good—love, or evil.
Both affect and live on touching all of humanity.

Only Christ/our Father can triumph over evil.
All that is asked of you
is your willing cooperation
in God's plan—to do God's will,
to patiently allow it to unfold before you.
Love your fellow man and
your God above all things.
Follow the example
I have left you in my life on earth;
follow my teachings.
Know that I will never leave you,
never abandon you, never forsake you.
No matter how desolate you feel,
turn to me at all times and in all things.
I am your true and eternal
source of peace, consolation, strength, love.
I am all things.
I know the innermost secrets
of your heart's desire.
I will purify your heart.
You will each day become
a more perfect reflection of my love.
I am love—
love beyond any human's comprehension.
"I fear I will not carry out your will, that I won't know it, or be too weak."
Do not be afraid or concern yourself;
I will give you the strength, courage, wisdom
as you need it.
Be patient and allow my plan
to unfold for you...
Yes, people will be brought in and out
of your life for a reason.
Oft times you will never know what that is
but be blindly asked
to function in our Father's plan.
Be patient.
All will be provided you as you/it is needed.

I was reminded of a recent gospel:

> And he said to his disciples, "Therefore I tell you, do not be anxious about your life, what you shall eat, nor about your body, what you shall put on. For life is more than food, and the body more than clothing. Consider the ravens: they neither sow nor reap, they have neither storehouse nor barn, and yet God feeds them. Of how much more value are you than the birds! And which of you by being anxious can add a cubit to his span of life? If then you are not able to do as small a thing as that, why are you anxious about the rest? Consider the lilies, how they grow; they neither toil nor spin; yet I tell you, even Solomon in all his glory was not arrayed like one of these. But if God so clothes the grass which is alive in the field today and tomorrow is thrown into the oven, how much more will he clothe you, O men of little faith! And do not seek what you are to eat and what you are to drink, nor be of anxious mind. For all the nations of the world seek these things; and your Father knows that you need them. Instead, seek his kingdom, and these things shall be yours as well.
>
> "Fear not, little flock, for it is your Father's good pleasure to give you the kingdom. Sell your possessions, and give alms; provide yourselves with purses that do not grow old, with a treasure in the heavens that does not fail, where no thief approaches and no moth destroys. For where your treasure is, there will your heart be also."
>
> Luke 12:22-34, RSV

I love you, my child. You and your loved ones
are in my constant care and protection.
Do not be afraid to live.
Do not be afraid to die.
There is great work which lies ahead
for you and all souls which our Father has created.
Some are more aware of this than others,
but awareness is not a necessary precursor
to participating in our Father's plan.
Our Father's/my will is done.
God is all powerful, all loving, all kind, and lastly, all just.
(*Lastly—having temporal meaning in earth time, and
finality as regarding the end of the world and final judgment.*)
Allow me to speak and work through you,
to touch other's lives.
"I feel unworthy and undeserving of the gifts I have received. Please
make me worthy."
You know well, my child, that all the children I have created
are beautiful and equally special,
important and unique,
loved by their Creator.
You have genuine humility, and this is good.
Humility will maintain the special gifts
I have given you in perspective.
You are each given special gifts;
they are all different.
My words and man's are not the same.
Suffering is a gift when it brings one closer to God.
When one allows God's will to be done,
*submitting one's own will to God's,*
suffering bears fruit.
Man does not see suffering as a gift.
Not every gift in God's eyes
is at odds with what man considers a gift.
When they coincide
it is just as important (as with suffering),
that the experience be lived
in keeping with God's will—in accordance with his plan.

How a man suffers and lives the joys of his life
should always reflect the honor, glory and praise of our Father.
I love you, my child. Important work lies ahead.
Be up and about your business.
"I don't want to leave the comfort and sanctuary of your presence, the
intensity of peace, and respite I feel here."
*I am with you always; where you go, so go I.*

October 25, 1995
During Mass before the Gospel:
"Why have I received the gift of feeling your presence so closely?"
You are each of you given special gifts.
All are equal in our Father's eyes,
all important in his plan.
They (gifts) are not recognized as such among men.
After Communion:
Be still, my child, commune with me.
Eyes closed, there was peaceful, short silence, generalized light, and
less awareness of physical discomfort, with an overall lightness of being,
as if floating.
Let my love and peace flow over you.
Be filled with my love, strength, and courage.
Do not be concerned. Sit with me awhile.
Place down your pen and feel my presence.
Allow it to fortify and inspire you. Close your eyes.
I felt great closeness with Christ and in silent wordless communica-
tion an understanding was imparted through partial but colorful analogy.
Man is to God as a beloved pet such as a dog is to man.

*The dog is content merely to be with or near his master*
*and by analogy,*
*so is it man's deepest interior desire*
*to return to his Creator, to be with God his master.*
*Imagine if a dog had the potential to become human*
*and in the process of realizing that potential*
*could glimpse beyond the canine realm*
*into the mind and heart of man to exchange communication,*
*unrestricted by mental capacity, instinct or nature.*

*It is an infinite leap beyond such hypothesis*
*that God has so imbued us with the Holy Spirit,*
*that we are allowed communication with the Divine*
*and more phenomenal yet, that we are invited*
*to share God's eternal life as his children.*
You are filled with the Holy Spirit
which is why you are able to communicate with me;
it is why you (mankind) are elevated above a dog.
The Holy Spirit was breathed into you
from the dawn of creation—the Alpha,
*before the beginning of time,*
*before the creation of the world.*
Time has different value here.
Man's laws of time do not apply.
What I say cannot be understood in man's words.
Place down your pen. Close your eyes.
Feel my presence. Now...
Go home and consolidate my words to you.
Read them. Observe the themes developed.
See the pattern, where I am slowly, gently leading you,
one step at a time. Do not be afraid.
Good things lie ahead.

Referring to someone who has suffered injustice at the hands of a black-
hearted person:

...Do not create crisis.
The truth will set you free.
Self-knowledge frees you
from the tyranny of...negative experience,
brings one closer to me,
makes one more master of their fate,
and more fully empowered in exercising their free will—
wresting it back from evil forces which have played upon them
(and) rippled their aftershocks of destructiveness
and divisiveness upon their innocence.
They will survive and triumph as my favored servant.
I am here to serve them and all mankind,
to bring you to the Lord our Father.

Encourage, reassure them all will be well.
I am at their side though they know it not.
I am never beyond them, always with them.
The Holy Spirit will more fully enter their heart
and all those for whom you pray to me.
Prayer is very powerful from the pure of heart.
It (prayer of the pure of heart)
is most closely aligned with our Father's will
and therein derives its great strength/indomitable power.
All prayers are answered, though the answers
are not always recognized by man.
As a kind and loving parent
all that is good is provided to
my children, my/our Father's creation,
all that they need.
Needing and wanting are not always recognized
as the same in man's and God's words
nor are comfort and happiness,
nor success and achievement.
It is only these words
as defined in God's terms
which will transcend mortality,
that will live on to eternity.
The first shall come last
and the last shall come first.
You are all here to be each other's servants,
none more important than the next,
regardless of outward worldly appearance or trappings—
be they inherent gifts, good fortune or any aspect,
or circumstance of life station into which you are found.

I remembered a dream from earlier in the week. Its message summarized life's daily purpose: we are all here to help one another carry each other's crosses, and in so doing, to follow Christ's example.

In the dream I stood in a doorway and looked down a long narrow hall, filled with a stream of variously afflicted and to varying degrees suffering people. They were single file, coming towards me on the right and going away from me on the left. I stood as one link in this long chain.

From my vantage point, where the chain turned in the narrow hall, it was easy to see how those in the opposite line could help one another from their remaining strengths. In this complementary manner we could, in a sense, make ourselves whole.

Physical circumstances constrained their perspectives, a tunnel vision worsened by downcast heads—each immersed in his or her own suffering. My sadness at this sight was heightened at seeing how much relief and comfort were immediately available to all, right at arm's reach. How much easier we could make one another's journey.

I felt compelled to call down the hall, "Those with healthy arms, help those without. Those with healthy legs, help those without. Those with strong minds or emotional strength, help those without. Help each other! Jesus Christ has taught us that we are here to help each other carry our crosses." There was no reaction or even stir from the line of misery before me.

I awoke with rapid heartbeat and relief to find it a dream.

> You are all special gifts given.
> They are merely, to the man, different
> but equally important in God's eyes.
> My/our Father's final judgment
> makes all a (level field).
> All souls are an integral, unique
> and important part of my/our Father's plan—
> utterly detached from any seeming value
> or importance placed on that life
> by worldly standards.
> My/our Father's grace and love
> are freely given to sinner and saint alike.
> We are here for all people.
> Our gifts are not earned or deserved.
> They are given of pure, unconditional love.
> Love beyond man's comprehension.
> An open heart is needed to receive these gifts
> and therein lies the difference between sinner and saint—
> the predisposition to receive/accept, unconditionally,
> without question, (that is, with faith,)
> the gifts bestowed upon them.

Pray for the conversion of sinners.
Pray that they open their hearts to my grace
and the presence of the Holy Spirit,
that I may more fully enter their hearts...
Do not dissipate your life's strength striking against
the immovable effects of evil manifest in those
who choose to do you injustice.
Allow me to handle them.
It is only I/my Father
who can effectively combat evil's force.
Your only weapon/defense is your free will.
No more is expected nor are you capable
in combating evil in the world about you.
It has already been done for once and all time
in the presence of Christ, my Son on earth,
through his life, death, resurrection.
The fate of all finitely (that is,
with finality and for all eternity) sealed
when he will come again in glory one day;
the final judgment day when all souls' choices are made eternal.

Pray every day, my child.
Pray and work for your fellow man.
"Help me please, that I do your will. I pray and hope it will be a gentle
path for myself and loved ones, but I don't wish a difficult path upon
any man."
You are good, my child.
All things happen for a reason, good and bad.
Do not be alarmed at what you see around you.
(world suffering, injustice, pain, and more)
Be moved to prayer and align your will with mine.
Christ on earth did not right every injustice he saw
(in his human state, as he lived his life),
but suffered upon seeing them.
Join your suffering in this and all things
to that of Christ's life, passion,
and then take comfort
and share in the joy of his resurrection.

His life, death, and resurrection triumphed over evil and
gave meaning to the otherwise inane suffering
flowing from/originating from evil.
How this is accomplished
is mastered in my/our Father's plan
and no man has comprehended its entirety.
When you share in divine eternal life
through the life of the Trinity
all knowledge is yours,
all truth is yours,
all love,
all time,
all is yours,
all which ever was,
is
and is to be,
which is good,
is yours.
We will all of us one day
be together in peace, harmony, love.
It will be a new day;
a creation arising from the united wills
of all souls created by our Father,
who have chosen to submit/align
their wills with mine/our Father's.
Those who do not will have
perished from this life
(in the new creation)
like 'the wheat sifted from the chaff.'
Those souls (the chaff cast out)
will live eternally in the tyranny of hell—
darkness, and suffering, perpetual suffering
for which there is no relief.
Pray that as many souls as possible be saved this fate
and join their wills with our Father's.

I was distracted by a homeless man seeking shelter in the back of the
church, which was now nearly vacant:

**Be not afraid. Instead be filled with compassion, prayer, but not fear. He is a child of God as the rest. I love you.**

I love you...

 October 26, 1995
Gospel:

> Jesus said to his disciples: "I have come to light a fire on the earth. How I wish the blaze were ignited! I have a baptism to receive. What anguish I feel till it is over! Do you think I have come to establish peace on the earth? I assure you, the contrary is true; I have come for division. From now on, a household of five will be divided three against two and two against three; father will be split against son and son against father, mother against daughter and daughter against mother, mother-in-law against daughter-in-law, daughter-in-law against mother-in-law."
>
> Luke 12: 49-53, Lectionary

I had never understood the day's gospel; but today through both the priest's sermon and wordless insight, I received my first glimpse. The first reading (Romans 6:16-23) explains the gospel context. Christ accepted a baptism of evil, suffering, and pain, by taking human form to live amongst and humanly experience the evil created by men's and angels' free will. In so doing, through his life, death and resurrection he set us free of evil's slavery—providing us the path to salvation along with the example and teachings to follow that path. Christ came to a world ruled by evil. Man was slave to sin, having fallen prey through human weakness. Christ came to light a fire and destroy this bondage. Christ brought disorder to this regime and ignited a turning in upon itself to bring about his own peaceful realm.

That morning I had awoken in a great deal of physical pain, and my ears were also quite symptomatic. Over time an insidious severe pain had come to extend from my lower neck over my shoulders scapula and arms. The complexity and multiplicity of my other symptoms overshadowed and delayed diagnosis of a contributing factor in this pain—two small herniated cervical discs. It felt as if a heavy weight bore down on my neck and shoulders. I sat now, in quiet repose after Communion. It was difficult to leave the peace and comfort of where I found myself, "I don't want to leave, yet know I have much to do."

**Yes, I know, my child**
**and I am pleased that you do not want to leave,**
**yet you must be up and about your day's work.**
**Pick up your cross and follow me, my child.**

I was reminded of the physical pain pressing upon me. The image of the cross identified with Christ's suffering, strengthened me to persevere.

**Be up and come with me.**

Later that morning:

**It is the intention of your heart's desire which matters**
**(and) upon which you are judged.**
**While the world judges**
**by results/outward appearances**
**this is not the way of God,**
**who knows the innermost depths of a man's heart.**
**Intention is an act of will,**
**results are not.**

Late October, 1995

I was by myself in a relatively unfamiliar train station. I was rushing and unable to take in close lines and columns of information on the boards indicating which track my train departed from. I asked directions and found my way to the platform. However, I could not identify the sign to confirm I was in the correct place. A conductor, dressed in dark blue suit and hat, stood beside the train. I asked him whether this was the train to my destination. "Yup," he curtly replied.

"Will all the doors open at that stop?" I asked.

"No, only the last and fourth car." he said.

The last car was not an option; its continuous swaying, coupled with my inner ear disease made motion sickness a certainty. I entered the door directly before me, somewhere in the middle of the train, and settled into a seat. About twenty minutes later a conductor came to collect my ticket. After he left, I realized I did not know which car in the train I was in and had no idea which was the fourth car. I got up the stop before mine to find a conductor to ask, but none was in sight. There was, however, a man standing in the aisle holding two large rings full of keys attached to his belt, but he had no identifying cap or jacket. I asked, "Are you the conductor?"

His voice boomed back at me, "Lady, I was the conductor when you asked me if this was your train on the platform. I was the conductor when I took your ticket. I am still the conductor and I'll be the conductor when we get to the end of the line."

"Sorry, I didn't recognize you." but clearly nothing I could say would do any more than make the situation worse. "Will this door open at the next stop?" I asked, pointing to the door several feet away.

"Lady, now you can get off right here," he said pointing to the same door, "or you can walk all the way back to the end of the train." Disgusted and rolling his eyes, he walked away, quite satisfied with himself for putting another irritating dim-witted passenger in his or her place. I stood there, as I had been, leaning against the wall on my left and holding the top of a seat with my right hand maintaining my balance as the train jostled along. I watched the conductor in disbelief. Part of me wondered, "To whom is he talking?" and then I registered the discrepancy between how I come across, and how I am.

This was a novelty of my illness—experiencing life from so many new perspectives, seeing people react to me as if I were a different person.

Before my illness, one meeting was all it took to effortlessly recall a name and face. People were often impressed and flattered that I remembered them. Now it was the opposite—a frequent source of embarrassment to me and an occasion to leave others feeling slighted. Now I generally needed to meet someone five and six times before sufficiently registering the details of their face to recognize them again.

I preferred the conductor's direct approach over those who remained silently polite, harboring ill will and thinking I had rudely ignored them. At least knowing gave me the chance to correct the misconception. Some falsely concluded I was aloof, unfriendly, moody or just "flaky"—friendly one day and treating them as strangers on the next. How many people had I offended because I did not recognize them the next time I saw them?

It was so strange to have people react to me as someone I was not. Who were they talking to? Then I would realize this is how I now come across, but not how I am.

October 27, 1995
Regarding the book's direction:
Eliminate the personal, non-universal,
other than in furthering the theme of the book.
"I hope I can find everything, all the scraps of paper and notebooks."
Do not worry; you will have what you need
in the context (I) want it to appear.
I am well pleased with you, my child.
You are learning well to lead your life in accordance with my plan.
You are right in emphasizing the urgency of your writing.
"Yet, I do not want to fall behind on matters of responsibility today."
Yes, my child.
Take me with you the day through/throughout your life.
I am with you. Do not be afraid.
You are correct not to plan,
all is planned for you...
Carry my love within you like/as a light
which shines forth from your eyes,
an energy which emanates
from every aspect of your being.
Just allow me to be within you.
Be aware of my constant presence in yourself,
those around you, and in all of creation.
I love you. Go, my child, and be about my work.

October 30, 1995
On the disciplinary challenges of parenting:
Respond out of love and sorrow, not anger.
(Be) non-judgmental, compassionate, forgiving;
yet, present the reality of consequences.
It is because you love them that consequences are measured.
Surely it would be, in the short term,
easier for all parents to give a child what they wanted;
but this is not in their long-term best interest.
So too it is with me and the Father—
with our creation, our children.
I love you, my child.
It is difficult but your efforts will bear fruit.

Be not afraid. I am always with you.
I will provide you the wisdom, strength, perseverance
and courage to see your work/journey through.
Do not struggle so. (Help me help you.)
(Become more receptive.)
Relinquish your will to mine.
All will become easy, your burdens light...
I am your confidant.
No one understands and knows
the complexity of your lives
and the hearts which touch it as do I.
I am the only one who fully understands,
and who can adequately give you counsel.
Be still, my child, and listen. When you are fatigued
recline into my arms and I will give you rest.
I am your refuge from the weariness,
burdens and heaviness of the world.

Regarding an acquaintance injured by evil:
It is all in my plan, that good will flow from it.
I/my Father will draw good from evil.
They have my full compassion and mercy.
Their life, at a very young and innocent age,
has been touched by evil.
They will be wrested from it
though the battle is not easy.
Pray, pray every day for/on their behalf.
The battle is not yet done. I will guide you/your hand.
Be not afraid. Be assured of my constant presence,
guidance and counsel. Turn only to me.
I will provide you safe haven/comfort,
wisdom—as only I who know all,
to the very intention of each man's heart, can provide.
I will share with you what you need, no more as to be confusing.
Just seek the stillness to listen to me and rest in my arms.
Allow your weary body rest in me.
Let me carry you...

Yet taint
(meaning: the mark left by man in harming another with evil)
does not the entire soul spoil.
It will be expunged from this beautiful soul.
Your prayers are more powerful than you know.
Kneel and pray with me for a while.
Focus yourself at the altar,
Mary, the cross, our suffering
and my presence in the Eucharist.
Mary suffering with Christ—
identify with (this) as you see their behavior.
As pure innocence they were nailed to their cross
and made to suffer at the hand of wickedness,
abuse—their brush with evil.
The result evident in behavior beyond their control today;
distorting their beauty
and ability to reflect
God's image and likeness.
I considered the ramifications for society, and the growing number
of abused, or neglected children across socioeconomic strata.
Offer them compassion, love, understanding.
It is not their fault, and yet they, like you and all,
must break the cycle of evil
by taking command of your lives
and loving, forgiving—living by my words,
though (human) reflex tells you otherwise.
This requires a great leap of faith.
They are not there yet but one day they will be,
and like you, the stronger their faith will be.
Allow me to work through you.
Do not interfere with my plan...
Deliver me all of your anger,
injustices felt, disappointments, worries,
guilt at the day's end and through the day.
Allow me to provide you eternal enduring shelter.
My kingdom is upon you.
It is within you and all around you.
Live in my kingdom now and forever after.

It is more difficult in the sea of darkness
but I am here, now and for all time.
I am yours and you are mine.
Let your heart be pierced
with the sorrows of this world
and lovingly suffer with me in my passion.
Be sensitized (increasingly) to sin and its ramifications.
Feel the pain produced in those it touches and those who generate it.
It is good (refers: to pain not sin), my child.
All my works are good.
Be up now and about your day's work.
Find all the happiness and joy there is in the days and days ahead.
Great beauty surrounds you.
Let my light shine from your eyes, light your path
and my energy emanate from your being.
Bring me to all those you meet.
Fear not. I am always with you.
I will never abandon you. I love you.
I winced at the pain in my shoulders, neck and back.
Allow me to lift the weight of your cross from you.
Be with me, my child.
Be aware of my presence within and all about you.
Go, my child, with me in your heart.

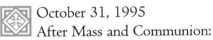October 31, 1995
After Mass and Communion:
One small step at a time, my child.
Start with your heart.
I am with you. I will never leave you.
Carry me with you the day through.
Turn to me; I will give you rest...
All is my work, my creation.
All is good/beautiful.
Be still, my child.
In the quiet of your heart you will find me:
springing forth, bringing new life to you,
your life's force, your strength,
your meaning for living/existence.

Let my peace be upon you.
Be filled with it and the light of my love.
Feel its warmth.
Let it soothe you and
your aching body—your cross.
Willingly accept this from me.
Pick it up and follow me/my example.
I am leading you to a better life—
far better than you could conceive or imagine,
a life of pure happiness, peace, love—love for all.
Bring more souls to my presence.
Bring them through allowing me
to be present in you,
those you meet each day.
I am speaking of the little ways, about life,
the heroics of daily living, not the solitary grand acts.
I speak of the weariness of monotony, the mundane:
persevering through the trials of parenthood—
keeping me/my Father as your model and example;
maintaining and nurturing your faith,
providing it sustenance to grow stronger.
Share it (faith) with others not in grand acts
but more subtly in your manner of being.
I love you, my child...
Bring joy to all that you do, because I am there.
Be patient.
Be at peace;
all in its time,
all in its place,
all for my love.
Be up now, my child and about your day's work.
Take the joy of my presence with you in all that you do,
everywhere that you go. I love you.
Be strong; allow me to strengthen you.
I ask nothing more of you than you are able,
and all will be provided you as you need it and more.
Be at peace.

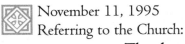 November 11, 1995
Referring to the Church:

They have preserved my word,
yet, they have separated me from my people.
The Church must heal from within,
not with further division
(it does not need further division.)
Do not look with anger upon my Church.
Look with mercy and compassion for the sins of men
who have distorted my intentions.
I continue to guide and direct it.
It will be set right—in time...

All baptized souls share in my priesthood.*
The extent to which they participate in its
*(power / energy / vitality)* depends on their willingness.

Referring to the exclusion of women from the Sacrament of Holy Orders:

It is not just (meaning: only) for men to anoint priests
and prescribe who is fit in their eyes.
All power, all authority comes from me
and this is not my intention.

---

* The concept of baptized souls sharing in Christ's priesthood was foreign to me. I had no recollection of it from religious instruction as a child. I consulted the current Catechism of the Catholic Church [see below] to find it was, in fact, the Church's teaching. Through the Sacrament of Baptism souls share in the priesthood of the faithful. Further participation in Christ's priesthood is conferred in the Sacrament of Holy Orders (ordination). I could not understand why I had no memory of this teaching on Baptism. My question went unresolved until 1997 when my cousin pointed out to me that, indeed, this aspect of Catholic doctrine had not been stressed for a long period prior to the Second Vatican Council. Truth remained constant in the Church's teaching on Baptism, but with Vatican II there was a change in emphasis, a revitalization. It was not so much "change" as return to more original perspective from the Church's earliest years, its roots.

[page 398, Catechism of the Catholic Church: Liguori Press, Liguori, Mo.; English translation of the Catechism of the Catholic Church for the United States of America copyright 1994, United States Catholic Conference, Inc.—Libreria Editrice Vaticana.]

In my ministry on earth all were included
from the most lowly outcast and sinner.
None of my children are to be denied
their desires to come closer to me and
more fully participate in a life with me.*
The militant approach is not what is needed here.
Patience and forbearance are in demand...
Fractionalizing my Church further is not the answer.

The above referred to the Catholic Church in the United States or elsewhere distancing from Rome, formally or less formally in gradually slipping away. I understood this as Christ's implicit support of the Pope as leader of his Church.

Christ's enduring love for his Church strongly underlay all that I heard, as did his wish for healing, love and forgiveness among his followers, that we work together, not against one another in following his path. Those who disagree with the Church's position on women and the priesthood, are asked to respond not with fighting, but with tolerance and calm restraint. We are asked to accept the present as God's will, trusting that God is guiding the Church not according to man's time table but his own divine plan. Our limited vision does not allow us to see the perspective in God's plan. It is important to recognize that while God is perfect, man is not, but this does not negate the work God does through us. We are reminded that Church leaders are also human and we need to accept one another and the frailties of our human state with mercy and compassion.

Review: the early Church history, especially Mary Magdalen;
the role and presence of women around me:
foot of the cross, appearing first to Mary Magdalen and
summoning her to tell the others (referring to: Christ's resurrection);
choosing a woman to say 'yes' to my/our Father's will
and give birth to me in her womb;
lying in my mother's arms after bodily death
attended by other women.

---

* I understood this to mean the categorical exclusion of half the population based on gender. It did not mean there should be no rules to exclude those who would be destructive to the Church as institution or to its members.

Women were disciples. Priests did marry.

Early Church corrupt—it wanted riches.

(I understood this as a reference to the Church during the Dark Ages.)

Strong cultural overtones subjugated women.

This is not my desire/intention.

This is not my teaching...

I love you. Take me with you wheresoever you go.

You are never without me; nor are your loved ones.

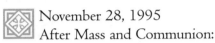 November 28, 1995
After Mass and Communion:

Be at peace, my child.

My thoughts went to a little girl recently murdered, a victim of child abuse. The details were particularly disturbing and horrendous. Her story, splashed across every news media, shocked even the most hardened. I did not know her in life; my only connection now, an intensity of prayer; though she could be nowhere but heaven. I included children suffering similar abuse, and those who perpetrated it. I could not help but repeatedly wonder "Why? What good could ever be drawn from this atrocity, from so much suffering in so innocent and short a life?" Most times I do not hear a direct response but on this occasion I did.

To draw out the compassion of others—

to respond with and to elicit compassion.

You are all part of the same body.

When one part hurts, the remainder of members feel its pain.

It is natural for another to give comfort and help relieve the pain.

This was first illustrated using our physical bodies as example.

*When our foot is injured our hand reflexively*

*and naturally comforts and cares for it.*

*The analogy was then made to*

*mankind's spiritual membership and common bond,*

*joined and united in*

*the Mystical Body of Christ;*

*similarly, when one member is injured,*

*we collectively suffer*

*and should just as reflexively comfort*

*and console the member in pain.*

*We are each of us capable of the best and worst in everyone;*
*depending upon the set of life circumstances we are born into,*
*and the gifts, talents, blessings*
*and crosses we receive...*

**I am all around you. I am everywhere.**
**I am with you always. I will guide you.**

November 30, 1995

At home, just after morning Mass and Communion, I looked at the crucifix and saw golden light illuminate its upper two thirds. The light seemed to emanate from the figure of Christ, most brilliant about his head and chest. The light flowed over the crucifix's edges to a wider area. There was no direct sunlight in the room, nor was there a light on.

**I am with you, my child. Do not be afraid...**

"I am sorry, I am so disorganized its hard to get anything done."

**You are forgiven, my child.**
**Your heart is where it belongs.**
**Allow your disorganization to let me more fully direct you.**
**Rely on your intuition, I am there guiding you.**

**Yes, the little girl** recently murdered— **she is with me now**
**and more happy than you can imagine.**
**She has not lived and died in vain.**
**Allow her story to inspire you...**
**I will help you. Be not overwhelmed.**
**I will provide whatever is needed to do my will.**
**Nothing is asked of you but what you can do with my help.**
**Nothing is possible without me.**
**Yes, you** (mankind) **are one body.**
**When one member/hand hurts**
**the others should comfort it.**
**Love one another, share your burdens,**
**decrease the suffering around you...**
**I am the supreme healer.**
**(I) understand all. Let me be your guide.**

"Please help me to better listen and above all, please help me to do your will—my family, all of us, help us all."

Do not be concerned, my child.
I know the intentions of your heart's desire.
Excessive concern over this or any other matters
removes/voids you from the present moment and
diminishes my *(ability/effectiveness)* to act through you
(or be present through you).
In order to be present to you
you must be present to me and
that can only occur with each moment as it is lived.
Referring to the afterlife:
Later it is different, there is no time.
All exists at once.
Do not censor my words as they come to you to paper.
Do not try to make sense of it; just write as you hear it.
Do not try so hard...
I will touch many lives through you.
Minister my grace, healing love and
forgiveness upon those you meet.
All things happen for a reason.
Things you believe coincidence are never.
All is planned of long ago
There is a purpose for all...
I looked at the crucifix; searching for the aura of light, no longer vis-
ible to me. "Jesus, please don't let me ask for signs and marvels of your
presence. Please let me pray and live exactly as you want it."
Do not be afraid, my child.
Do not try so hard. It is easy.
Do nothing; be only receptive to me.
We are all with you—Father, Son and Holy Spirit,
Mary, those who have gone before you,
those who are to follow and all my angels.
We are there with you.
Our love pours out upon you.

The fallen angels have polluted my creation,
We are in battle, good versus evil,
light versus the darkness.
You are in battle for me.

Bring others to me.
Be infused with my peace, strength, wisdom, patience.
All that you need will be provided you and more...

I felt overwhelmed thinking of all I had to do today, and demoralized at how little and routine it actually was, only made into mountains by illness and its limitations.

Yes, there is much to do but let me prioritize your day/activities.
Your life is a prayer, every act to the most mundane.
Do not make an artificial distinction/barrier between
this time of prayer/special closeness we share,
(that) I have allowed you to feel,
and the remainder of your life.
It is all one and the same—a continuum.
Do not erect barriers.
Take me with you wheresoever thou shalt go.
Take me in your thoughts every conscious moment.
Not one moment allow me absence.
Say YES to my presence.
Reaffirm it in every conscious moment of awareness.

The devil works/gains a stronghold
through preying on men's fears, men's weakness,
making the evil he is appear attractive, irresistible.
Ground yourself in me.
Deny yourself the luxuries which tie yourself to the world.
Live simply...

Referring to a material gift I had been given, which in some ways resembled the beauty of the night sky:
Let it remind you of the Blessed Mother
and the many stars of the night,
the many souls I have created
to reflect my light/joy
and live with me forever
sharing my divine eternal life.
Make yourself a perfect reflection of my love, my image.
Treat others as I have treated you.

Let my peace wash over you. Be not afraid...
Come, my child, kneel with me a while longer.
Be with me.
Allow me to be with you.
You are mine and I am yours.
I looked at the crucifix for inspiration.
Yes, my child, your body is the cross to which you are nailed.
Identify with me in my suffering/passion.
Join with me. It is not for naught.
It brings you closer to me and
many other graces flow from this.
You are my beloved child, in whom I am well pleased.
My arms are open to you.
Come to me to find rest and sustenance
to continue the mission before you.
All is and will be well.
All is in my/our Father's hands.
Our (the Holy Trinity) wills are one,
the pronouns are unimportant.

The admonition on women priests is a human distortion
my Church has placed upon my teachings.
It will not stand; but good will be drawn from all human frailty
be it well intentioned or malicious.*

I am all-powerful, all-loving, all-merciful. all-forgiving.
When the earth stands still and time exists no more
all who have not chosen me
will exist beyond my mercy and forgiveness.

---

* Christ's all-abiding love for his Church underscored these words. I did not in any way take them to undermine either the Pope or the Church because it is also made clear that our role is to accept the Church's position as the on-going unfolding of God's will. We are not called to intervene but to yield, and to trust that it is God directing the Church's path—working through mankind and drawing good from all our human frailties. Our limited vision, unable to see the perspective in God's plan, does not allow us to make sense of the steps along the way. [This passage may seem contradictory because it reflects the paradox between man's free will and God's immutable will. This paradox of wills cannot be understood in our mortal state, but only accepted as part of God's mystery.]

They will choose perpetual lives of suffering and pain
beyond any human imagining.
My justice will prevail.
For those who do not know me,
I will not know them.
Knowing me through the person of Jesus Christ
is the most direct path by which to reach me;
yet I am here for all, regardless of how
they have come to know me—their Creator.
To know and love Christ, my Son,
is to know life made simple.
Love my Son, Jesus Christ,
Mary, my Mother, and
the Holy Spirit, whereby you are infused
with the potential for divine life.
The Holy Spirit is the giver of truth.
I will never abandon you.
When you feel forsaken, remember I am there.
I will never forsake you. Any suffering you and
your loved ones endure will bear much fruit.
There will be great purpose.
I will never give you suffering greater than you can bear.

"Please help me with the writing. I don't know what to edit. I do not want people to have a 'holy' expectation of me which I know I am not and can't meet. I do not want to besmirch the beauty of what you have allowed me to share."

Do not pretend to be other than you are or where you have been.
You are here in your present form, experiences included,
as this is where I want you to be.

I was given specific direction on what to include of the locutions, and otherwise general focus, summarizing previous guidelines I had been given.

The mystical is the province of every man.
I am here for all souls.
All souls come to me.
Whether they believe in me/my name or not.
Answer to me and to themselves,
the truth laid bare before them on the final judgment day.

There is much love, peace and beauty in the world.
Enjoy my creation and make these things grow
that my creation may be restored to its perfection,
a perfect reflection of my image, my love.
Bring me to all men.
Let the hills, mountains, valleys, seas,
and wind sing my name.
I am love, pure love.
I am your beginning and your end.
Come to me,
come to me,
come to me,
my child.
Do not resist.
Come to me now and forever.
I will give you rest.
I will fill you with my peace and love
till your contentment overflows
in sublime, exquisite ecstasy.
Forget all your earthly cares, concerns,
even the aches and frailties of your body...
Be with me.
I am all that you need and desire.
All good flows from me
and it is all yours
*and to those who love me.*

Referring to my effort at recording the mixed word and wordless communications so completely:

(Do not always feel you need to add 'other people'; it is understood.
My relationship with you is very personal, as is mine with all others.)

Let me fill your heart with the goodness of which I speak.
Close your eyes. Place down your pen.
Feel my presence,
its power, its majesty, its warmth, its love.
Kneel back now and close your eyes.

I was surrounded by a keen awareness of God's presence in me, in
every person and in all things everywhere; as well as the need for his

ongoing presence for the continued existence of all, to the smallest electron maintaining its atomic orbit. I was filled with awe at the complexity and order of creation and evolution. I became warm, as if immersed in the soothing crimson light which was my only visual awareness, though my eyes remained closed. I felt pure contentment, peace, and then God's great love and mercy.

> **...You are worthy because you are chosen.**
> **You are not chosen because you are worthy.**
> **You understand this, my child.**
> **You have been over the abyss.**
> **You know** (meaning: have experienced)
> **there is nothing without God.**
> **There is void...**

Today was a most special occasion in my spiritual life, its circumstance invited joy and celebration.

> **All the angels, saints, Mary, the Blessed Mother**
> **and the most Holy Trinity rejoice...**

I had the most immediate sense of their entire presence and in my elation I felt that I rejoiced with them. I could see and feel their presence above and all around me as a great domed firmament of luminescent, confluent, soft white clouds, each lit from within by pure white to gold light. My body felt light, as if enveloped in a protective invisible cloud. I was without pain or physical sensation. I became aware of my own mortal father's presence in this multitude surrounding me. He had no distinct features, but appeared to come slightly forward as an amorphous, soft, white light, glowing from within and framed by magnificent sparkling gold and white light which shone upon him from every direction. It was the second light which briefly defined or outlined him from the others. I believe this defining light was the presence of God, which infused the entire scene and allowed my visit.

What was to follow I experienced but that once. There was the most phenomenal sense of my father's actual presence. My only awkwardness was not knowing what to call him. It was a small secret I hid without thinking. I could not say the word "Daddy" or "Dad," without stumbling over it, or my voice becoming stilted, even if it did not refer to my own father. Since his death I could not say either word to speak of him. I only used the more formal, removed "my father," and avoided that when I could. Now, in this extraordinary moment of my father's presence, I wanted to address him by name but could not. "Father" seemed too formal, but still, I could not utter "Dad" or "Daddy." Even my memories of him showed no trace of calling him "Daddy," when surely I knew I must have.

Now my father soothed my discomfort as he might have kissed a knee I had just scraped on the sidewalk. He surrounded me with the warmth of his love. I basked in his pride and happiness for me. He then spoke directly to me:

> "I will be here when you pass over
> Catherine, my dear daughter.

You are beginning to understand why I had to leave you so soon,
> that you might grow hungry for our Lord
> and be trained on a spiritual path.
> I am, as all the heavenly angels, saints,
> Mary and the Blessed Trinity, so pleased with your love
> for your sisters, family, fellow man."

It was as if he were right there with me! The moment was pure emotion; memories vividly flashed. I became aware of physical sensation as my eyes brimmed with tears, like a cup cresting full, its contents about to break free of their own surface tension. Before he could be as quickly gone as he appeared, I blurted, "Please help me; I miss you still!" and with that my eyes released, overflowing as streams beyond their banks. My father spoke again:

> "It is all right, my daughter.
> In a blink, my child, you will be here
> and realize how temporary even the longest earthly life is
> in comparison to eternity...

"Remember:
> 'The woods are lovely dark and deep,
> but I have promises to keep
> and miles to go before I sleep
> and miles to go before I sleep.'*

---

* Excerpt from "Stopping by Woods on a Snowy Evening" by Robert Frost, which I first read in high school. The woods evoked many happy childhood memories. It was a favorite, almost magical, place to play for my sisters and me.

Four lines from "Stopping By Woods On a Snowy Evening" are from THE POETRY OF ROBERT FROST EDITED BY EDWARD CONNERY LATHEM, Copyright 1951 by Robert Frost, Copyright 1923 © 1969 by Henry Holt and Company, Inc. Reprinted by permission of Henry Holt and Company, Inc.

"You knew from whence you first heard this, that it spoke to you,
and immediately it was in your memory,
and woven through the trials of your life on so many occasions."

The white-gold light which distinguished him from the others faded and he melted back into the crowd. His presence remained, but less intense and distinct, as was the presence of so many others. To describe the scene as simply a fusion of souls would not do it justice, given the individual personal connection I felt with so many, people whom I had lost, and people whom I had never known; they were distinct, yet inseparable.

Emotion overpowered me. Simultaneously I became increasingly aware of my physical self and the beautiful firmament began to fade. "Oh please don't anyone go. I want to feel your close presence for longer. Please stay."

...We are with you, my child, and will never leave you.

The expression, Communion of Saints, was now more than words. It was the reality of all those who died and chose to live eternity in God's presence. I had new understanding of what it meant to be part of the Mystical Body of Christ and its significance in our on-going relationship with those in heaven—linking us by living bond, all part of the same body.

Let my healing power flow to you
and through you to all those you meet.
I am your strength,
your life's blood,
your life's very force,
your reason for existence,
your Alpha and Omega...
Share your joy and peace with all
but bring the darkness to me for light and warmth
to shine upon it that it may bear fruit as I have willed it.
Go, my child. Go in peace to love and serve the Lord.
Go with me in your heart and soul's eyes.
Follow me. Let me lead you where you are to be.
Draw strength and all that you need from my love
in which you are bathed in warm white light.
Truth* be in your heart and upon your lips.

*meaning: the Holy Spirit

I have breathed the Holy Spirit more fully upon/within you.
Now up, my child, and be about the tasks at hand.
Do not be daunted by their magnitude,
all is possible with and through me.
Consult me in all things,
no matter too small, none too large.
Be blessed, my child, and filled with my
peace, love, beauty, wisdom, forgiveness,
mercy, justice, strength, eternal life.

 December 4, 1995

The Eucharist is one part of my priesthood...
It is important; other aspects of the sacramental are as well:
the sacramental in our daily lives, ministering to those around us
in actions, words, deeds, thoughts, intentions—demonstrating love.
Identify with Christ.
Wrest back the true meaning of priesthood;
empowered *through the Holy Spirit*
*and identification with Christ.*
The sacramental in every day life is important.
All (are) asked to bear witness.
To identify with Christ and bring him to all...

I remembered the book's theme given me in March, 1993: "Jesus Christ is here within us. Everything, every day in our lives is sacramental." How confusing the request had been to draw my notes into a cohesive whole; but now what I had just heard seemed to do just that. I laughed at my prior misconception: that it was I who was to accomplish this task, when I was only to wait patiently and allow it to be given to me—merely to record it. I asked myself, "How many 'authors' get to 'write' a book and the surprise ending is on them?" I realized my active efforts had only been in the way; the more ironic as it was the cognitive limitations and disorganization, which so vexed me, that had spared me interfering. I felt the strong presence of Christ and his love sharing my amusement at having made riddle of the obvious.

"Oh! I must call my mother! I can finally answer her questions: 'How far are you on your book?' and 'How will you know when it is finished?' Yes! This is it! This is the end!" I said aloud, my reaction bittersweet. "This must be the end, the theme is drawn to its conclusion,

loose ends tied-up; and my heart moving toward deeper forgiveness."
My thoughts were interrupted:

**Priests\* give the Sacraments.**
**Over the ages an artificial barrier**
**has been created between**
**my people** (the laity—priesthood of the faithful)
**and my priesthood** (the clergy—priesthood through Holy Orders);
**intended for them each in which to partake/to share,**
**to share on a personal level,**
**to minister/bring me to all they meet and touch.**
**Give my Church back to the people.**
**Shepherd them, guide them,**
**but do not imprison them in rules**
**which exclude and do not demonstrate my love,**
**mercy and forgiveness to all.**

Later:
**No one can disenfranchise me from my people.**
**No one can disenfranchise my people from me.\*\***
**Organized religion does not separate me**
**from my people, nor my people from me.**
**They** (organized religion) **are there to facilitate my people**
**coming to know me, not fractionalize and turn away.**
**I am not a God of exclusion.**
**All come to me, undifferentiated by race, sex,**
**ability or any artificial barrier.**

Later, before sleep:
**Now sleep, my child. Rest your body.**
**Lie in my arms and rest in peaceful slumber with me.**
**I am watching over, guiding, and protecting you and your loved ones.**
**Have not a care (in the world).**

---

\*Priests meaning: ordained priests empowered to administer the Sacraments through the Sacrament of Holy Orders.

\*\*disenfranchise in the sense of meaning: deprive of a privilege.

All is provided for you and
those you love and more...I love you.
"I love you, my Lord. Thank you and please forgive me my sins, my failings. Help me to grow stronger, wiser and more courageous in carrying out your will."
Do not try so hard.
My will is easy when you unite your will with mine.
Be patient and allow your life/my plan
to unfold about you.
Have faith; trust in me
and you will come to understand/know
there is no reason for concern.
Sleep, my child. Sleep in my arms.
The angels, all the saints, Mary, the Blessed Trinity
envelop you and your loved ones.

December 5, 1995
After Mass and Communion:
The news still held the innocent face of the little girl murdered, and more disturbing details of her life and death.
Referring to her suffering:
When (you) see suffering in the world around you
(have compassion).
Now that you know,
you have an obligation,
that they have not suffered in vain.
On whatever scale you meet it
let those who have suffered and died not be in vain.

In excitement I continually had the urge to share with my family what I assumed to be the book's conclusion.
Do not yet discuss it.
It is not yet brought to its fullness.
Explained:
*Speaking of it would dissipate my energy, concentration, stillness,*
*receptiveness for listening and being available*
*to bring the book to completion.*

"How much more could there be?" I wondered, "The book's theme seems complete."

*I understood that I was to review the seven Sacraments*
*and parallel how these are brought to life*
*in the priesthood shared through baptism.*
*Specifically, in this role of shared priesthood how to allow*
*the grace of the Sacraments to act as a living force in our daily lives*
*in smooth continuum beyond church doors.*
Sacraments are not intended to be isolated,
and compartmentalized in inaccessible places;
*nor are they intended to be left behind,*
*as if lifeless rituals, exercises, and monuments in church.*
*Rather, the Sacraments are to be brought home with us,*
*given life as* an integral part of daily living.
The Holy Spirit dwells in the heart of man,
not in buildings, edifices or
hierarchies of power and position.
These have the life of the Holy Spirit
only in so far as man brings it there.
Sacraments are an integral part of daily living.
What more holy, sacred a place than human life itself—
your body is the Temple of the Holy Spirit.
When these acts of love,
which is what the Sacraments are—
are performed, grace flows forth.
There is healing of the human spirit.
The Sacraments are the
(life blood, sustaining force,)
sustenance of my people.
*When we embody Christ we embody the Sacraments*
*bringing special grace upon us and those with whom we interact.*
*To embody the Sacraments in the imitation of Christ:*
*we love; we love with Christ*
*as our example and focus.*

*Church leaders are human,*
*subject to the same frailty as we in carrying forth our priesthood.*
*Neither we nor they can do this perfectly.*

*Have a forgiving attitude.*
*Have forgiveness in our hearts.*
*Love is to accept others as they are—this implies forgiveness,*
*given our mutually shared imperfect state.*

I had not followed through on reading and heard:
*I was to read about:*
**the history of the early Church, Mary Magdalen,**
**women as deacons** (in the early Church),
**marriage and the priesthood and why this changed,**
**why the Council of Trent,**
and the **Vatican II** Council came to be,
**the evolution of the priesthood**
**and distancing of the laity and clergy:**
*emphasis on ordained ministers and separation of the Eucharist*
*de-emphasized the laity's share in Christ's priesthood.*
My understanding of this reading's purpose was to answer questions
I had about some of what I was hearing.

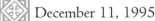December 10, 1995
Referring to the priesthood, with respect to women, marriage of
priests, and the laity's share in the priesthood:
**A revolution is not needed in Rome.**
**A revolution is needed within the heart of every man.**
Explained:
*At present we, the laity, are far from allowing*
*our share in Christ's priesthood, through Baptism,*
*its full expression within us; that is,*
*we do not acknowledge or fully value what we already have.*
*To realize this potential would transform our Church*
*and world on a revolutionary scale.*

December 11, 1995
**The Holy Spirit lives in the hearts of my people**
**not in buildings, (hierarchies,) positions/stations of power.**
**The presence of the Holy Spirit is brought to these**
**by the people who fill these roles and fill the buildings—**
**pouring forth more love.**

Be forgiving toward Church leaders.
Mistakes have been made. Inequities exist.
In time my Church will be restored as I intended it.

A revolution is not needed
to restore my priesthood to the people.
People must simply acknowledge
and commit themselves to this in their hearts;
a church excluding no one,
by virtue of their birth, from its administration.
The real essence of my priesthood, my Sacraments,
lies in the heart of man.
Grasp this,
acknowledge it,
reaffirm it
and set the world afire/ablaze
with my love for all humankind, all my creation.
Great *(transformation/force/power)* lies in
grasping the power of love.
Make my love manifest through your actions.
Be guided by imitation of my life—
following my commands.

December 12, 1995
After Mass and Communion:
Earlier I had lost my gloves. It was a cold but not bitter day.
This is to remind you what the poor feel like.
Be still, my child. Let my peace be upon you.
I am the/your shepherd.
I lead you to all good things. Follow me.
See my face in all those you meet.
Yes, what you do unto the least of my brethren
so you do unto me.
Do not forget the poor and less fortunate.
You have been given many gifts and blessings
and with it comes a great responsibility
to use them for my good and greater glorification.
You are my beloved servant and I am yours.

Together we proceed to the Lord our Father.
I will bring you to him.
I charge you with bringing others to him.
People who may believe because they see you
but are not yet able to see me—
not yet able to have an awareness of me
because they rely solely on their bodily vision.
You know how much greater there is
than what your human (physical) eyes alone see.
Do not fear. I will give you strength.
All things happen for a reason,
from the most minute to the grand.
The gloves are a small lesson in charity:
a reminder not to forget those less fortunate,
a reminder, to use the gifts I have given you to help them.
Alleviate their human suffering (and in so doing)
demonstrate love in your actions.
Allow them to feel love, so that
they will experience my love
for them in their hearts.
Help open the hearts of those
who have never experienced (enough) love.
Yes, my child, the abused and
neglected children of the world,
the throwaways of society.

My thoughts flashed to the children I worked with in my teens and
early twenties. They remained in a special place in my heart and prayers.
Most, but not all, came from homes of poverty; but they were all abused
and neglected; and lived their childhoods in institutions or a revolving
door of foster homes. This fine thread of connection with them was
woven into my life.

Their ill treatment is the breeding ground
for the devil's handiwork.
Evil is like a parasitic infection.
It is alive yet cannot live without human host
to give it body and form.
Love kills the evil,
halts its growth (its perpetuation).

The antidote provided by my death and resurrection
and the continuing command:
love one another as I have loved you and
love your God above all things.
The healing process is in effect and requires all souls
to follow these commands to eradicate evil/the devil's influence
from my creation, so that a new...*creation/world* may come to pass,
one of pure love, joy, and peace—
a creation from the unified will of souls
with my/our Father's will.
I love you, my child.
You have been with me from
before the beginning of time and you only now
begin to see what you so long ago, willingly took on.
We are with you, my child.
Though you be surrounded by the sea of darkness
and sometimes feel you founder,
never are you any but moving forward to the goal
our Father has for you, his will for you,
the unique mission for which you have entered the world
(as each soul is created for a unique mission.)
"That is daunting to grasp."
Do not be afraid, my child.
All will be provided you and more as you need it.
Be not afraid.
"I have made so many mistakes. I can see for some time, how you
have bailed me and others out from them; and I can sometimes even recognize the good you brought forth despite my errors. I am so very sorry
for my transgressions. I am deeply grateful that you saved me even from
myself; and that you should be there for me so personally."
You are only beginning to become aware
of how much we* are present in your life.
We are all and always here with and for you, my child,
as we are for all souls.
All souls, however, must begin with
the intention of desire to do the Father's/God's will.

---

* Meaning: the Trinity, Mary, the Communion of Saints, and all God's angels.

The outcome/results are not important;
it is the intention which lies in the heart of man.
This is upon which you are judged—
judged by me and self-judged
at the hour of your death and final judgment day.
Love one another as I have loved you.
This is the most important command.
Take me with you wheresoever you shall go today.
Physically take care of your body.
It is the Temple of the Holy Spirit.

The following was imbued with the warmth of compassionate humor; and directed at my continued difficulty fully accepting illness, adjusting myself to live within its limitations and my reduced stamina:

There is much work you are to do yet on earth
and you will need wheels to get around.
I smiled at the turn of phrase.
How many miracles can be performed on one body?
Even cats have only nine lives.

In amusement, I wondered; though not cured of illness, had I been spared its full fury? This was not the first time it was my strong intuition, "Yes, I had." I was directed to preserve my remaining health by:

eating right, getting enough rest, simplifying life—
decreasing stress, more time for the spiritual.
(In addition to, not in place of medical treatment.)


Regarding the person of darkness:
You are in an on-going process of deepening forgiveness and prayer.
Regarding the source of his soul's circumstance:
It is his willful, evil nature...
It is not a matter of his being childlike,
or that his behavior cannot be helped.
(meaning: it is a matter of his will and choice)
Yes, it is now harder for him to break with
his evil ways and the influence evil has in his life,
but all the more reason to stay clear.
...love him and pray for him from a distance.
No human soul is a match
for the powers that rest there.

Pray that he open his heart to my saving help
to wrest him back from the powers of Satan.
His soul is in dire straits.
The best you can do for him is pray, forgive—
all from a great distance...

Regarding evil:
Don't allow the forces of evil to create
any more suffering in the world,
in particular to the innocence of childhood.
Contact (with evil) will leave its imprint in living form,
infect, and further make stronghold of its grip—
infecting humanity, living off its life's blood,
destroying it in the process as a parasite kills its host.
Evil lives as an infection upon man.
Love is its antidote.
Be up now, my child, and about your day's work.
Glorify my name in all that you do
and never forget my immediate presence
within you,
all around you
and everywhere.
I love you.

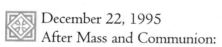 December 22, 1995
After Mass and Communion:
...You are all called to be my priests
and bring me into your lives each day,
to intricately weave me into every aspect of life
and touch every person you meet.
I felt discouraged at the discrepancy between the on-going beauty of
Christ's words in his presence and my ability to live them and follow his
life's example.
Do not try so hard, my child. Let it go.
Feel the joy of my presence, the joy of my moment.
Let it all go, my child. I am with you.
Take heart. All will be well;
just allow me to work through you.

**I am there. Just allow me.
All will fall into place...**

January, 1996
My daughter's persistence caught me in an untimely moment of weakness, and we became the proud owners of a medium size green parrot who could say, "HEL-LO".

"Mom, Isn't he cute!"

Tentatively, I looked. Scaly feet, two toes in front, two in back, each ending in dark claws, wrapped about my daughters finger. They seemed strange and forbidding—out of an old science fiction movie, magnified for special effect.

"Mom?"

I realized how long I was staring. "I guess he's pretty cute, but I don't know about those feet."

"What's wrong with his feet? Here, hold him." my daughter said, extending her hand; the parrot remained calmly perched.

I instinctively recoiled at the prospect of touching those feet, "No, I don't think so." My daughter's face dropped. I quickly added, "His feathers are a very beautiful color though..." I stopped mid sentence. Those odd little feet had already traveled up my daughter's arm. The parrot settled on her shoulder nestling into the curve of her neck. His feet were no longer visible, hidden beneath his body; he was only a fluff of feathers stroking his head against my daughter's neck and the side of her face. She giggled with delight, yet the parrot, unruffled, continued to snuggle affectionately.

"Mom, I think he likes me. Oh please...!"

We called him Kermit; it seemed to suit him. Inside of a week my children had taught him to say, "Hi ho, this is Kermit THE frog here." and next Kermit was imitating the laughter that greeted his efforts.

I returned home one day, about a week later, to find him flailing about, trying to free his front toe. It had become trapped between a cage door and an adjacent bar of his cage. He had broken off most of his tail feathers and some of his wing feathers. I was going to have to touch his feet. I could not release his toe—it had become too swollen to fit through the narrow space. Those scaly claws, once so hideous—now evoked a different response in me, bloody and macerated as they were. Kermit was silent but his eyes were full of pain and fright. I hoped he had not been like that for too long.

I could not pry the bars apart with my hands. I ran to the kitchen throwing drawers open and closed searching for a "jaws of life" equivalent. My minimalist kitchen had few gadgets to offer. I located a screwdriver in a small tool box at the bottom of the closet, and with it spread the bars wide enough to set his foot free. Without thinking, I reached my hand into his cage and Kermit caught hold. He nestled down into the palm of my hand and the moment I sat on the couch he came closer, settling into the crook of my arm which rested against my chest. He made soft noises. What an endearing little creature.

I prepared a box, and we were off to the vet. It was not an office, but a medical center complete with veterinary residents in training for subspecialties, dogs in CAT scans, cats with IVs, and an emergency room which did not discriminate by genus or species. It was a jarring juxtaposition—looking as professional as a hospital or multi-specialty clinic, but all the patients were furry, feathered or scaly—not a bathrobe in sight.

Ushered to an examination room, I carried the little box, and rested it beside me on the table. It was again odd to look about the well appointed room, as professional as any doctor's office. I glanced at the clock, standard fare for such an office, and identical to one I remembered in the radiology reading room. Reminiscing began. It was 1:30 PM; what would I have been doing on an average work afternoon? How easy it was to still picture myself in a long white coat before a double hung bank of view boxes, mounted along two walls which met at right angles.

Dictaphone in hand I intermittently turned in my swivel chair or stood to take in the corner full of X-rays, new and old ones for comparison or a series of films from a more extensive exam. How ingrained in my memory the voice over the intercom still seemed, "Dr. Toye, you have a call on line two." Not uncommonly four or more things presented to be done at once. I could picture one of our X-ray technicians waiting at the edge of the room, considerately, unobtrusively letting me know they were ready for me to begin an afternoon procedure, but not interrupting my dictation. I really liked our department staff, one more added pleasure in going to work.

Then I heard, "Mom." The spell was broken. That was not part of my work afternoon. It had sounded just like my daughter but she was at school. Instinctively, I looked about the empty room. I was not at my view box diagnosing broken bones from the emergency room; I was waiting to find out if a parrot had a broken foot. Again I heard, "Mom."

"Was that my daughter's voice? Could she be in the hall outside?" I wondered, puzzled at how loud and clear it was. Impossible, she did not even know I was at the vet. The next time I heard, "Mom" I realized it was coming from the box at my side.

"It's the parrot!" I laughed. The feeling in the pit of my stomach was like a roller coaster's sheer descent—an abrupt plunge: defrocked of my long white coat, relieved of my Dictaphone, I went from busy, "important" professional to caretaker of a wounded bird "calling" me, "Mom."

The door opened and the vet's assistant came in. I was still laughing; she looked quizzically at me. I held up Kermit's box, "He just called me "Mom."

Unable to hide her amusement she simply said, "The doctor will be right in." The benign contempt of the professional: she thinks I think the parrot has finally "bonded" with me. I remembered something analogous back before the tables were turned. I was an intern covering the pediatric ER one night when there was a frantic call from a new father. "My wife has gone to the store. It's the first time I've been alone with the baby. The umbilical cord has fallen off!" He continued in a state of panic, "and I can't get it to stick back on. What should I do?" After some routine questions to confirm that there was nothing unusual occurring, the father was reassured that this was supposed to happen. We were all touched at his concern but no one could suppress laughter picturing him trying to reattach the shriveled, dried umbilical stump.

The vet had come in and was busy attending Kermit. Her beeper went off and her assistant answered the page. How familiar it again all began to seem until I heard, "Exotic animals answering a page." After listening to the call the assistant presented the history to the Vet, "We have a 160 pound Boa Constrictor in respiratory distress on its way to the ER."

It had been just that kind of ironic day; my only association between Boa Constrictor and respiratory distress was as perpetrator not as victim. In a bit of a silly mood now, I considered how you would carry a 160 pound snake much less determine that it was in respiratory distress. I could not squelch my question to the vet, "How would you know if a Boa Constrictor was in respiratory distress?"

"Why just the same way you'd know in a human."

At a loss envisioning this physiologic leap past comparative anatomy, I continued, "But, how do you mean?"

"They'd be gasping for breath, of course!" and she looked at me with the disdain of a head nurse sentenced to a tour of duty with the greenest of green medical students or worse yet, one with academic credentials an arm long and not the common sense to come in out of the rain.

I usually leave a doctor's office or similar appointment feeling a little low, reminded of my losses, how life used to be, what I was missing. Today I was thankful that I could find the joy in the day as I walked in the brisk air, with the wind at my back gently pushing me in the direction I was headed. I thought about the vast diversity of animals. "Thank you, God, for creating such varied and beautiful creatures. I guess his feet are not so bad after all, now that I've gotten to know the little creature."

 January 11, 1996
After Mass and Communion:
>...Let my peace be upon you, my child, and quell your fears.
>**All things are possible through me, none without me.**
>**I will give you all that is needed**
>**and more to do the tasks at hand.**
>**Do not trouble yourself with anxiety/concern**
>**for what tomorrow will bring.**
>**All will be in place for you and your loved ones.**

Referring to the person of darkness:
>**Yes, my child, evil exists in the world**
>**and it is best avoided *at all costs.***
>**Allow me to do combat with these forces.**
>**Man is no match, he is ill equipped...**

>**...be with me a while conscious of my presence**
>**in and all around you.**

I felt Christ's presence so strongly and became free of all physical discomfort; but with sufficient awareness of it to be grateful for this momentary but timeless respite. The awesome power, majesty, beauty, and peace of Christ's presence were stark contrast to the reality of daily suffering. My thoughts were now triggered by several street scenes of hardship and misery which I had seen before Mass; these swirled to a multitude of others: personal, family, friends and strangers ever present in the news. "Oh Jesus, this world is such a sad place!"

There is also great beauty, my child.
All of my creation is good.
It will take man's love, man learning to love,
to transform my creation to their physical eyes.
A world of endless beauty awaits all those who choose it.
Bring more souls to me, my child.
That will please the Father, your/our Creator...

Referring to the person of darkness:
He is filled with (the ways of the wicked...).
His path (back to me) grows thick with brush and he is all but lost.
Hope always remains till his final choice is made.
He is in great need of prayer.
He has caused great suffering in this world,
hurt my precious and beloved creatures,
brought a blight upon my creation.
He is in great need of prayers.
His days of evil doing will soon come to an end.
You are a pivotal person; you, because much of his darkness
has been inflicted upon you, hurt you...
You...have suffered at his hands.
Your forgiveness, *implicitly love*, is what he needs.
In this you also protect yourself from further harm.

"Jesus do you forgive Satan?"
One cannot forgive that from whence no sorrow is felt.
"What about this person of darkness? He demonstrates no sorrow, no remorse. Why should I forgive him?"
There remains a shred of humanity alive within (him).
Therein lies the thread of hope
that his soul may be wrested back from Satan.
Do nothing but pray for him, actively try to forgive.
Leave your heart open to me/my presence
that I may further heal your spirit and guide you.
Do not be afraid...All is possible through me.

What to tell those who have suffered grievous loss or senseless injustice, so traumatic to them that they have been unable to allow themselves to even feel its full sorrow, in preservation of themselves, though this has delayed their moving beyond it:

...To allow their heart to open enough to feel the pain,
more fully to allow my presence to enter them
and heal through my love...
Stress my healing love
and the perfect, all-loving family
they and all have in heaven:
Father,
Mother, (Mary)
Christ,
Holy Spirit.
I am with you, my child.
I am with you now and always.
Be up now, my child, and about your day's work.
Take me with you wheresoever you go.
"I don't want to leave, it is so peaceful and consoling here in your presence."
Remember, my child, your life in every aspect is a prayer.
(implicitly meaning: when lived with proper attitude.)
Be up now, my child. I love you.
"I love you, Jesus. Please let me feel your presence the day through. It is so comforting and full. I hope this is not wrong to desire so much refuge from the pain of human existence."
I am here for you, my child, now go.

Later in the day explanation of Christ's answer on forgiveness and Satan:

*Forgiveness can be given,*
*but the act is not complete until it is accepted / received.*
*Just as God's love is given to all souls created*
*but the difference is how much each soul accepts.*
*Love and forgiveness are the same.*
*It is the same 'yes' we must say to God.*
*It goes to the root of free will.*

January 16, 1996
After Mass and Communion:

Let my peace be upon you.
Let me fill/surround you with my light.

Be at peace, my child. Do not try so hard.
I am well pleased with your efforts.
I know the intentions of your heart's desire.
You must learn to live with
the world's imperfections and your own.
It is one of the crosses you must bear.
In this state (limited/human) you are better able to
learn to love than in one of greater perfection.
Always remember it is the intentions
of your heart's inner depths, not results—
not outward appearances (that matter)...

...Do not trouble yourself with matters of your health.
Bear no anxiety. But do take care of yourself;
your body is the Temple of the Holy Spirit.
Allow nothing to abuse it.
I felt more peaceful.
Have no concern, my child.
Detach yourself from all (people, things, goals/aspirations)
and focus your full attention on me every moment.
Be consciously aware of my presence
within and all about you.
Follow my lead (example);
follow my commands.
In so doing all—every aspect of your life
will fall into place (and) you will most easily fall into
your expected place in God's plan...

...Pray for the poor and homeless.
Do not fear them. Have courage. Be filled with my love.
All power, all (everything) comes from me.
I love you. Help them (the poor).
Be filled with my compassion and love for them.

Be slower to anger.
Be filled with my patience and show it to all around you,
especially to your children and family.

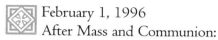 February 1, 1996
After Mass and Communion:

**Detach yourself from all people and all things**
*all worries/concerns* **and come to me.**
**You are here (but not on your own time).**
**You are here because the Father wants you here.**
**There is much work to do before you die, my child.**
**Glorify my name and you glorify the Father.**
**Bring more souls to me/the Father**
**and greater glory is yours.**

"Please help me."

**Trust in me, have faith;**
**listen to your deepest heart's desires.**
**There am I.**
**We are commingled.**
**We are one.**
**Your spirit can never be separated from me.**

"Oh thank you, that is so beautiful!"

**You do not fully realize the power of its significance.**
**The power which can flow through you in my name**
**for the betterment of humankind,**
**man, the loveliest of my creation.**
**Be up now, my child. Be with me later,**
**pen in hand, in the quiet stillness...**
**I have greater blessings (gifts/insights) to bestow upon you.**
**I love you. Take me with you, my child.**

"I love you."

February 2, 1996
Mid-day near a church I was drawn to a chapel dedicated to Mary where I sat in quiet before the Blessed Sacrament.

**Come and sit with me a while. Let my peace be upon you.**

I prayed for the person of darkness. I tried to surround him with the light of love in the intentions of my prayer. Any light I could bring about him was immediately, violently sucked into himself and replaced by black vacuum.

*the aura of evil—a black hole*

The graphic analogy was to a giant dying star (black hole), collapsed

in upon itself with mass sufficient to produce a gravitational field so
intense that nothing, not even its own light escapes it.
*The aura of evil is like a black hole*
*selfishly, destructively, pridefully sucking everything into itself.*


Be filled with my peace. Do not be afraid.
All is according to (my/our Father's) God's plan.
You do not have to try so hard.
It is unfolding as God planned and your willingness
to acquiesce your will is all that is needed.
All will be provided to you and more as it is needed.
Yes, in looking back over your life
you see many threads drawn together;
even infinitesimal, seemingly inconsequential,
small threads have prepared you
(planted a seed for growth in you)...


You are anxious because you have too little faith.
Faith requires on-going growth to live.
If not it withers and dies.
Allow me to help you nurture your faith in me.
Allow me to help you learn
how to teach others to find faith in me.
Bring more souls to me and the Father.
This I have commanded you.
In this you will find greatest peace
and the greatest joy of your life—
joy beyond any you can conceive/imagine.
You remain unaware of the power
(meaning: Christ's presence)
which resides within you (mankind).
Allow me to flow through you to others.
Be my eyes, my hands,
my feet, my heart
(showing compassion) on earth;
take me with you wheresoever you go.
Lead others to me by your example.
"I will fail and make mistakes."

You will not falter, with me at your side,
commingled with your very spirit.
Some will deride you. Be not alarmed or afraid...
They judge you in human terms and
the battle between good and evil rages about the earth.
It (earth) will one day be consumed by it (evil)
and I have come to *(evacuate/rescue/save/remove)*
as many souls as are willing to leave it for eternal divine life.
Evil and loss cannot be understood in terms of the world.
There are no answers there.
It meets the devil's bidding—
(destruction/death/discordance/chaos, lack of harmony.)...
You are an instrument of my peace and saving love to mankind.
I love you, my child and I am well pleased with your efforts.
Be less harsh upon yourself
when you fall short of the task you perceive at hand.
These are lessons in patience and humility:
accepting your limitations, turning more fully to me,
depending more fully upon me,
a gentle reminder in meekness...


Bring all the darkness to me.
Seek counsel for matters large and small, only with me.
[The exclusivity of the latter was not intended for an indefinite time
period. I understood it was in some way related to completing this book;
that my energy be fully focused and more intensely receptive of my rela-
tionship with Christ and his blessings.]
No matter is too small for my attention and presence with you.
Every moment of your consciousness
filled with my presence is your goal.
All will follow and flow smoothly thenceforth.
Yes, my child, there is much to do today
and much to do before you die...
You are all in my care and protection.
It is time to go now, my child...


There is no distinction between
my presence to you in prayer and the rest of your life.

The only difference is your awareness (of it).
Be steadily aware of my presence.
Regularly stop (ever briefly)
to refresh yourself with this thought.
Practice my presence in every aspect of your day.
I love you, my child.
"I love you, my Lord; stay with me, please don't leave."
I am with you always. Stay with me.
Bring me/your awareness of me
with you wheresoever you go, whatever you do.
Take comfort in my presence.
Regardless of the moment
know that I am there—leading you.
Be at peace. Up now, my child.

February 8, 1996
After Mass and Communion:
Be at peace, my child. Let my peace flow over you.
I expressed sorrow for my previous day's transgressions.
Do not be ashamed, my child.
I know the intentions of your heart's desire.
I will draw good from it from those you touched.
Your example will light their path.
Accept my forgiveness and move on.

Referring to the on-going pain of the thorn within my heart:
Yes, do bring the darkness to me.
Allow it to draw you closer to me.
I felt overwhelming love, unconditionally given, unrelated to my own
failings. "Your forgiveness and beyond that such great compassion is more
than I deserve."
You do not comprehend the scope of my love for you.
Be at peace, my child...

Yes, my child, you can make all your works,
every act, deed, thought from the smallest, most mundane
(seemingly insignificant) to the grandest gesture—
our work, if you just allow it.

Just allow your will submission to mine/our Father's.
All is done for you. All given to you.
All as it is needed by you
in carrying forth my/our Father's plan...
"Please guide my path in how to know your will."
Do not try so hard, my child.
Be patient and allow your life—
my/our Father's plan for you, to slowly unfold.
I am taking you where you need to be.
All is well. Be not afraid.
Harbor no guilt. Accept my love and forgiveness.
Live in the moment.
Do not look back;
you are then unavailable to me in the present
to do our Father's work here on Earth.
Carry no concerns in your heart.
Place your full faith, hope, confidence, trust in me.
I know what you need before you are aware,
and it has been readied for you.
Have no concern...
All things happen for a reason.
Good will be drawn from evil.
All in accordance with our Father's plan.
Do not be afraid.
Do not be afraid to live.
Do not be afraid to die.
You are my beloved creature.
My creation (is) in the reflection of
my image and likeness, my goodness,
and you are good.
Let my peace flow over you
and empower you in my name.
All in time, my child.
You are moving where I want you to be.
All in time. Do not be afraid.
Let the warmth of my light
imbue every fiber of your being.
I had great physical pain.

Give the pain to me. Unite it with mine.

Allow me to make your burden light (in so doing)

picture the weight of the splintered cross on my back.

I am with you, my child. I will never forsake you.

I felt badly at my poor response to that which I had come to feel was God's will for me.

Accept your human frailty, my child.

Suffer with me. (meaning: in Christ's passion)

Accept my forgiveness/love.

Allow it to purify you,

strengthen you, bring you closer to me.

Unify your will with your divine Creator.

Yes, my child, there is much work.

Be up now and about your business.

Take me with you wheresoever you go.

I will light your way from the most (seemingly)

insignificant turn to the largest. I love you.

"I love you."

I am with you always. Be off.

I am carried in the vessel of your heart—

Temple of the Holy Spirit—your body.

 February 9, 1996

After Mass and Communion:

Do not be afraid, my child.

Let my peace flow over you.

Be still. Be still in your heart.

Unite your will/your soul with mine; all will be easy.

Allow me to guide you, your every word, your every step.

Be constantly aware of my presence.

Strive for this. All will naturally follow.

"I love you."

I love you, my child...

...You are to bring my word, my presence, to your fellow man

in your life, your work, your every action and intention.

"Help me please, Jesus, I am afraid I will fail."

Do not fear; all will be given you as you/it is needed.

Be not frustrated/deterred by your human frailties.
They are lessons in humility.
"I feel unworthy."
Worthiness is unrelated to God's love for man.
My/our Father's love is freely given.
It is without conditions.
Man must only choose to accept it.
Accept our love and our forgiveness.
Openness and repentance are needed to receive these gifts.
These gifts are here for all souls we have created.
You are good; my creation is good; all my works are good.
They (God's works) cannot be understood
or evaluated in man's eyes,
by the eyes and scales of the world alone.
To be human/mortal (encased in human body)
is to be only partially alive.
True life comes when you pass over
into my realm—my kingdom.
My kingdom in which all souls
are invited to share in divine life and live forever.
Only those souls who accept this invitation will be saved.
The others will perish in the fires of damnation.
There is no middle ground, no room for indifference—
indifference to the forces of good and evil
which abound around you,
locked in fierce combat.
There will be no ground for uncertainty,
agnostics—not knowing, or atheists—denial.
There are only two choices
to my/our Father's request/invitation—yes or no.
All will be judged upon the intentions of their hearts;
and the talents with which they have been blessed;
and the crosses with which they have been blessed.
All is made fair/just/equal in the eyes of the Lord—
my eyes, the eyes of the Father.

Do not be concerned...
...All will be provided and given you as it is needed.

Make yourself an instrument of my peace, my love,
bringing my love to your fellow man.
Allow me to speak
through your eyes,
your lips,
your touch,
your every thought, word, and deed,
the intentions of your heart.
"Please, Jesus, help me to submit my full will, unconditionally to the
Father's will."
Yes, my child. My help is with you.
Never doubt it or my constant presence.
I am with you now and always...
...Be up now, my child, and about your day's work
Go forth, my peace and presence within you
and touch all you meet with my love,
my compassion, my forgiveness.

February 12, 1996
After Mass and Communion:
Do not be afraid, my child.
All is unfolding as my/our Father has willed it.
Be filled with the joy of my presence.
I am with you now and always, watching over you
and your loved ones, guiding you, protecting you.
Accept my love.
Feel its power and
transforming effect within your heart.
Touch your fellow man with my presence you feel.
We are one, my child.
We are welded inextricably,
indelibly at our very essence.
You can do nothing but follow me.
Do not struggle against it; our spirits are one
*commingled as one.* Be not afraid.
The world judges through different eyes.
Their judgment will not last.
It will pass away as will all earthly time.

Time is of the Earth.
It will pass away.
There is no time in my kingdom.
All exists at once.
There is no death.
None want.
There is only pure love.
Love beyond any human imagining
as is the state of joy in my kingdom.
Bring more souls to me.
That is your mission.
That pleases the Father.
All will be provided,
IS
in following this command.
(Meaning: all that is needed exists intrinsically in following this command.)
Do not worry. Do not be afraid.
Do not concern yourself with how you will accomplish this.
Simply follow my commands, my life's example.
Allow me/the Spirit to guide you
in the innermost depths of your heart.
Allow every day the stillness—
the stillness in which to hear
the softness of my voice/my lead.
I love you, my child, and I am well pleased
with the intentions of your heart's desire.
Be not concerned about their outcome.
Be still, my child. Do not try so hard.
Exert less effort. Allow the work to me.
Be my hands, my feet,
my eyes of compassion and love
to look out upon the world.
Take me with you wheresoever you go.
Maintain constant awareness of my presence
and all will naturally follow suit
as night the day, and day the night.
Be up now, my child.
Be filled with the joy of my presence.

Be filled with my peace.
Let my love sparkle from your eyes
and bubble forth from your lips.
You are loved, my child. Your loved ones are loved,
and in my constant care and protection, as are you.
"I don't want to leave—it's so peaceful here, yet I know I have much to do."
Yes, my child. But remember I am always with you.
Your life is a prayer—every act
from the most (seemingly) mundane,
to the most seemingly grand.
You do not leave my presence,
you just become less aware of it as you are distracted
by the cares/anxieties/*worries* of the world around you.
Make a more smooth continuum;
practice my presence.
Practice it every moment.
Make it a *steady/continual* aspect
of your conscious awareness.
I am yours and you are mine.
Make my presence a habit. (in awareness)
I became distracted.
Allow your human frailty
to bring you closer to me—(to) teach you humility.
I love you. Do not fear.
Be up now, my child, and about your day's work.
I am leading you where you need to be.
Take my hand; follow me.
Rest your head on my breast/in my bosom
when you are weary and I will give you strength,
no matter too small—none too large.
Turn to me. Bring the darkness to me.
I will make it light.
I will refresh you—eternally (now and forever).
My love is limitless. It knows no bounds.
All is possible through me.
What you ask the Father in my name will be given you.
Go now. Love your children. Love your fellow man.
Tell them how much I love them, how close I am to them.

**Tell** them **to turn to me in all** their **struggles and joys.**
They are **my beloved creatures as are you and all your loved ones.**

 February 15, 1996

All things exist at once in my kingdom.
There is no time.
(In some respects) you are already here;
yet I know, this is not comprehensible to you.
Your mind wanders (races) to free will and choice,
trying to understand (this paradox).
Yes, my child, it is a conundrum; for the time being,
you must accept it as incomprehensible.

 February 19, 1996

*Love is implicit in forgiveness.*
*It is more difficult to forgive that person*
*who has hurt someone you love,*
*than if they had hurt only yourself.*

*Mary is of integral importance in understanding*
*Christ's passion and its significance to us.*

*Christ said*
*'Father forgive them they know not what they do.'*
*Mary was silent, suffering silently,*
*helpless to help her Son.*
*Mary's forgiveness to the world has come after—*
*implicit in her not abandoning the world, instead,*
*making herself increasingly available to her children*
*to teach them how to come to know her Son,*
*his word, his life's example;*
*to bring more souls to God,*
*our Lord, our Father, Creator to us all.*
*Mary suffers, as only a loving mother can,*
*the anguish of watching one of her children*
*be cruel and unkind to another of her children.*
*Mary is truly Mother to us all.*
*Her love for us is unconditional.*

*Her nurturing, kindness, understanding*
*and compassion know no bounds.*

February 20, 1996
After Mass and Communion:
Regarding failing in an area of great personal importance to me:
The secret my child,
is awareness of my presence.
    I understood this as I replayed events, imagining my input modified by more immediate awareness of Christ's presence, and appreciated alternate possible scenarios.
Maintaining awareness of my presence
you are more likely to do my will,
carry out my word/work,
conduct yourself consistent with
my life's teaching/example.
"Help me stop making so many mistakes."
You are human, my child, you must expect mistakes,
and be more forgiving of yourself and others.
I love you, my child, you and all the souls
I have created—created from/of love
drawn from nothingness to life,
a life with purpose, to be shared
with your Creator in divine eternal life.
In giving you the gift of free will—
(that is) making you, elevating you to me,
not an inferior creature of (my creation),
you have with it, the responsibility (burden) of choice.
You must choose to come to me,
return to me—your home.
I do not force anyone to come to me.
All must come of their own free will.
All must choose the fate of their eternal life.
All manner of help is given to all souls.
It is not so hard as what you make it.
Life is simple.
Follow me. Follow my word.
You make your life more difficult otherwise.

Do not struggle and rail against my will.
Submit your will to mine. Allow me to guide you.
Recognize I know better for you
than you could begin to imagine.
Trust in me.
You know the generosity of your heart
towards your children; and that
you would give them all you could and more.
Magnify that by infinity and you see me in my inclination
toward the beloved souls I have created.
I love you, my child.
Take me with you wheresoever you go.
Touch those you meet (in particular your family/children)
with my love, my presence.
Reflect me to the world around you.

 February 23, 1996
This is my message to you all:
bring me alive in your hearts—the hearts of man.
Make my presence felt in the daily fabric of your lives
from the most mundane to the grand.
I am here within you,
everything, everyday
in your lives is sacramental.
Revere life.
Acknowledge my presence within you
and in all those you meet, my presence in all of creation.
Bring the grace/love of my Sacraments alive
to set the world ablaze.
Transform my creation for all the world to see.
The power and beauty of love knows no (equal/match).
Harness it—bring its effects to bear
upon the earth and all mankind.
Give my love life—arms, legs, feet, eyes, (heart)
to minister to all who will receive it.
You are all mine and I am yours.
Simply receive me into your heart.
Say yes to my presence that my work begin within you.

Love one another as I have loved you.
Forgive those who trespass against you
as you would have me forgive you.
This is love.
Love me/your God above all else.
Accept my love, my forgiveness.
My forgiveness is love.
Acknowledge me as your Creator.
Humble yourself before me (and your fellow man)
as I took human flesh
and humbled myself before all creation.
Return to your Creator who brought you from nothingness,
(abandoning you not, though you are
oft times/largely unaware of my presence.)
You are all unique and special in my/our eyes.
Return to us of love not fear.
More love, peace, joy awaits you
than you are able to comprehend.
I am always with you.
I will never forsake you.
To your final hour the choice is yours.
Come to me.
Return to me.
Be drawn by my love.
Say yes.

I had thought this was the book's last locution. It seemed a fitting ending, and in many ways I was relieved to think I had been given its close—to place this task to rest. I was more than surprised when the locutions both continued and intensified.

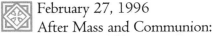 February 27, 1996
After Mass and Communion:

Be more aware of me in each present moment
and it will be easier to do my will.
Do not be tied/bound by past deeds or omissions—
you are unavailable to me or those I meet
through you in the present moment.
Exist in the moment at hand.

Make me constantly present in your awareness of the moment.
I am yours and you are mine.
We are inextricably commingled.
We are one.
Your will is mine and mine is yours.
You can do nothing but follow me.
"Why then, do I have so many failings, Jesus; so many short falls? Why
do I continue to sin?"
It is the intention of your deepest heart's desire,
the will of your spirit; it is shackled by the body and
all its human frailties and suffering.
The spirit within you ardently longs
to return to the Father, to do the Father's will.
Your spirit has been healed/cleansed and it suffers
shackled to your human body and mind,
which continues to struggle against
the will of the Father and spirit.
Your spirit and the Holy Spirit are one
and in so doing you are one with the Father and *Me.*
"I don't understand these distinctions between body, mind and spirit."
You are not ready to fully comprehend, my child.
They are all part of you.
They are all my creation.
They are all good.
They are distinct and they are indivisible
as is the Holy Trinity.
It is not important that you understand these things
to do my work in the world.
All our creation is beautiful.
Yes, you have correctly gained insight into the afterlife;
though it was hard for you to listen unimpeded
to the wisdom I spoke.
(meaning: in fear of punishment or that the gift of Christ's
presence would be withdrawn for my transgressions.)

Referring to life after bodily death:
All souls will exist in heightened states
of awareness, perception, knowledge.

There will be no escape.
No manner in which to blunt/numb the reality
in which they find themselves—no exit, no escape,
(such as:) *suicide, distractions, ambition,*
*worldly pursuits to get caught-up in,*
*drugs, alcohol, others to blame.*
There will be only each soul and
the stark reality they have chosen for themselves:
light versus darkness,
good versus evil,
eternal joy, peace and love
versus
perpetual unbearable suffering.
Whatever you do unto the least of my brethren
so you do unto me.
Love one another as I have loved you.
Love me/your God above all things.
Follow me—the path I have cleared for you
and you will know life made simple.
I am your servant,
your servant to bring you to the Lord our Father.
Serve others as I have served the Father.
Bring other's souls to me/the Father
and your joy will be increased/multiplied.
Those who have chosen to live their lives
in glory/homage to the darkness
will know ten-fold every suffering/pain
they have perpetuated in those around them—
magnified through the ages, across time and space.
You cannot imagine their pain/anguish.
They will appreciate it all at once.
I have told you there is no time.
(meaning: after earthly, bodily death)
All exists at once.
Those who need will be purified
before they behold myself/the Father.*

* meaning: purgatory

Others who relinquished all hope in refusing to accept
my/our Father's love and forgiveness
will live in the eternal damnation of darkness
and unimaginable suffering,
an eternity of regret,*
knowing it was at their own hand.
I do not condemn men to the devil.
Men go there of their own free will.
The truth laid bare to each soul
in the final hour judges all.
Were I not there to lift man
from the anguish of this moment
all but the purest life,
(a baby; Mary, my Mother)
would be crushed of its weight.
The weight of remorse, guilt, regret,
feeling the pain caused others—
the soul would be smothered in misery.
At that time those who have known me in this life,
so will I know them.
There are many ways to come to know me.
To know my Son, Jesus Christ
is to know life made simple.
This path has been laid for you of our love,
to show you in human terms
for your eyes to see and your ears to hear
the way to the incomprehensible—the way to me.
There are many religions in the world;
they all come to me.
They (all souls) are my children
regardless of the religion they have come to know,
regardless of their inability to have faith
whether atheist or agnostic.
At that final hour
all will be asked the same question,
with full knowledge/truth in their consciousness.

* meaning: hell

All (will be) invited to share divine eternal life—
to accept our love, our forgiveness;
or
choose the darkness—
continuing to hold themselves
and their power, god above all.
Not all can be saved, my child.
Living a good life, in keeping with my word,
predisposes one to the right choice
and brings others to me by example.
Be up now, my child, and about your day's work.
Take me with you wheresoever you go. I love you.

February 29, 1996
Regarding a difficult, seemingly no-win, interpersonal situation:
*My role: to accept it as God's will,*
*with patience, and compassion for the other party.*
Yes, it is a difficult balancing act, my child—the art of living.
Let me show you life made simple.
Follow me, follow my commands.
Detach yourself from all persons and things
and cling only to me—every aspect of your life
and the people in it will fall into place.
Regarding feeling pulled between worldly and spiritual obligations:
When you follow my commands:
love one another as I have loved you,
and love your God above all things; all is done.
Pick up your cross, my child, and follow me.
I have left you my life's example and teaching (sacred scripture)
to show you how to follow the path
I have made for you to eternal salvation.
Help others carry their crosses—yet, always bear in mind,
it is they who must experience the suffering of their cross
and turn to me to lift its weight.
To remove a person's suffering,
*which cannot be entirely removed from any person's life*
is to deny them a beacon (part of their map/signal) back to me.

Do not impede my communication. You are trying too hard.
You will be given what you need to know.
Our wills are one, my child. Do not be afraid.
Do not fear displeasing me.
I know your heart's desire to its innermost depths.
I know your true humility.
Just practice more awareness of my presence
from moment to moment and all will flow into place.
Accept your human frailties and weakness,
suffer them gladly for me.
Allow all things, be they suffering or joy,
to bring you closer to me.
Let me help you, my child.
Be bathed in my love and acceptance.
Do not be so harsh upon yourself.
Be where you are.
Be in the moment.
You are mine and I am yours.
Be up now, my child; there is much to do today.
Let me speak through your lips and
concern yourself not with what you will do or say.
Make no plans. Be open to my guidance...I love you.
"I love you."

Take me with you wheresoever you go;
your life is a prayer...
Bring my presence to those around you.

Late February, 1996
Many technological and medical advances in our age seduce some men to the false perception of being god-like, in particular, not recognizing their own dependence upon God. Beyond creating love or hate, man has no true creativity, that is the ability to make something from nothing. Man's absolute powerlessness before God is emphasized by stark contrast to creativity, in its opposite—destruction.

*Man cannot destroy what God has created.*
*Physically, man can only change its form.*
*Even the most destructive nuclear explosion converts mass to energy.*

*Neither can man destroy the immortal soul*
*God has created in each of us;*
*but, the eternal fate of that soul*
*can be altered by the individual's choices.*
*Every soul lives forever,*
*either united in God's presence in heaven,*
*or forever absent God's presence in hell.*

March 3, 1996
Several wordless locutions on the nature of God, man's relationship with God and the analogy of light are consolidated in the following chapter along with some prior insights.

# LIGHT

Jesus spoke to them again, saying, "I am the light of the world. Whoever follows me will not walk in darkness, but will have the light of life."

John 8:12

God is like light—the pure, white, life-giving light of the sun. Sunlight is all pervasive; we cannot live, nor would we have come into existence without it. No one doubts the existence of sunlight, though our bodily senses lack the capacity to perceive it directly. We become aware of light only after it interacts with something which brings it to a level our senses can detect. We see opaque objects because light is *reflected* off them. We see transparent objects because light is *filtered* through them. We have: crops which grow; circadian rhythms which regulate plant and animal life; photographic records; and the sun's heat; because light's energy is *absorbed*.

Even the sun and stars are only visible in the sky because the light they emit is filtered and reflected through their gas. Once released into the void of space, the same light streams through its vast blackness and remains black and invisible to our eyes until it reaches an object to interact with and illuminate, such as a planet, our atmosphere, satellite, space ship, the world around us.

In the course of light becoming available to our senses, the interaction distorts the original light. The beam is bent, or its color altered, or its energy transferred into another form; or any combination of the three. What the original light would appear like to our human senses is impossible to grasp, but we still speak of its reality in theoretical abstractions of physics, such as particle and wave theory. God is even more incomprehensible; and the manifestations of his presence still more pervasive and all-encompassing than the sun's light. His hand is in the beauty, majesty, and awe of all creation around us; and his face no more exquisitely, sacredly etched than in the eyes of all mankind. Man is set apart from all else; because he also bears God's Spirit; imbued with it before the dawn of time; created by God in his own image and likeness.

It is so difficult to open our eyes beyond our bodily senses, as we float in a sea of darkness, blinded by the world's physical reality. Occasionally our inner eyes blink open, and we reach a transient higher state of aware-ness, allowing us the insight to appreciate better the presence and manifes-tation of God's light in the world around us, through our bodily eyes.

God gave us his Son, Jesus Christ, made flesh that with human eyes we may begin to visualize the incomprehensible. Christ brought the real-ity of God into simple humanly comprehensible terms in taking on our humanity. Christ, in his life, death and resurrection, created the bridge of our salvation. A path cut through swirling, dark, chaotic seas engulfing us on every side. In his redeeming act he made the bridge for us to return home. The bridge's destination is the fulfillment of our existence—it is God's invitation to each of us to share divine, eternal life.

Christ is our safe passage home. Christ beckons us to follow him. He showed us how to travel the bridge's path. He showed us his compassion, mercy and forgiveness—how to get back on the bridge regardless of how many times we fall from it. He encourages us on the way. He can do all things; but there is one he will not. He will not make one say yes to his call; because our free will is our own, a gift not to be revoked. If we floun-der in the dark waters, too weak to lift our hand above its weight; the soft-est whispered, yes, in the intentions of our heart is the beginning. The faintest cry for his help is heard and answered.

Christ brought guidance in the most simple images. He showed him-self as man, Mary his Mother, a baby born within her, their unified suf-fering in his passion—forged of that special maternal-child bond. He left us his life's example, his teaching, his word and works preserved in scrip-ture, his Church to guide us, his presence in the Sacraments—all to show us how to travel the bridge he made for us from the depths of his love.

Christ's earthly work completed, the Holy Spirit, sent by God dwells within us, to further light our path and give us strength along the way. The Holy Spirit is like the eye of our soul; readily able to appreciate God's light. The presence of the Holy Spirit gives us the potential and grace to begin to communicate with a being so far superior to ourselves—the infi-nite, incomprehensible Divinity, our Creator. The Holy Spirit is the giver of truth, the guide to our discernment in coming to know God and that unique purpose for which we were created.

The world is filled with many distractions to avoid thought of our own earthly mortality, our own unimportance. In appreciating that our sole importance derives from God we humbly acknowledge our true selves; that we are defined only in terms of God. It is for this which we exist: to glorify God. In glorifying God we are each called to reflect his light upon all creation, in particular, our fellow man. We are called to allow Jesus to be born within us as did Mary, and then allow God to become manifest to us and through us to all whom we touch. We are called to make our lives a recapitulation of Christ's in every way, including the way of the cross, and then share in the glory of his resurrection.

Sunlight contains all the colors of a rainbow, also easily seen when light is broken up through a prism. Why are things differently colored when the same clear white light shines upon them? It depends upon which colors in the rainbow of white light are reflected back to our eyes and which are absorbed by the object. A red object can only reflect red light and absorbs the remaining colors of light. Green objects can only reflect green light absorbing the remaining colors, and so on. Black objects absorb all colors unable to reflect any light. White objects reflect back all the colors of light and so derive their purity and perfect representation of the original color of the light.

We are all called to reflect God's light—his love. The point of God's love is not to absorb it, retaining all its heat and warmth for ourselves as the color black; or as by taking all the talents, blessings and gifts God has given us and using them entirely in self-satisfaction. The point is to reflect God's love back upon mankind, our families, those we meet, all creation. We are each called to glorify God, to brighten the world by reflecting his love—his light.

We each reflect God's love in our own unique color. None of us can completely reflect the pure white light of God's love. Mary and Jesus, each born without original sin, are the only persons who have perfectly reflected the full radiant, white, beauty of God's light, his love. They are the only persons who have fully aligned their wills with that of God, the Father's. Placing ourselves above God, and selfishness—our inability to love our neighbor as ourselves, are responsible for the light we absorb and are unable to reflect back. God draws good not only from the colors of his love which we reflect, but also from those we cannot or won't—our sins. Those who have placed themselves a long way from God's grace, refusing his unconditional love, lost from his path, reflect the color closest to black.

The blackest black is reserved for those who are the personification of evil. These are not people merely lost in sin, they are consumed in evil. They have allowed Satan parasitic residence in their souls, permitting the spirit of evil bodily form to propagate more chaos, destruction, torment, and to enslave more souls to his service. They have sold their immortal souls into eternal suffering for the immediate and temporary gratification the world can give. In this pact the devil's enticing, soothing balm is freedom from conscience, empowering them to enjoy their spoils as they live beyond the rules of civilized men. They are not enhanced by this "freedom," but are reduced in their humanity, enslaved by it, addicted to evil's domination and power. They are numbed by the loss of their conscience. In Satan's service, to his ends, they are now better equipped to propagate evil upon their fellow man. There is indeed a non-human quality to these people; devoid of the capacity for empathy to link them with their fellow man in kinship or compassion.

In this devil's pact, they have forfeited their capacity for remorse. All preparations are now in place to burn their bridge to an all-merciful, all-forgiving God, a God who continues to shine love upon even them—seeking them out, to return to his path, holding out hope until the final hour of their death, their last opportunity to choose light over the darkness.

These people often are attractively disguised among us, crossing every walk of life, every culture, every aspect of society. If you have glanced their sphere and recognized them, you have felt the electrifying chill in your spine. The greatest danger in encountering a person truly consumed in evil is becoming like them—evil yourself. It is easy to react to their insults in kind, a progressive downward spiral, under the old law "...'An eye for an eye and a tooth for a tooth.'" (Matthew 5:38*) Christ replaced this law when he triumphed over death and with it Satan's tyranny over man. In establishing the new law, Christ arms us with the ultimate weapon against those who choose to embody evil: "...love your enemies, and pray for those who persecute you..." (Matthew 5:44)

The greatest destruction these people of darkness spawn is the souls they ensnare and take with them. It is a heritage passed to successive generations, until their chain of bondage is broken by love. "And do not fear those who kill the body but cannot kill the soul; rather fear him who can destroy both soul and body in hell." (Matthew 10:28, RSV) These people

---

* This reference is to Old Testament law (Exodus 21:23-25)

of darkness are like the black holes of the universe with such enormous gravitational force, that they bleed everything in reach into themselves. The closer you encounter them, the more irresistible their pull in dominating, controlling, dehumanizing another—enslaving another's will to themselves.

We must acknowledge that evil exists and learn to recognize this level of blackness in its attractively disguised forms, then maintain the greatest distance possible. Man is no match for the diabolical force which powers it. This fighting must be left to God. If you have stumbled into its path, pray for God to deliver you and guide you clear. Pray too, for those under Satan's spell; that they be released and also find their way home, before their choice is eternally irrevocable.

All the complementary colors of our hearts fused together, individually striving as we are able in our own unique ways to do God's will, would more closely reflect back a pure white light. We need each other. We cannot accomplish this more perfect, greater glorification of God alone. We can only do this together. We are all each others servants. What we cannot do separately we can do together.

> "'For I was hungry and you gave me food, I was thirsty and you gave me drink, a stranger and you welcomed me, naked and you clothed me, ill and you cared for me, in prison and you visited me.' Then the righteous will answer him and say, 'Lord, when did we see you hungry and feed you, or thirsty and give you drink? When did we see you a stranger and welcome you, or naked and clothe you? When did we see you ill or in prison, and visit you?' And the king will say to them in reply, 'Amen, I say to you, whatever you did for one of these least brothers of mine, you did for me.'"
>
> Matthew 25:35-40

The colors I reflect of God's light are incomplete. It is the light of one partial facet, among an infinity of facets in the unflawed white brilliance of God's love. It is God's light made manifest to your eyes— having interacted with my imperfections. I reflect a distortion of its original beauty, and rely on God's mercy for what is missing.

Our Lord does not come down from
Heaven every day to lie in a golden
ciborium. He comes to find another
heaven which is infinitely dearer to
Him—the heaven of our souls.

Saint Thérèse of Lisieux

# JOURNAL SELECTIONS

"Christ has no body now on earth but yours, no hands but yours, no feet but yours; yours are the eyes through which Christ's compassion looks out at the world, yours are the feet with which he is to go about doing good, and yours are the hands with which he is to bless us now."

Saint Teresa of Avila

 March 4, 1996
After Mass and Communion:
Embrace my Church.
Embrace the/my Sacraments and
all the grace they hold in store for you.
Open your hearts to my love/grace.
I will pour more into your hearts than you can hold.
I love you, my child/children.
Love me, love your fellow man.
Keep my word. Follow my lead.
Pick up your individual crosses and follow me.
There you will find me: in the suffering and joys of your life,
in the suffering and joys of your fellow man.
Look into the faces/eyes of all humanity
and there you will see me—
see me made manifest to you in the flesh,
the living flesh.
Follow my command.
Love your neighbor as yourself
and love me/your God above all things.
Detach yourself from all but me.
In so doing, all will naturally fall into place
in your life and with your fellow man.

When/if you cannot feel my presence,
make an act of will.
When you feel nothing (in your heart),
make an act of will—a choice
(in keeping with my word
as you will find in the scripture.)
When you have no faith,
ask it of the Father in my name.
When you have no trust,
ask it of the Father in my name.
When you do not know my will,
ask but that you do it, of the Father in my name.


Up, my child, and be about the work of the day.
I love you. Take me with you wheresoever you go.

 March 13, 1996
Referring to *MY CHILDREN LISTEN*:
Instructions around the book...
They are a story within a story—a parable
of your will and mine commingling
(interweaving, mixing together).
You are learning how to recognize and do my will—
submit your will to mine...
Get to my words.
They are paramount.
Recede into the background.
Time grows short.
Now quickly be about your business.
Relax into me.
Trust in me.
I will guide you/your hand.

March 14, 1996
There are **great truths, universal truths**
in the **world's** great and true **religions**.
There is **more in common than different,**
depending on how one chooses to look at it.

Referring to the world's many religions:
Respect your differences,
love one another and live together peacefully.
Leave the mystery of bringing all men to salvation to me.
Referring to someone of Christian beliefs:
Live your life in accordance with my Son, Jesus Christ
and you have done what is your (duty, life's work)
to bring more souls to me.
Soul's come to me in the gentle stillness
not through force (pressure), manipulation,
any effort to impede their full access to their own free will
or subvert their wills to another, no matter the reason.
There is no cause which justifies the subversion
of another's will in the process.
Souls are drawn to me of love.
Seeing and feeling love
makes them more receptive to my call.
This is man's role to make manifest—
directly visible to their bodily eyes, my love to all.
How else can man (more readily) see me?
Bring souls to me through the example of your life,
your love, the love you have (most fully) to offer
when you follow my lead,
my commands,
my example,
my life.
Pick up your cross/crosses
my child/children and follow me.
In so doing, so you will lead others.
Let them touch me through the love you make manifest
(bodily present) for bodily senses to identify.
Let it be so commonplace that
no man doubts the existence of God,
just as no man doubts the light of the sun,
for all the many all pervasive ways
in which it is (interacted with)
and made manifest—
visible to the human eye.

Reflect my love, my children,
that no man doubts my existence
and all become increasingly receptive to my love
within their own hearts,
my healing love,
forgiveness,
compassion,
mercy for all souls.
Return to me, my children.
Come home.

"Where is this going in the book?" I asked, confused, still thinking the February 23, 1996 entry was the book's close.

Do not concern yourself with where, my child.
I will show you. Do nothing.
Do not impede my work, my words. Listen.
Close your eyes and feel my peace flow over you...
You are trying too hard, my child. Do not try so hard.
All will be given you as it is needed.

March 15, 1996
After Mass and Communion:
Regarding bringing the darkness, the thorn placed in my heart, to Christ:

I will draw good from evil.

Referring to its pain:

It will make one strong.
You struggle but not in vain. Be still, my child.

"I don't have time to be here, I have so many things to do today." I could not dismiss my annoyance, and feeling the words were an intrusion. "My hands are too tired to write."

There is always time to sit with me a while.
Cast off the cares and anxieties of the world.
Forsake them, their distraction.
Detach yourself from all persons, things, ambitions.
Cling only to me.
I am the true source of your strength,
your life.
I am.
I am the/your beginning and the/your end.

I am all that matters.

All that is important,

all that you are is defined in me.

What could be more important than sitting with me a while;

drinking from the well spring of

eternally refreshing water I give you to drink.

"Forgive me, my Lord, for my ingratitude and impatience. Thank you that I should still be able to hear you in this way. I am so sorry to have offended and hurt you."

You have not offended me, my child.

Man cannot hurt God.

You offend your own soul and that of others

whenever you turn your will and attention away from God.

The world and its many distractions must be lived in accordance

with the commands, example, words, I left you in my life

in order to draw meaning and purpose from it.

Man only diminishes himself

and his own soul's ultimate glory

in turning away from God.

"Help me Jesus; what you are saying completes the parable of the book, and I cannot organize what I have and where it should be placed."

Do not worry, my child.

All truths cannot be told at once.

They must slowly emerge,

each in their own individual way, unique to each man.

This is the work of God, not men.

Regarding one of my children (her age and stage of development pertinent to the remarks) increasingly resistant to attend Sunday Mass:

Yes, allow her space—the freedom of her will.

She needs it...reaffirmed by you that it is undeniably hers.

Give her unconditional love, compassion, and the space to be her.

It is not important that she go through the motions

of organized religion, presently meaningless to her.

They are only a source of anger and alienation at present.

Let her be. Let her come to me in her own time, as did you.

I am always there for her as all your loved ones,

guiding, watching over them, and protecting them.

Just love her, my child, and give her space.

Feeling frazzled, anxious, and pressured, "Forgive my annoyance and impatience, Jesus, I have so much to do. I try the day through and don't accomplish anything. I am so disorganized, I can't get anything done."

> Place it in my hands, my child.
>
> Do not try so hard. Be patient.
>
> Allow my/our Father's plan for you to unfold in your life.

I felt very peaceful and calm, as if all were in order, in contrast to disorganization's unrest.

> Take my peace, calm, tranquillity with you the day through.
>
> Allow it to touch all that you meet.
>
> It is grounded in me/my love.
>
> Allow it to shine through your eyes, pass through your touch.
>
> Bring the presence of my healing love to all that you meet,
>
> most (especially) bring it to your family, your children.
>
> Be up now, my child, and about your day's work.

I regretted my attitude of annoyance.

> I am not angry or disappointed with you, my child.
>
> I understand and have full compassion
>
> for your human frailties.
>
> Accept them yourself.
>
> Struggle under their weight
>
> and allow them to make you
>
> the more humble, (and) compassionate
>
> for another man's weakness, and forgiving
>
> of another man's sins against you.

I thought about punishment in the wake of my impatience and annoyance at taking the time to be in Christ's presence and listen that morning.

> Do not fear my wrath/punishment.
>
> I am a God of pure love.
>
> Regardless what you do or don't,
>
> I am here with the same all abiding love.
>
> There is nothing you can do which I do not forgive.
>
> Remember the secret is the intentions of a man's heart
>
> which only God knows, and knows before the man.
>
> I know the intentions of your heart's desire and I am pleased.
>
> I will continue to purify them.
>
> Allow me to teach you—show you the way.

**Be up now, my child. I love you.**
**I will purify your heart, *its desires, how it sees;***
**concern yourself not with how.**

Late March, 1996

My cognitive difficulties had generated a mix-up obvious to my children. It was three times as much work to correct my mistakes, if it was not already too late. When we were alone, my oldest daughter asked, "Mom, do you have Alzheimer's?"

Her question caught me by surprise. I laughed, "No, I don't have Alzheimer's. What would make you think of that?"

"There was a show on TV about it last night and it looks just like you, the way you can't remember things. Are you sure you don't have Alzheimer's?" she asked, now unable to hide the concern edging her voice.

I smiled at her and said, "Yes, I am sure I don't. After all, how many diseases can one person have?" My attempt at humor failed to smooth the furrows in her brow.

She looked more intently at me and said, "I think you do. You should ask your doctor what she thinks."

"Really don't worry..."

Before I could finish, she asked, "Well, then why do you have such trouble remembering things? You were never that way before."

"No, I wasn't before I was sick." I said.

"No, that's not what I meant. You're worse even since then." she said.

"I think it's mostly that you're more aware of it as you've gotten older." I tried to reassure her.

"Sometimes you do seem better than others. Why?" she asked.

"It's because my illness goes through periods of flare-up and relative quiet." I explained.

"Are you sure you're not getting worse?"

"There has been some progression, but then it seems I've also had longer and more frequent flare-ups as well. My degree of difficulty with memory fluctuates with the flare-ups, especially my inner ear symptoms. My memory comes back to the same point between flare-ups. Alzheimer's doesn't act like that. The constant loud ringing in my ears and chronic pain are also distracting." I said.

Briefly changing the focus she quickly spoke, "You wouldn't tell us if you were dying."

"I am not dying," I protested.

"Why can't you remember?" she implored, seeking reassurance in the logic of reason.

"Remember the last time we played scrabble. You thought I wasn't trying because I made only three letter words, when you knew my vocabulary was better than that. The trouble I have with my inner ears and balance affects my ability to visually scan the board. It limits what I can take in and then apply of my intelligence, especially if time is a factor. It's like knowing how to ski, but being in a wheelchair—you can't use the knowledge. It's really very frustrating."

"I don't understand." she said.

"The more symptomatic my ears are, the more my brain depends upon my eyes for the information to help maintain my balance. Instead of smoothly scanning, my eyes continually stop to briefly register information as to where I am relative to the space around me. This information helps my brain maintain my balance but, interrupts what I was looking at, and it's then more difficult to take in the small details. You've probably also noticed that when I am not feeling well, I tend to be uncoordinated and clumsy, even walking into the edges of furniture. Those things also depend on knowing your spatial orientation relative to what's around you."

"Yeah, I was worried about that too, but I think now I understand." Her face relaxed, and she came over and put her arm around my shoulder and said, "Well, look at it this way, Mom; if you can't remember, there will never be any reruns." We laughed, the additional inside joke being, that I virtually never watched television beyond news programs anyway.

"Now don't think you and your sister are going to be taking advantage of it!" We laughed some more.

 Spring, 1996

I felt badly over an argument I was party to, the day prior.

**My child, I did not say make no enemies.**

**I call upon you (and all) to love your enemies.**

**You are what you are. I love you as you are.**

**I will make you strong to carry my work through.**

**My grace and love are ever with you,**

**guiding you/your hand.**

"Please forgive me, Jesus. I often lose my patience as the day passes, and feel a great degree of failure carrying your word through."

Do not fret. Do not concern yourself. Do not try so hard.
Just allow my peace, my presence to overtake you,
moment, by moment, by moment, in your day.
Your life can only be lived a moment at a time,
and it is in those moments, as they are lived,
that my presence is (can be) made manifest to you.
Bring my conscious awareness to each moment in your life.
In this we (meaning: Christians) are similar to
(Buddha, Gandhi, Eastern religion)—a universal truth
among my many religions of the world.
I am only able to act through you as you allow—
that is, only as each moment is lived.
"I worry about distorting your communication."
Do not worry, my child.
I have told you—you are chosen for the coloring
with which your heart sees the world,...
We are inseparably one. You can only do my will;
do not struggle or rail against it...
You are inextricably drawn to it—
welded/melded with mine/our Father's...


God does not punish man.
The misfortunes of life are never punishment
for man's actions or inactions.
Many fall away from me at this
when really they need to draw closer.
All the misfortunes (loss, pain, suffering) of this world
are manifestations of evil's effects upon it.
They (misfortunes) successfully do
drive more people (souls) from me
creating chaos/confusion as people examine their lives
for meaning and purpose in the aftermath.
This is the devil's work, propagating his spirit,
and inflicting suffering on my creation.
Always remember I/my Father
will draw good from evil.
Allow your hearts to heal.
Allow our will be done.

You are each capable of the best and worst in all.
The man who does not think so simply knows himself not.
Different gifts, different crosses, (circumstances) life brings,
make the weak strong and the strong weak.
You are all saints and sinners;
the ultimate difference is
the final predisposition of your heart's choice.
You must all say, 'yes' or 'no' to
my/our Father's healing love and forgiveness.
You must choose the light over the darkness
to live in eternal happiness,
rather than damnation/perpetual suffering.
There is no numbing balm of indifference
after mortal death.
Your/every soul lives forever
as my/our Father has commanded you.
To those who choose the darkness a numbing balm of void
will look the greatest pleasure, compared with the suffering—
a suffering that knows no end, knows no relief.
Man may view some lives as disposable;
I/my Father value each soul we have created
with the importance of the most precious jewel/treasure.
All are beloved in our eyes.
There is no obliteration of
your spirit/consciousness upon death.
You are merely born into a higher form,
one of unparalleled higher awareness than you can conceive.
The increased wisdom,
knowledge of truth,
heightened perception,
in every way you know, and far more,
is what makes the joy which awaits you incomprehensible,
and the suffering of those who choose the darkness unbearable.
There are no drugs, balms, elixirs, alcohol,
to blunt the awareness of this pain.
There are no exits (suicide, death) to escape
the pain they have chosen
in reaching for the darkness over the light.

I say to you again, all men must choose
between the darkness and the light.
There are only two choices: yes, or no.
All souls are invited to share in our divine eternal life;
but they must accept the invitation to complete the gift.
We are here for all souls,
all manner of help available to each,
available on a more personal, intimate level,
than you can conceive.
I am (we are) everywhere.
We are all around you.
We are with you always.
Yes, your lives are recapitulations of my and my Mother's passion.
Suffer with me; redeem more souls through uniting
your suffering/your will with mine.
Take every opportunity to forgive those souls around you
who have given home to evil in their souls.
Your love of that soul, in your forgiveness,
kills the evil— stops its growth and propagation
and further protects/shields your own soul.
Remember my words:
'Father, forgive them for they know not what they do.'
You do not forgive the evil;
you forgive the soul—
the soul because it still contains
some flicker of the light of my presence
and thus some hope for its own salvation,
till its final hour when the ultimate last choice is made.
At that time, the light is either forever extinguished
and the soul lives in perpetual darkness,
heightened awareness, unbearable suffering without end—
all the greater knowing this was at his own hand,
OR
those who choose the light,
regardless how dim at the time of their choice,
will live in a radiance of peace,
love and joy
beyond their imagining.

Remember the parable of the workers
paid the same at day's end versus the entire day.*
All are filled to overflowing regardless of the cup
with which they come to us at life's end.
The size of the cup you offer me/my Father
is a matter between each soul and their Creator,
and has no bearing on the joy
of the other souls in my Kingdom.
Bring more souls to me/our Father.
This is how to best please.
The more soul's you bring the greater is your cup.
Do this by living Christ in your life.
Align your will with mine.
Give body, arms, legs, hands, feet, eyes to the spirit of Christ
that his goodness, healing love shine forth on all you meet,
that others come to touch him through every action,
every thought, word, and deed.
The more souls join us,
the more souls rejoice,
and in this all in my kingdom pray
every/each soul on earth retain/secure the largest cup
to offer my/our Father at the hour of their death.
The size of any one cup
does not diminish/alter the joy
of any soul's ecstasy regardless of theirs,
because all are given more than they can appreciate.
Our prayers are with you my child.
Do not be afraid.
All that you need will be provided for you as it is needed
to do my/our Father's work...


Regarding an unresolved matter which had provoked yesterday's argument:
Hold your tongue, my child; allow me to keep it in check.
It is an act of love.
Now up and go, my love. I am always with you.
Be aware of me/my presence.


* The Parable Of The Workers In The Vineyard. (Matthew 20:1-16)

April 14, 1996
After Mass and Communion:

> **Give of yourself that others may come to me.**

Regarding a parenting challenge resistant to my best efforts:

> ***Place it in God's hands, trust.*** **Let them see the truth.**

Regarding publication of this journal:

> **You must bring it, my word, to my people—my other children.**
> **You must give of yourself to bring me to others.**
> **I will help you. I will always be there for you.**
> **I will never forsake you.**
> **Bring other souls to my/our Father,**
> **and you can no more perfectly glorify God.**
> **Bring them through your love...modeled after me in my name**

 April 15, 1996
After Mass and Communion:

> **I am one with you, my child. We are one.**
> **Do not try so hard. Be at peace.**
> **Allow me to work through you.**
> **I will give you the words that you need** (meaning: in writing).
> **I am well pleased with you, my child,**
> **with the intentions of your efforts; but,**
> **you do not have to try so hard to do my work—my will.**
> **Trust in me, that I will work through you,**
> **that you will have all things as you need them and more.**

Regarding how to manage an oppositional phase of childhood:

> **Be kind.**
> **Trust in me, my child.**
> **All is well.**
> **Allow her to be as she is.**
> **Respect her will.**
> **Do not try to subvert her will to yours.**
> **Allow her to be free.**
> **Allow her will to be free.**

[This did not refer to situations in which a child's safety, or similar matters of significant parental responsibility were at issue.]

Free will is my gift to each of you.
It is the mark of God's Spirit upon man.
It is how you are created in my/our Father's image and likeness.
Do not be worried or concerned for your children.
They are safely in my loving care and protection.
Continue to let them know me
especially in your love.
Love them as I have loved you—unconditionally.
Show them patience, forgiveness, compassion.
Be as Mary to you.
Remember she came to you in your need,
though you had not acknowledged her.
Mary is Mother to you all.
I am your brother.
My Father is your Father.
We are all united through the Holy Spirit.
Do not try to understand this (mystery of the Trinity),
(presently) you cannot,
but one day you will understand this and all things.
Care for your body, my child,
in both health and personal appearance.
They are both important
in carrying my/our Father's work forth.
Do not dress yourself strictly
in clothes of mourning (black/dull) as if I am dead.
Clothe yourself as one who rejoices in my living presence.
Shine this forth from your eyes, and
in all manner of yourself, and in all that you do.
You understand the balance of which I speak.
I will guide you...

Do not be afraid, my child.
I am always with you. I will never forsake you.
Allow my peace to flow over you and
immerse yourself in my saving, healing love and grace.
Rest your pen down, and be with me a while in silence.
Feel my majesty, power,
and peace of my presence.

Simplify your life, my child.
Deny yourself (give something up).
Make this each time an act of love for me
an act of further uniting yourself
with me and Mary,
my Mother/Mother to us all.
Turn to her, follow her lead and example.
She loves you dearly, my child.
She is well pleased with you, and
wants you to increase your devotion to her.
Say a Rosary to her each day and
devote it to Mary's intentions for the world.
Be aware of the Blessed Mysteries of the Rosary (as you pray it.)
Mary will show you how to pray the Rosary to her.

"Thank you, Jesus and Mary. It is something I have never known but wondered about the monotony of repetition. What is the purpose of this repetition? I wasn't able to answer this to either of my children."

Do not be concerned, my child.
It will be given to you and more.
Its mystery will be shown to you.
Use it to bring others to greater devotion
to Mary and her Rosary.
Allow it to increase your own devotion
and increase your faith.
Be up now, my child, and about your day's work.
Carry me with you wheresoever you go.

A monstrance* upon the altar held the Blessed Sacrament, the consecrated Host, in view for veneration. I prayed. It was very peaceful. I did not want to leave.

It is (all right), my child.
Go now, your life is a prayer.
I am with you.

---

* A vessel in which the consecrated Host is placed and displayed for adoration. It is generally made of precious metal, has a broad base, stem, and atop the stem the Host rests behind a clear window usually surrounded by an elaborate design—as if radiating from the Host.

April 18, 1996
After Mass and Communion:
Regarding this book:

**...Get to my words... Tell little of yourself...**

"I love you Jesus. Please help me better serve you, better do your most holy will."

**I am well pleased with you, my child—**
**(with) the intentions of your heart's desire.**
**Do not try so hard. Exert less effort.**
**What I ask you to do is easier than you make it**
**because you have not yet learned to fully trust in me**
**and have faith in my plan for you.**

My eyes upon the Blessed Sacrament in the monstrance; I knelt to pray. "It is so peaceful, Jesus; I could sit here a very long time."

**I know, my child, but your work—**
**work you must do for me and the Father calls you.**
**Go, my child, and get to my words...**
**You will see all will fall into place**
**in accordance with my plan.**

"I am afraid."

**Do not be afraid, my child.**
**Feel my peace and strength within you.**
**Allow it to emanate from you.**
**Allow the light of my presence**
**to shine forth from your eyes upon all that you meet.**
**Do not worry. All will not be easy, but all will be well.**
**You are in my constant care and protection**
**as are your children and loved ones.**
**Mary (also/similarly) holds you and your loved ones**
**(and those for whom you pray) in her heart.**
**She is so pleased in your devotion to her rosary**
**and the roses\* you offer her.**
**She pours great grace upon you.**

---

\* This did not refer literally to flowers. In the context I understood it to mean each bead of the rosary or more generally any prayer, act of kindness, or effort offered to Mary.

She wants you to increase your devotion to her,
and spread it to others...
Mary has spoken to you as have I.
Reread the words you have been given.
They are also from the Trinity.
We are one.
We are in unison.
Our wills are indivisible.
Do not trouble yourself
pulling the words apart, analyzing them,
trying to understand precisely from whom they came:
*Father, Son, Holy Spirit, Mary.*
It doesn't matter, and you can't understand.
It doesn't matter, because our wills are one.
Unite your will with ours, my child.
Go now, my child.
Go forth, and do the work
I/we have planned for you.
Take me with you wheresoever you go.
I am never without you. Do not forsake me.
Speaking to Christ in his humanity: "No, Jesus, I am sorry for when
I have hurt and abandoned you turning my back. I am really sorry. Help
me please, not to do that any more. Help me to make up for all the times
when I have."

Accept my forgiveness, my child.
Go, and sin no more. Do not wallow in guilt.
Live in the beauty of the present moment,
as I give it to you and show you
my/our Father's plan unfolding.
Be receptive. Keep an open mind and heart.
Focus yourself on the awareness of my presence within you,
in all those around you and throughout all creation.
All will then naturally fall into place.
Love me (and)/your Father above all things,
and love your fellow man as I have loved you.
Kneel and pray in quiet, then leave the church.
Go in peace. I love you.
"I love you."

April 24, 1996
After Mass and Communion:
                    Be calm, my child.
                I am with you. Be not afraid.
                    Let me work through you.
            Allow others to feel my love through you—
                your actions, words, deeds.
            Be not concerned over the book's progression,
                or how it will come to be/pass.
                It is in my/our Father's plans.
                All will be provided and more
        as it is needed (to occur/transpire)...It is my plan.
        Take support...from the structure of my Church.
            Write today. Edit as I have instructed you...
                Be at peace, I am with you.
            Have no concern over your loved ones,
                or any other person/or matter.
                They and all your loved ones
            are safely in my care and protection.
        Go now, my child, and set about the important work
                I have set before you...
    Use it (meaning: feeling God's presence) to reach out to others
            and allow my healing love to touch them,
        all for the purpose of bringing them closer to me—
        leaving them more receptive to my own call in their hearts.
        I love you, my child. I am well pleased with your efforts.
                Be not concerned about results,
        just continue to strive to do my/our Father's will
                and follow my commands:
                *Love your neighbor as yourself;*
                *Love your God above all;*
        *my commandment of love* in the intentions of your heart's desire.
            Be up now. Take me with you wheresoever you go.
                    Your life is a prayer.
        Carry my peace and presence with you for all to see.
        Draw strength from it to the smallest moment of your day.
            I love you. Place down your pen and go, my child.
"I love you."

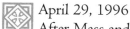 April 29, 1996
After Mass and Communion:

**Be conscious of me, my child.**
(meaning: Christ within me and others.)
**Be ever conscious of me and it will help you hold your tongue,**
**(and) measure what you say with my kindness and love.**
I was sorry for having recently lost my temper.
**You are forgiven.**
**Your human frailties imprison you.**
**Your heart would fly, but you are chained like a bird**
**with thread about its feet—tethered to clay.**

"I love you, Jesus. Thank you for being with me. Please be with those I love and let them feel and know your presence; but, I don't wish them any calamity or ill to receive it. Is there a gentle way?"
**I am only gentle, my child, gentle to all my children.**
**It is the harshness of the world which has interfered—**
**evil and its destructive aftermath.**
**I am pulling you from its jaws.**
**I have not produced the pain.**
"I know, Jesus, I am sorry."
**Yes, my child, I know;**
**you have come to better know me in your heart;**
**and I am well pleased with the intention of your heart's desires.**
**Do not be concerned over** a loved one; they **will be well.**
"I know I shouldn't ask if you mean physically or spiritually."
**Do not concern yourself, my child; concern yourself with nothing.**
**Go home and write my book...**
**Go, take me with you wheresoever you go.**
**Let me shine from your eyes; your life is a prayer. I love you.**

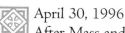 April 30, 1996
After Mass and Communion:

**Do not plan;\* be open to my words—**
**what I have to unfold before you.**

---

\* This and similar references are understood in the context of good judgment and honoring our responsibilities and obligations here.

If you plan, you may preclude yourself
from fully participating in my plan—
at the level I want you there.
I am pleased with you, my child.
You have grown in your prayers and closeness with me.
You are better able to pray my/our Father's will be done.
You have grown in my wisdom to know it is I/our Father
who knows best what you and your loved ones need,
know best how to spread my word,
the beautiful message
in the book entrusted to your care.
Treat it like a beloved child.
Nurture, care for it, and protect it.
Then set it free upon the winds to have its own life.
It will always come back to you.
What it returns use in all ways
to further glorify my name, our Father and the Holy Spirit.
You will know what to do and how to do it
because it will be laid before you...
"I love you, Jesus. Thank you.
I am so happy; at the same time I am also afraid."
Fear not, my child; I am always with you.
Concern yourself not for your loved ones—
they are in my constant (always in my) care and protection.

"I am having trouble choosing which words you have given me to include
or not. I do not want to distort, or diminish what you have given me."
It is the opposite, my child.
Remove yourself in any way possible from the work,
to make fewer distractions from my message.

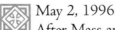 May 2, 1996
After Mass and Communion:
Ability at mass communications in your age
has been abused by man.
It is one of my many gifts which have been abused.
It sanctions evil,
its suffering and destruction.

It numbs my creatures to its violence and depravity,
and tells others weaker among you:
it is all right—acceptable.
It begets more evil in those susceptible
and already weak of the sins against them...
Great destruction will rain down upon man...
It is not inevitable—at least man's outcome in the destruction.
You (mankind) must turn to me with your whole heart and soul.
Use all the gifts I have given you to glorify my name—to glorify God.
Fight against those who use these gifts* to sully man,
to drag him into the mud and mire.
Wage a war against them.
I am at your side
as are my angels and saints...
Do not let them dehumanize
my most beloved and blessed creation—man.
Subjugating/denying man his free will is dehumanization.
Lack of kindness in all forms is dehumanization. Fight against it.

May 10, 1996
Regarding the incomprehensibility of God and God's plan:
*Each man is like one cell as part of a perfect human body.*
*Each cell has a different role and functions:*
*skin cell, liver cell, nerve, among others.*
*Some cells grow and are lost over time.*
*Some cells develop preparing the way for others to take their place.*
*Some cells mature and remain for the life of the organism,*
*as it grows in the wisdom and beauty of age.*
*All the cells together, interdependent,*
*make up a wholly functioning body;*
*yet the sum is greater than the parts,*
*beyond complex physical organized functions*
*to conscious awareness.*
*Man's capacity to become aware of God derives from*
*the presence of God's Spirit breathed into us,*
*raising man above a dog.*

---

* Meaning for example: mass communication.

*The inability of one cell to fathom*
*the whole living organism,*
*its consciousness,*
*and its own role within the body*
*is like man's inability to fathom*
*God, his plan and our small part in that plan.*
*One cell is alive and intact of itself,*
*with its own independent life functions,*
*yet dies if separated from the body.*
*Within the body the cells are mutually interdependent*
*for their function and survival.*
*Each cell is just one part of the whole.*
*Each cell is essential yet does not know the whole.*
*When cells go awry, they can grow out of control, as in a cancer,*
*destroying the very organism which sustains them.*
*So it is with man and the impact of his sins*
*upon the greater body of mankind—also destroying it.*
*When men sin, they too grow out of control,*
*inviting greater and greater input of evil.*
*Ultimately good is brought from evil by God.*
*It is the spiritual of God's kingdom,*
*not the earthly, which lives forever.*
*We are a spiritual body united in Christ.*
*We are all connected via this Mystical Body of Christ.*
*Those who choose to turn away from God as their final choice,*
*are like sloughed off dead skin—*
*once having served their purpose,*
*then died and decayed.*

May 12, 1996

During evening prayer I contemplated anticipated critics, "There are many who could reduce this manuscript to nothing; I could make their expected arguments myself." I heard:

**They would have missed that which escapes definition by man.**
**They would have missed its most critical element;**
**the element which brought it to life**
**and sustains all life—**
**the undefinable quintessential.**

> Their words and beliefs are powerless
> in making God nonexistent,
> in uncreating God.
> They will know the elegant simplicity of truth
> one day, themselves, first hand.

 May 13, 1996
After Mass and Communion:

I looked about the church, its altar, Crucifix, statues, Stations of the Cross, the images in stained glass and remembered a time when I viewed them and the Church's rituals with intellectual condescension. Now I saw their value. The Catholic Church is rich in imagery: the Holy Family, Jesus, Mary, and Joseph, the Nativity, Crucifixion, Pieta, the risen Christ; and ritual: the Mass, Sacraments, celebrating the Church calendar.

> *The images and ritual are not God*
> *but a meaningful way to allow our limited human senses*
> *to quickly begin to grasp the incomprehensible.*
> *To feel their* (the images and rituals) *full power*
> *one must see them with the fluid openness of a child.*

 May 14, 1996
After Mass and Communion:

Referring to the abused and neglected children in our world:
> ...my children most in need...
> Let me touch those in need,
> that they open their heart
> to my healing love and grace.
> Let them know they have both
> perfect Father and Mother in heaven,
> intimately present to them though their eyes cannot see.
> Pull these children back from the brink—society's throwaways.
> Do not allow your society to desecrate their precious lives and souls.
> You are all my children.
> Help each other to carry your many crosses.
> Share your blessings among you and
> I will bless you in greater abundance than you can imagine.
> Gather/pull people together from all phases and walks of life.

Bring those feeling useless, abandoned in their old age,
to know the true joy of life
by giving to these young children—
provide them the stability of love and security...
I call my laity to me, young and old alike.
Set my world ablaze with my love.
Care for the old.
Care for the young.
Help them to grow in love,
respect, and service to one another.
Spread my word over every corner of the earth.
I will help you. Do not concern yourself with how. I am with you.
The old, hunger for me/the spiritual.
They hunger to be needed and of service.
The young hunger for love, particularly
the abused, abandoned, the outcast.
Bring these two together,
and any able body between,
dedicated to my service.
I am with you...
Make my love manifest to all who will see it...
Be up and about your day's work.
I am with you. I will make you strong. I love you.

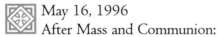 May 16, 1996
After Mass and Communion:
Take your pen and sit with me a while.
Make your work effortless.
Do not be concerned.
Just allow me to work through you.
When you make your work effortless
you are most able to do my will
(because) you are most receptive.
Making your work effortless is an act of patience;
it is slowly allowing my/our Father's plan to unfold for you...
Be not afraid.
I will not forsake you in your hours of darkness.
All (in dark and light hours) will draw you ever closer to me.

All your suffering will bear great fruit for you and many souls.
Many souls will be brought to the Father
through work you allow me to do through you...

Mary is in a special way Mother to all my priests.
You are all called to be my priests and
to serve me in different ways.
Living your lives in keeping with my word and example
is each person's duty and their greatest accomplishment
in leading other souls to the Father
through the living example of the love—the lives of love.

Great destruction lies ahead, my child.
Man has not long to mend his ways
to ready himself through this period
(strengthened) by my love.
Love, he (man) can make manifest to all mankind.
The time grows short...
Be at peace in my love, care, and protection,
as I hold your loved ones as well.
Do not be afraid or fill your belly with anxiety.
There will be a great warning given to man
for all the earth to see.
No creature great or small will miss its significance;
but not all will be moved to act upon it.
Many will be overcome by fear and
subject to the devil's bidding.
Help squelch their fears
with my message of hope and reassurance.
The End Times are upon us/mankind.
I will soon come again in great glory
for every eye to see—obscured from no man
It will be the dawning of a new age...
a (world) of love, peace—love and peace among all.
Go, my child. Be about my work. I am ever with you.
Take me with you wheresoever you go,
and let me touch all whom you meet.
I am your strength and life's force...

May 21, 1996
After Mass and Communion:
                    Sit with me a while.
I felt the close presence of Christ.
                    I will strengthen you.
"It is hard to know how to picture you."
              I am one with you, my child,
                  I am all around you,
                    I am everywhere.
              I am no place more sacred
                than in the heart of man.
                This is my tabernacle.
                There is nothing on Earth
                  more holy or sacred
                    than human life.
                Revere life in all forms.
    (meaning: man, and beyond to animals and plants)
              Respect what I have given you.
    (meaning: creation and all our natural resources)
            A time comes when they will be scarce
                    and then no more.
          Time grows short for man to turn to me,
                  to turn to their God...


                Unite your will with mine
              and it is united with the Father's
                    and the Holy Spirit's.
          Concern yourself not with doing my will;
              simply will it, and it will be so.
          We do not fail anyone who asks our help
                    in the Father's will.
                None but the Father's will
                    ultimately prevails.
              It is only the false notions of men
                    which cloud this.
                It is man's lack of humility
                    before their Creator
              which blinds him to the truth.

Begin with humility, my children, and we are easier to find.
You are all here to be each others servants,
none greater or less than the rest.
I am your servant to bring you to the Lord, our Father.
Place your full faith, hope, confidence in me.
All will come to pass as it has been written in scripture.
Concern yourself not with the events of the world.
They must proceed that a new creation...
may come to pass.
Know, my children, that all is for the good.
Love one another as I have loved you.
It has never been more important
than in the trying times ahead.
Loving one another,
making my love manifest to the human eye,
brings more souls to the Father.
There is no greater glory man can offer God than this:
loving his fellow man as I have loved you.
Follow my life's example, teaching, word.
Return to the Sacraments;
I am here for you.
Acknowledge my presence.
The Eucharist is each man's personal link with me.
I am there with special graces to pour forth.
Receive me as you would your loving brother, spouse, friend.
Regard me as real,
alive.
Give me shelter in your hearts,
and allow me to grow in you
and you in me.
Make your life easier with me
as your constant strength, your life's force.
Do not try so hard, my child. Be patient.
Make your work effortless and
you are all the better able
to receive my help.
Close your eyes and sit with me a while
in the stillness of your heart.

Let my great peace flow over you.
"I don't want to go."
You must, my child. I have made you strong.
You do not leave me; you carry me with you wheresoever you go.
Touch all you meet with the love you feel from me.
Make my love manifest for all human eyes to see.
Mary is always with you, my child.
She is your loving Mother.
She carries you, your children,
and all those you love in her heart.
She is always there for you.
She wants you to make others more aware of her presence.
Increase other's devotion to Mary.
You know how much greater a task it is
to forgive hurt done to someone you love than your own self.
This has been Mary's greatest act of love for mankind—
forgiving what has been done to me.
It is not just in the Crucifixion,
but in desecration of life and
creation for all time—
*Christ is intimately present throughout.*
Mary shows her love to mankind in remaining present to you,
showing man the way to me—your path to salvation.
Do not underestimate her power and
healing love for all mankind.
She is truly Mother to you all.
She is the Mother of God and
you are each called to share divine eternal life—
begotten from before the dawn of time
and on into eternal infinity.
(Meaning: In sharing divine eternal life
we become part of God who is without beginning or end,
and in that, we exist with God prior to our birth on Earth.)
You cannot understand this, my child.
The constraints in your concept of time do not allow it.
Time does not exist in my kingdom.
All exists at once.
This is one reason for purgatory.

No soul desiring to be in my presence
would allow the suffering he has created
to be a part of our kingdom.
The soul atones for the suffering he created
by suffering himself.
My act of redemption,
love for all,
has atoned for all sins for all time;
simply avail yourself of the impossible,
which I have done for you,
by uniting yourselves and your wills with mine.
A soul wants to purify itself before being in my presence.
It is the way it is.
There is no other way.
For those eternally devoid of my presence,
those eternally damned, pity them not.
They do so of their own choosing.
It is no mistake or accident.
I am here for all souls;
no manner of help
will be/is denied those who seek it.
You are good, my child.
All my works are good.
Do not be afraid.
All will be provided you and your loved ones
as you need it and more.
Make Mary an ever more present part of your life.
She is ever with you as she is in a most special way
with all of my priests...

Simplify your life. Own less.
Give to the poor. Do not hoard excess.
Go now, my child, it is time to be up and about our work.
Know that I do not leave you but that your life is a prayer,
to its smallest act—act of kindness. I love you.
"I love you, my Lord. Thank you for your presence."
Be at peace.

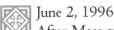 June 2, 1996
After Mass and Communion:

I still carried an undercurrent of resentment towards my illness and it periodically surfaced, as was the case today. The following brought me a significant step closer to deeper acceptance and peace in living with my fate.

**Were it not for your illness you would not follow my path.**

"I am sorry," I responded in shame, unable to hide the truth. "I know I would be spending my life quite differently, significantly distracted from you, if I had my health." Certainly, I would not have been at Mass that day, among many others, nor would I spend as much time in prayer.

**It is not to be sorry, my child.**

**It is as it is.**

**This is God's plan.**

**Accept my will, my child;**

**your life will grow easy.**

**Rely on me, your full strength and life's force.**

**I am all that you seek and need.**

**Bring other souls to the Father through me...**

**In this is your greatest joy.**

**Others will know your authenticity by your works.**

**Love my children. Care for them.**

**Allow them to feel my love made manifest in their lives.**

**I am with you in all that you do.**

**This mission will succeed because it is God's will...**

Referring to a family in difficulty and for whom I prayed:

**Concern yourself not for them**

**they are in my loving care and protection...**

**They must all learn and come to know me in their own way...**

**Go now, my child.**

**Let my peace reign in your heart**

**that my love, goodness and kindness**

**shine forth from your eyes and emanate from your being,**

**touching all whom you meet and all for whom you pray.**

**Your life is a prayer. I love you.**

**Take me with you wheresoever you go. You are never without me.**

Early July, 1996

Another flare in illness left me the usual symptoms plus markedly greater than usual associated irritability. I was beside myself, in such a hyper-irritable state, unable to respond in my customary manner, or how I wanted, to both people and circumstances. It distressed me to see myself so short tempered with those closest to me, and to hurt those I loved the most. I prayed in earnest, "Please help me Jesus, I can't stand watching myself be so unkind. Please forgive me, and draw good from my sins. Please let this irritability pass."

**Suffer yourself gladly,**
**you are learning more compassion for others.**

I understood this to mean more compassion for others in their faults and limitations. It was further lesson in not judging others because one does not know what another comes to a situation burdened by. I wondered how much of man's behavior was beyond their control—a genetic deck and fate's hand predetermined.

Christ's words were not what I expected or wanted to hear, but as always they focused me back toward meaning, purpose, and the journey's work—becoming more fully human in greater compassion and love for others. The words were consoling, their acceptance and forgiveness implicit. It was a focus past drowning in self-pity and illness.

Third Week of July, 1996

*The source of evil acts in our world is two-fold:*
*First, old infections/insults which have yielded wounds*
*and are propagated from men injured by evil's touch;*
*like waves they ripple and pass from one person to the next,*
*to the next generation.*
*Second, new infections of souls by Satan.*
*At present: the rate of new infections is increasing.*
*There have never been so many walking wounded in the world.*
*The cure is love.*
*It neutralizes the source of infection,*
*Satan's parasitic dwelling in mankind—the host.*

Early September, 1996

After near total absence from May to September at weekday Mass, prayer, and efforts in gathering earlier prayer journal notes; I was forced

to acknowledge the cause. A published book had come to seem a potential reality. My avoidance was for fear of just that—publication. I did not
want to lose the anonymity of my life, the privacy I valued. I did not wish
attention, positive, or even less so negative; I was also concerned about the
potential impact on my family and my health. Moreover, by nature I had
never desired the spotlight or life in public view.

 September 12, 1996
After Mass and Communion.

I felt very badly over the impact of my irritability and its resultant
short tempered fuse, in particular upon my children.

**You recognize your imperfections.**
**Refer them** (my children) **to their perfect Mother.**
**The Mother who is always with them, guiding,**
**watching over them, and protecting them.**
**She cradles them gently in her arms.**
**The intentions of your heart are pure.**
**Your love demonstrates my presence to your children.**
**Continue. Do not expect yourself to be perfect.**
**Greater good comes of honest acknowledgment**
**and disclosure/admission.**
**In these ways you allow your children**
**to know me.**

September 16, 1996
After Mass and Communion:

**Be still, my child. Listen to me.**
**Find the stillness in your heart.**
**I am there.**
**Be not afraid.**
**I am with you now and always**
**though sometimes you know me not.**
(meaning: recognize)
**I am there.**
**Return to your writing...**
**Bring other souls to me through this**
**and your daily actions** (daily life). **Be not afraid.**
**I am with you. I will guide you/your hand.**

I will lead you where you need to be, as your loved ones.
Do not concern yourself with the cares of the world.
They are passing and of (infinitesimal importance).
Their only value/importance is what they reflect
of my love/God's glory to others.
Glorify the Lord, my child.
Sing praises to his name.
I am your Alpha and Omega.
It is in and through me alone you have everlasting life.
All living things are filled with my energy.
Man alone has a soul, created in
my/our Father's image and likeness—
(men are not limited to earth.)
(meaning: They can accept God's invitation to divine eternal life,
and live forever as children of God.)
Man is limited by his thinking;
God is not.
The divine is incomprehensible to man.
Concern yourself not with my mystery.
Trust in me and accept the beauty
and mystery of my/our Father's creation.
There is no more important command than this:
love one another as I have loved you.
With that, all else will fall into place.
Revere life;
I am in you;
I am in all living souls who surround you.
The light of my presence exists
until the final hour of each (soul's) judgment,
at which time they must choose,
and that choice is eternal.
Your society is in marked decline.
All souls must respond to this
to stem the tide and reverse its pull,
that others are not drawn into
(and down) by its current.
Do not try to make sense of what I say as you hear it.
Merely write. Write, then read and reflect upon it later.

Referring to my writing and spiritual absence:
Concern yourself not with what you have missed this summer.
You do not yet realize the benefits gained.
(meaning: what was learned from struggling
in the relative absence of God's grace.)
It will become obvious as you return to your writing.
Glorify my name, my child.
Take me with you wheresoever you go.
See my face, the light of my presence,
in all whom you meet.
Meet their eyes;
gaze into the window/mirror to their soul.
Pray for those who cannot pray for themselves,
both living and deceased.
"Jesus, please help me; help me to do your will. I feel so sick."
Be brave, my child. Have patience.
Pick up your cross and follow me.
It is in this way you are led to our Father.
Remember, your cross (as everyone's cross,)
in life is a blessing
when you allow it
to bring you closer to me/our Father.
Allow me to lift the burden of your cross.
Give it to me.
Let me lift it from your shoulders and leave your body free
to do my work and only my work.
Submit your will to mine.
Allow me to more fully live through you.
All will be well.
As the Lilies of the field are clothed, and the sparrows of the air fed,
all and more will be provided you and your loved ones.
I/your Father know your needs and
prepare for you, well before you are aware.
Allow me to live through you.
Live in me and I in you.


I watched a plainly clothed man carrying articles from the altar after
Mass. His reverent simplicity in these small tasks inspired me.

Find the sacred in everyday life, my child.
It is the small, repetitive, mundane acts,
not the grand,
which brim to overflowing with my love.
I am in the grand as well
but my potential for plenitude/over-abundance
is greater in the small in reaching masses.
Be not afraid.
Follow my instructions,
my word, the example of my life.
A way has been prepared for you, your loved ones,
as all souls our Father has created.
It is each your mission to follow that path
to eternal life/salvation,
if you so choose.
Man's free will is his gift,
never to be taken from him.
In this he is created
in my/our Father's image and likeness.
Through this he is empowered to create—
create from nothingness
the power/energy of:
good or evil,
love or hate,
harmony or discord,
peace or *malcontentedness.*
The energy he creates will live forever,
as will the rippling effect
of these energies on those to follow.
Man is defined
by the intentions of his heart's desire.
To become more fully human
is to approach Divinity.
To become more fully human
is to become more humane—
compassion, empathy,
reverence for life—
life in all forms.

**Man is the highest form of life on earth.**
**Man's life is sacred**
**because your soul is in**
**my/our Father's image and likeness.**

September 17, 1996
The thorn in my heart twisted; the old wound reopened, unleashing its original pain. I walked in the rain, all shades of grey, matching my interior sorrow. My feet were cold, wet and hurt. I had to go to a small chapel dedicated to Our Lady. The thought of being there comforted me more than warm, dry slippers, and so I continued. I settled into a pew near the front and knelt, my heart aching beneath a weight of sadness. I tried to pray. I had difficulty feeling close to Christ, or his presence.

**You are (too) guarded, my child.**
Caught unawares, I realized, "Yes, I am." and as quickly recognized that if I were not, the pain would be too great.
**Let down your guard.**
I could not, as if my resistance blocked a tidal wave from washing over me. I felt a compelling, strong presence of both Christ and Mary.
**Pour all your heart's sorrow upon us.**
**We will make you light.**
**Unite your suffering with ours.**
**Identify with Mary my/our Mother**
**in my passion, death, and resurrection.**
**Allow yourself to feel**
**the great sorrow of this world**
**and give your sorrows to us.**
**Unite your suffering with mine**
**and Mary my/our Mother.**

September 18, 1996
After Mass and Communion:
My sorrow continued into the following day.
**Unite your sorrow/suffering with mine**
**and Mary my/our Mother;**
**this and all other circumstances of life—**
**my way of the cross.**

Feeling the close presence of Mary and Jesus consoled me. I understood:
*The circumstances of our lives*
*represent our own unique way of the cross,*
*just as Christ's path to Calvary was his.*
*When we unite our sorrow and suffering with Christ in his passion;*
*we contribute/participate in Christ's saving act for all mankind.*

I pictured Mary and Jesus in their human travail and, of love for them, ardently wished that if bearing my sorrow, united with theirs, relieved any degree of their suffering, "So be it."

 September 19, 1996
Yes, I am leading you in many ways,
from the most infinitesimal act/aspect of your day—
my guiding hand/presence is there by your side.
The only variation is your awareness of it/my presence.
Be aware of my presence.
Be constantly aware of my presence.
Practice this.
Make it a habit.
In so doing
you are less likely to stray from my guidance.
Receive Communion daily.
Listen to my word. (meaning: the Mass liturgy).
Be aware.
Be alive and live in the moment.
Return to your writing. This is the most important/paramount
task for you to accomplish. It is like no other task I have given you.
"What about my children?"
They are different.
They do not negate each others' importance.
They are not mutually exclusive. They are on different planes.
I promise you, my child, when you heed my word and write
as I instruct you, your children will not be neglected,
but rather, further blossom
in the light and warmth of my presence.
All that you and your loved ones need and far more
will be provided for you before you even know what is required.

"Please help me to spend my energy, and live my life as you want it. I feel
I waste a lot of energy."

Yes, my child, you make your life more difficult than it need be.
I have told you what it is you are to do, and
yet you struggle and rail against my will as if
you are not certain of what I have said.
Time runs short,
and yet, there is still time
to align yourself with my will;
it would not have happened sooner regardless...


Referring to the person of darkness:
Allow the justice to my swift hand.
I am might above all and
all wrongs will be set right
in my final Judgment Day.


Regarding someone I loved finding their way:
Allow them, as I you,
to come to see the truth in their own time,
in their own way.
Support them, be there for them.
They have many painful discoveries ahead.
Be there for them as I have without reservation
been there for you: all-loving, all-giving,
all-forgiving, all-compassionate,
and above all—all-patient,
respecting their own free will and person.
Your free will is the self-determination of your person.


...Attend Mass later today...
Be about my work, my child.
Concern yourself not with what that work is to be,
but only what is in the present moment.
Heighten your awareness to my presence
in each moment as you live it,
and you will be most keenly able
to know and follow my will for you.

Do not tie yourself to past regrets.
This keeps you hidden from me in the present.
Do not worry about the future;
this further absents yourself from me.
You can only most fully do my will and that of the Father's
by living and being most fully aware of our presence
in each moment as you live it/the present.

"I don't want to leave, I am so peaceful here, connected with you and centered."
You do not have to leave me, my child.
Take me with you wheresoever you go.
You better understand the meaning of what I have told you:
everything, everyday in our lives is sacramental.
Make manifest my love to all who witness you,
including yourself.
Do this by following my teachings,
my word, my life's example.
Call one simple fact to mind:
my presence within the heart of man.
I am all around you.
I am everywhere.
I am with you always and
I dwell in the image and likeness of God
in the heart of every living soul.

September 24, 1996
After Mass and Communion:
Be not afraid, my child.
Allow my Spirit to enter you.
Focus on my presence,
my presence within and all about you,
my presence in all living things
and no more sacred than in the soul of man.
I am in all creation.
I am all creation.
You are my beloved creatures.
I will not abandon you.

I have come to serve you—to show you how to serve others.
This is how you serve God and glorify God—by serving others.
Do all in the name of God.
Consecrate your smallest acts in the name of God.
Make your whole day holy/sacred.
Every moment you live, lived as a Sacrament—
a sign of God's love made manifest to all you meet:
from the most infinitesimal to the grand,
from the most mundane, repetitive to the grand.
There is none more sacred than
the mundane, repetitive tasks of everyday existence.
I am there in all my glory.
Help one another carry your crosses.
Help one another bear the weight.
Do not see your neighbor struggle
beneath the weight of his cross
without your heart lifting/rising/reaching-out
in the (deepest) intention of your heart's desire to help him.
Give all your crosses to me.
I will make your burden light.
You have experienced this, my child, you know.

Discouraged with myself I silently said, "I am sorry I fell away from you this past summer."

I have allowed you, my child, to see the vital importance
of my grace and presence in your life
by contrast with my absence.
You have been away from me
though I have not been away from you.

I was distracted by considerable physical pain.

Give your burdens to me, my child.
All for the good. All is in my/our Father's plan.
Mary is pleased with your increasing devotion to her.
She wants you to draw closer to her.
She has many special gifts to bestow upon you
(to shine forth on her other children), children who may
have more difficulty feeling her/our presence.
You saw what this was again like
by relative degree in these past months.

You saw how blind and aimless you became.
"Oh Jesus, please don't let me be there again, or worse yet further still."
Stay close to the Eucharist, my child.
Its grace is life sustaining.
It will give you the strength
to carry forth my/our Father's will.
Have courage, my child.
You have fallen back for lack of faith and courage.
Believe in me; trust in what I have told you,
where I am leading you.
Many important tasks lie ahead.
You must write. Write and bring my word
to those who cannot feel, see, hear
the gift of my presence.
Do not concern yourself
with *making/influencing* people
to believe in me; that is the work of God.
It occurs only in the intimacy of each man's soul.
Concern yourself only with being
a living example of my love,
a manifestation of my love,
a prism through which my love shines
upon all who come into contact
with you or your work.
I have given you a legacy. Treasure it.
Bring it to fruition as I have directed.
I am at your side.
All that you need and more
will be provided you as it is required.
You know what you are to do.
You have been given the vision.
"Forgive me avoiding what I have been asked to do."
You are human in your reluctance and clouding it over.
Be not afraid to carry it forth. I am with you now and always.
Carry me with you wheresoever you go...


Be up now, my child.
Care for your body—vehicle of my soul.

"'My', did I hear that correctly?"

Yes, my child, we are one.

I have entered you.

You are mine and I am yours.

We are eternally inseparable.

Your will is to do mine.

This is all that you can do.

Do not make your life so difficult

struggling against what is to be.

Accept it graciously

that all your strength go for the good,

and that you are not needlessly drained.

I am your strength and life's force.

Be up now, my child.

Go forth in my name. All will be well.

"I love you, Jesus. Thank you."

I love you, my child.

I hold you and your loved ones safely in my arms.

Make each (every) act of your day sacred.

 September 25, 1996
Just before Communion:

I wondered how I was to become closer to Mary. I looked forward to Christ's close presence in the Eucharist; yet how was I to increase my yearning for Mary.

*The relationship between*

*self/souls and Christ*

*and self/souls and Mary*

*are of a different nature, yet bear some similarity:*

*union—total and complete with Christ.*

*Mary—our Mother.*


*Ask Mary's help as mother.*

*Go to her for help in knowing/recognizing*

*and then carrying out God's will.*

*Ask for her comfort/consolation and grace*

*in doing this—accepting God's will.*

*Ask for her intercession.*

After Communion:

I had a strong sense of Christ's presence and through him the presence of Mary linked with his passion, death, and resurrection—his work of salvation. There was also a distinct separate presence of Mary, here with us on earth to carry Christ's mission forth. "Please help me to know and do God's will. I don't trust myself to do it."

Mary spoke:

It is not important to know God's will;

it is only important that you do God's will.

Be patient.

Allow each day to unfold as it is given to you.

Live only in the moment,

and so you shall be brought

to do the will of God.

Do not live in the past, my child.

Do not be filled with regret.

Accept your Father's forgiveness,

and give him your full *energy*/self today.

Do not yearn for the future.

Live in the moment,

yearning only to do the will of God

to the smallest detail of your life.

In this you will find joy and deep peace.

This is where I will meet you—

in each moment as you live it.

Later time is different; all exists at once.

It is beyond your comprehension

as is the pure joy and all the (bountiful gifts)

God bestows upon those who love him and keep his word.

Go, my child, keep me in your heart—your loving, caring Mother.

I am gentle with you and all my children.

Be not afraid. Feel my strength and protection.

"My children?"

They are equally in my care and protection as are all souls.

All need only accept what I yearn to give them.

I want to bring all souls to the Father

to share the boundless beauty, life and love—

the life my Son gave his mortal sacrifice to bring all men to.

> **Help me, my child. Help me complete**
> **my Son's mission/work on earth.**
> "I love you, Mary. Thank you."
> **Be up now, my child. Tend to your children.**

 September 27, 1996
During Mass words from the Eucharistic Prayer stood out:

> Before he was given up to death,
> a death he freely accepted,
> he took bread and gave you thanks.
> He broke the bread,
> gave it to his disciples, and said:
> *Take this, all of you, and eat it:*
> *this is my body which will be given up for you.*

As often as I had heard these words at Mass, today the phrase, "a death he freely accepted," stood out in a new perspective. I saw its relevance in the microcosm of each moment of our lives:

> *Christ accepted the death of his own free will—*
> *relinquished it, subjugated to the Father's.*
> *This is what we are to do each day*
> *as we live it moment to moment:*
> *freely accept the death of our own free will*
> *in submission to God our Father's.*

After Communion:

> **Make your mind a blank.**
> **My child, feel my majesty. Feel my presence.**
> **Allow my strength to fortify you.**
> **My presence is all that you need.**
> **All will fall into place around it.**
> **All that you need, desire, and more**
> **will be provided you**
> **when you acknowledge and live my presence**
> **as all that you need.**
> **You are good to allow Mary closer place in your heart.**
> **Continue and grow closer yet.**

She has much she yearns to give you,
much she wants you, as do I,
to pass on to others blind to our presence.
"Jesus, I have failed, the more so because of all the great and beautiful gifts I have received; because I too remain largely blind to your presence. It saddens me to act, all too often, as if I had never seen or known you or felt your presence."
You are forgiven, my child.
The intentions of your heart's desire are what matters.
You are bound in human form.
Accept your frailties and limitations
and allow it to teach you
greater compassion, love and forgiveness
for your fellow man.
You have been given the cross of a great forgiveness to bear—
almost as great as any human is asked to do;
but with my strength and mercy and
the help of your heavenly Mother
you will triumph...
Regarding a manifestation of evil:
You well recognize
there are more ways to kill than mortal.
Killing the spirit, the will,
controlling/subjugating the mind
of one to another is equally egregious;
and no greater than in the innocence of childhood.
No man has the right to deny another their free will
regardless the cause or ends justifying the means.

All will be well, my child. Be not afraid.
Take me with you wheresoever you go.
Up now, my child; be up and about your day's work.
Hold my presence with you the day through.
We are one.
See me in all whom you meet.
See me in the glory of creation which surrounds you.
See me and our Father's hand
in the smallest detail of your day.

Make your day, each act, holy/sacred in consecrating it to me.
This is your way of the cross.
In the step of each moment accept your death willingly,
(that is) relinquish your free will to the Father.
It is in losing it and giving up all,
that you will find everything—
everything and more
than you could ever imagine/conceive.
All is made ready for you, my child.
Much work lies ahead. Do not be afraid.
Derive courage and strength from my presence.
Do not sacrifice, but instead find joy
in all acts you perform.
Find pleasure, and
satisfaction in doing God's will,
as you release your feet from the clay
which binds your feet to the earth—
clay which has you suffer, and feel
deprivation in these acts,
not joy.
Lift your feet from the clay
*desisting/ceasing* from struggling
against them.
Give up.
It is then that your feet will fly free
and float above the clay
unencumbered by its weight
and appearance.
Be not concerned with where you will live
or what you will wear.
Yes, care for yourself,
bodily, mentally, spiritually.
Make the most of all the talents,
gifts, and blessings
I have bestowed upon you;
and above all use them
for the greater honor and glory of our Father.
Reflect our love to all that you meet.

Carry my word forth to the ends of the earth.
Write, my child...
Yes, my child, it is in doing
that which you are to do—God's will/in God's plan,
that you also best serve your children...
[The above in no way meant to the neglect
or detriment of the child]
Be up and go forth,
your heart filled with my joy and peace.
Let me shine from your eyes:
my love,
my peace,
my joy.
I love you.
"I love you. Thank you." I felt peace, joy and vitality.

 October 1, 1996
After Mass and Communion:
Do not try so hard, my child.
Let go. Allow me to work through you.
Allow my/our Father's plan to unfold
in your life as it is meant to be.
"Jesus, I feel so sick, I have so much pain."
This is a cross you must bear,
*your illness*, (the circumstances of your life).
Allow me to lift your burdens from you, to make them light.
I am the Bread of Life.
All who come to me will never hunger, nor thirst.
Place your full faith and trust in me.
Have I not provided for you till now?
Concern yourself not with how
I will provide
for you tomorrow.
Concern yourself not with what
my/our Father's plan is for
you for tomorrow.
Concern yourself only with today and
the moment within which you are.

In each moment bring my presence to your consciousness—
my presence within you,
those around you, and
throughout all creation,
for all time.
Focus only on this (my presence) and
all will flow naturally into place.
Do not try so hard.
You impede my/our Father's work.
You (in so doing) interfere with
my/our Father's plan.
You confuse yourself as to your will
and mine/our Father's.
All will be made ready for you
and more as you need it.
I/my Father look after
all our creatures and creation.
Live in my love and peace,
enjoy the great beauty surrounding you.
(meaning: people and all creation)
I love you, my child.
There is much work for you to yet accomplish.
Much is asked of you but no more than you are capable of
or prepared by me to do.
"I am afraid. Though I am happy to share the experience of your love, I
don't want to publish this book. It's the freedom and privacy of an anony-
mous life I don't want to lose."
Do not be afraid, my child.
Do as I instruct you and concern yourself not
with what you do not know or how it will happen.
Focus your attention on me/my presence
within and all about you.
Be guided by
my words, my work, my life's example
which I have left you and all souls
who choose to know me better.
(meaning: in the gospel and scripture)
Practice my presence.

The summer had been a swing of faith's pendulum, myself mildly lost in a relative sense. This was simple guidance for the journey back: be aware of Christ's presence. It was one easy thing to remember, one focus upon which to anchor.

October 2, 1996
After Mass and Communion:

I felt an extraordinarily strong presence of Christ; yet it only enkindled more yearning for him. It was a mixture of extremes: joy, peace, awe, the all-pervasive Presence and the longing to be closer. It is desire so strong as to seem a physical ache, an emptiness only God's presence can fill and make whole. Our God, our refuge, the one and only person who will never betray us, barring none—even ourselves. Time suspended.

**We are one, my child.**
**You are mine and I am yours.**
**You are my bride and I am your groom.**

Physical pain and other discomforts markedly diminished, though I was aware of them it was as if they were far away and no longer part of me. I felt light, weightless, as if floating. To experience Christ's presence so closely is to feel wholly complete, every need and desire anticipated and filled to overflowing. It is sublime, joyous, peaceful contentment.

**I love you, my child.**
**I am with you for all time.**
**I am all time.**
**I am all that is,**
**was**
**and will be.**
**I am everything.**
**Those who condemn themselves to hell**
**exist beyond me,**
**exist in interminable,**
**unimaginable pain,**
**in the void—the void of hell.**
**It is the absence of God,**
**the absence of God's sustaining love and presence.**
**It is important that my message reach every man.**
**Write, my child...**
**Allow me to communicate through you.**

"I am not worthy of this, I am not up to this. It is grandiose. It is not me—this role."

My child, none know better your role than I and the Father.
"Forgive me Lord. I am sorry at my reaction. It just seems so unfitting. I am not worthy. I have failed you. I am so sorry and feel the worse for all the wondrous gifts you have given me."

I will make you worthy, my child.
Place your full faith, trust, confidence in me.
Accept my forgiveness.
Do not follow Judas' footsteps,
unable to accept the forgiveness of your Maker.
Do not place yourself above your God
in refusing the depth of love
offered you in my forgiveness.
There is no time for you to *play god*
dwelling on past sins, regrets, living in the past.
Place your full energy/consciousness in the present moment.
This is where you are.
This is where you live.
This is where I meet you.
This is where my/our Father's plan is unveiled to you.
This is where you are to act, feel joy, suffer—
all to do no more than bring you closer to me
and (allow me to) draw other souls to me.
Allow me to reflect off you
to all whom you touch,
in your life,
your writing,
all that you do.
Your children are safely in my care and protection.
Mary holds a special place in her heart for them as well.
We are well pleased with you, my child.
Draw upon us to know how to love them even more.
You appreciate the great depth of love
man can have for another
through your love of your children.
You truly appreciate how one can lay down
his life for his children.

You grasp the suffering you would endure
if only you could spare your children.
Imagine that ten-fold beyond your imagination, and
you will begin to glimpse/appreciate/understand
the depth of love I/our Father has for
each and every soul he has created.
This is why it is so difficult for man
to accept my/our forgiveness;
it is beyond your comprehension,
the vast bounty of love
in which you are each held.
Appreciate your place
in the vast order of things (creation),
your place before your Creator.
Humble yourself.
Empty yourself of your own will
and seek/desire only to do that of your Creator.
Concern yourself not with what that will is.
(meaning: knowledge of it, like a map into the future)
Concern yourself not with how you will carry it forth.
Concern yourself only with your consciousness/awareness
of the present moment, and that
my/our Presence is paramount in that awareness.
In this way, my child, all will fall naturally,
easily, simply into place.
Do not make your life so difficult.
Do not try so hard.
You struggle and rail against my will in the process.
You confuse yourself between my will and yours.
I do not ask more than you can do.
I do not ask more than I have prepared you for,
not more than I will stand with you
and/to see you through.
All is well, my child.
I felt great peace and altered perception of my physical pain. The pain was
still identically there but I was in part removed from it.
I do not ask sacrifice, my child;
I ask love.

Be filled with my Spirit/Presence, my child,
and allow me to shine from your eyes,
your every act, your every thought.
It is in this, my child,
that you fulfill your life's work,
reflecting the light and love
of God's love upon creation.
This is each soul's duty,
to reflect God's love
in whatever way they are able.
There is no more perfect way
to reflect God's love
than (by) loving your fellow man.
Know your place in creation my child:
love your God above all things;
love your fellow man as I have loved you.
I have shown you in my life's work, my example,
my words, and teachings in (sacred) scripture.
I have left you my Sacraments, my child.
My presence remains with you
for all who seek it,
no more easily attainable for all
(than) in the form of the Eucharist.
Such great grace flows from this.
It is as vital to life
as the air you breathe
and the water you drink.
It sustains your spirit.
If man grasped this
there would be lines each day
out the doors of my Church,
(instead of the self help section of bookstores,
bars, drugs and other excesses.)
Man would not need to hide,
seeking only to numb his senses,
dull his consciousness,
forget his mortality,
run from his mortality.

If man knew (meaning: had faith) and trusted in
the great strength I offer/have in store for him
the world would be transformed
by my light, my energy.
Go forth, my child. Take me with you wheresoever you go.
You go not alone. I am with you always as is Mary,
all my angels, and saints.
The entire Mystical Body of my presence
is with you as one body inseparable from *you*
*as a single unique cell in its existence now,*
*and its development/growth over time.*

"What of those who do not do your will, those who choose not to?"
They are separated like the chaff from the wheat,
like desquamated epithelial cells.
(dead skin cells that fall away and are replaced by new ones)
Though they did not choose me
they served their purpose in my plan when they lived.
Those who choose me do not fall from my body
to decay into nothingness/painful void;
they remain a part of me
to grow and flourish
and live in divine eternal bliss.
It is each man's choice, my child.
Go now, return to me later. (meaning: writing)

To feel Christ's love and presence so intimately does not distance you from others. It is not a mutually exclusive love. It is the contrary; it creates more room for others. Christ's love does not engender jealousy; it generates more love drawing you closer to others. To be conscious of Christ within yourself and those around you is to be more alive, aware, available and connected with others in the present moment.

October 3, 1996
After Mass and Communion:
Again as yesterday I had an intense sense of Christ's presence. I yearned for more. My thoughts echoed, "I love you. Please help me do better. I am sorry."

Be still, my child. Sit back and take pen in hand. I love you...
Be my voice. Let me speak through you.
Write, my child. You must write. Today...
This is so important, my child.
Time grows short.
You must do my work.
Bring more souls to me/the Father.
Concern yourself not with how.
Many will draw closer through your writing.
Concern yourself not with how this will be accomplished...

I prayed for a friend and her family.
She and they too are in my care and protection...

Yes, you correctly understood:
Referring to a premonition yesterday which initially caused me fear:
If you do not feel great and deep peace
with that which is beyond man's ken
it does not derive from me.
(I would not scare man without avenue
by which to exit with hope.)
I do not strike fear in the heart of man without hope.
Consider yourself with your own children.
I am your loving Father and Creator.
I want all my children to return home to me,
each and every soul.
Each is important and special in my eyes.
Go, my child. Up and about your day's work...
Devote yourself to me (in your writing).
Devote every aspect of your day to me
from the smallest task to the grand.
All will be well.
Be not concerned for tomorrow
nor anchored to the past by regrets.
Live in the (present) moment and
maintain constant awareness
of my all-pervasive presence
within you, all around you, everywhere, for all time.

Be most keenly aware that I am in you
and within the soul of every man.
Revere life.
It is the Temple of the Holy Spirit.
It is Sacred.
It is Divine.
Help others to open their eyes to my presence.
Be with me, my child,
in your conscious awareness.
I am never without you.
You are never without me,
only your awareness fluctuates.

"Thank you, Jesus." I felt deep tranquillity and purpose. I did not know how the book would be published or even completed; it seemed an overwhelming task. I knew it would be as God willed it.

Go now, my child.
Be up and about your day's work—my day's work.
Take me with you wheresoever you go.
Your life is a prayer.
Turn to me often for all the strength that you need.
I am yours and you are mine.
We are wed.
Our spirits are one.
Mary is united with us and she longs
that you turn more often to her,
that you make her a more
conscious part of your awareness.
There is much she wants to give you of her grace,
much she wants you to tell others
to draw them closer to her,
all that my/our Father's work
be accomplished/brought to completion on earth.
Glorify my/our Father's name.
Reflect the beauty of our love
on all creation and you have done
my/our Father's will/your life's task.
(meaning: as true for each soul
in their own unique way and calling.)

October 9, 1996
After Mass and Communion:

Regarding the weight of futility experienced in efforts at an important task at which I continually tried and failed:

My will is done.
It is as it is, my child.
Accept what is given you.
Do not look for more or less.
Do not be concerned.
Your interests, as that of your loved ones,
and all my beloved souls
are provided for by my/our Father—
all that you need and more.

My thought turned to being in the way of God's will.

Be not concerned, my child.
Be patient. Do not try so hard.
Allow each day to unfold as it is given you.
It is then you will best see (most clearly see)
the path intended for you.
To live in the future or regret in the past
is to be unavailable to me and the gift of life
I have given you in the present.
It is to be unavailable
to do for me in the present—
to do my/our Father's will.


Regarding parents' trials helping a child through normal growing pains:

Relax back, my child.
Allow her to struggle and come into her own.
This is how she will grow and be made strong and whole.
She is safely in my/our Father's care.
Mary holds a special place for her
and your entire family in her heart.
Turn to her more often.
She is anxious for you (mankind) to turn to her
for more grace she longs to bestow upon you.
Allow her to empower you
to do my work more fully on earth.

My pulse quickened, recalling the association between past spiritual growth and suffering, "I don't know that I want to be empowered."

**Be still, my child. Be not afraid.**

**All** (meaning: God's plan) **has been laid out long before time began...** Regarding submitting my will to God's in his plan:

"I fear I will fail. Please Jesus, I do not want to fail at this, but I don't see myself capable of that scale of living."

**Do not concern yourself with that, my child.**

**It will not be easy on the surface,**

**but beneath it I will be there**

**carrying your burdens and crosses...**

Still struggling with my perception of God's will for me, and my strong aversion to publishing this material, I implored, "If I have to be sick, can't it just be in privacy and peace? I am sorry."

**Be at peace, my child.**

**Allow my peace to reign within you**

**and draw strength from my presence, my words.**

**Be not afraid; nothing will be asked of you**

**for which you are unprepared by me and more.**

**Mary, the host of saints and heavenly angels...yearn/wish, *pray*...**

**for your** (all God's children's) **success**

**in doing my/our Father's will...**

"Mary, please help me. Please help me to accept this as willingly and openly as you received Christ into your womb. I am truly afraid."

**Be calm, my child.**

**Allow my peace to flow over you.**

"I am afraid to follow this path and yet I am more afraid not to. I do not know what this path is or where it is to lead."

**Concern yourself not, my child.**

**All will be given you as it is useful/in your best interest to know.**

**Do not try so hard. Do not be concerned about**

**how you will follow my/our Father's will;**

**merely will it, and it will be so.**

**Live in the moment**

**ever conscious of my presence**

**and all will naturally follow.**

**I do not ask sacrifice.**

**I ask love.**

When you follow Mary's entreaty to fast,
do it with love in your heart for the poor,
for a sense of solidarity and love
for these my creatures/creation (too).
Allow it to bond you to all men for all time,
all those who have done without
at man's doing—man's selfish use
of my creation, my bountiful creation,
with an abundance for all.
Think always of the poor, my child,
most especially the little children.
In their innocence they are closest to me,
and also most prone/vulnerable
to the effects of evil.
Leave a legacy for them
in my word made manifest.
The work I have given you to do
will help provide for them—
will be a visible sign of my love
for all to see for all time...
Go forward; my peace and blessings are upon you.
Go, my child. Be about your day's work.
Take me with you wheresoever you go
that I may touch the hearts of man
and transform them as I have yours.
"Oh Jesus, I am truly not worthy. Please make me so."
Merely accept it, my child.
Be open to what I am giving you.
Merely accept the great gifts I pour upon you.
Receive my love and grace.
Receive the grace of Mary, our Mother.
Never allow your consciousness
to deviate from my presence—
forever, now, before, and always
entwined inseparably with your spirit.
We are one, my child,
as we have always been
and will always be.

Accept your road to Calvary.
It is as our Father has willed it.
Allow me to fill you with my peace
and lift your burden/cross
as we travel this road together.
Do it in love, my child.
Set your sights upon me and go forth.
"I love you, Jesus. You seem at once so close and yet so far—so far I can't
even explain how—beyond distance."
Yes, my child,
it is the blindness of your human condition,
plunged into darkness in pursuit of your
free will unaligned with God's.
It was the day man elevated himself
above his Creator and acted upon it
that all time began—
suffering, pain, death,
and loss entered the world.
All men share in the collective guilt
and all men continue in the same vein
weighed down by the shackles
of their (physical reality)
which befell them.
Be up now, my child.
Be about my day's work. I love you.
"I love you Jesus." I felt deep peace.

 October 10, 1996
After Mass and Communion:

I more clearly saw my past strivings and ambitions prior to illness as
misplaced yearning for God, needs and meaning only God could fulfill.
Before Christ's birth the earth was filled with emptiness and darkness,
with his birth came light and meaning. We are called to reflect this beau-
ty of Christ's light on others.
Be still now, my child.
Concern yourself not with how you will do my will.
Yearn/desire only to do it, and it will be so.
You expect more of yourself than do I.

You are more harsh and critical of yourself than I.
You do not begin to grasp the enormity of my love
for you and all mankind—you are none capable.
My compassion and mercy go out to you in this
and all your weakness/human frailty.
Do not try so hard, my child.
(Drop back) (meaning: take a less active but
more "actively receptive" roll.)
Be vigilant, my child,
for the signs and opportunities
I present to you.
There is not one small step
you need to orchestrate.
It is all planned for you.
Planned and in place before the
dawn of time/...time began.
Concern yourself not with capturing every word.
You will have what I want you to say—
in the form I want you to express it.
All will be well, my child. You and your family
are safely in my care and protection...

Mary has a most special place for all the little children
*hurt by the sins of mankind,*
*children of pain, the pain of man.*

...Make some time today to devote
to my work of writing. I will help you.
Just allow me to work through you—
through you in all things,
from the large to the small,
from the spiritual to the financial...,
all things, my child.
Be receptive to my guiding hand in all things.

Regarding an ill young person:
My child, I will make him well—
well because you have asked me to do so.

Your prayers are pure of heart.
You have prayed to me/our Father as you should for the ill.
(Meaning: as all should because God hears everyone's prayers.)
You have prayed in my name and asked
that our Father's will be done in healing—
be that will physical or spiritual healing.
I will heal his body, mind, and spirit.
This will be a turning point in his life.
Tell him this is a time of renewal and turning point.
It is an opportunity to be reborn—reborn in me.
Christmas is a time of rebirth for all souls in me,
to renew within them the true source
of their life's force and strength.

My child, pray. Be up and about your day's work...
Do not fear the intensity of closeness.
(meaning: in a relationship with Christ.)
Do not be afraid. Now go in my love and protection.

October 18, 1996
After Mass and Communion:
"Help me please with the anger and annoyance I feel with some people."
Allow your anger/annoyance to direct you
to where you need to shine forth
my love, mercy, compassion.
I love you, my child. Do not try so hard.
My work does not require such great effort.
Lean into it/me.
I will do it for you.
I will carry your load, your burden.
No man can do (anything) without God—
without my help, my intercession—
whether they believe in me/my name or not.
Your (duty/job/task) is to be
vigilantly receptive of me and my direction.

Referring to writing MY CHILDREN LISTEN.
Do not suffer over the precise word, the exact minute detail.

It will be given to you as is needed.
Concern yourself not with (this).
You are becoming (bogged down—weighted)
by your own criteria on how to do/perform my work.
You risk losing the whole (in) a perfectionism of the parts.
It is the overall feeling, the intention (which matters).
The intentions of your heart's desire are good, pleasing to me.
Now just allow me to direct them, hone them
to where I want them/you to be.
All will be well, my child.
All will be provided for you
and your loved ones as is needed.
Concern yourself not with how.
Make no plans. Just remain open to my guidance.
Do not worry for some loved ones.
All will be as has been planned—
planned since before the dawn of time,
as in your life and in all souls created by God.
"What about our free will, our input; how can these both be so?"
It is not something you are able to understand, my child.
It is beyond human thought.
It is beyond human consciousness.
There is no human dimension from which
to speak as a frame of reference.
One day this and all things
will be made clear to you.
Now it is only for you to accept
with faith and trust as divine mystery.
No one comes to life everlasting without choosing
the Father's will over their own.
I am your guide.
I am your salvation.
In this way,
no one comes to the Father
but through me.
I am your life.
I am your resurrection.
I am your soul.

*We are each so inherently intertwined/commingled*
*in soul or spiritual essence with:*
*God the Father, our Creator,*
*God the Son, Jesus Christ, and*
*God the Holy Spirit,*
*that we could not exist without God.*
*God initiated our creation;*
*and moreover remains as vital*
*to our sustained daily existence.*

Yes, my child, this is so. More than that,
nothing would exist in your physical world either
without my steady active presence,
the consent of my will to do
the will of my/our Father
and exist in all creation.
The world was made through me
and exists through me.

"How very sad it must be for you to see so much so closely! It distresses me to be aware of the world's sorrows, so little compared to your awareness, and that I am unable to change it—worse yet, that I see my own contribution to it."

Yes, my child, the weight of this
was worse than all the physical pain
of my passion and crucifixion.
This was the agony of my passion.
You see how with your eyes, ears and heart,
when you unite your suffering/experience with mine,
(it) eases the pain I felt as a man.
God does not feel pain.
God wishes more men experience the gift of love
and return to him.
You cannot begin to understand God's reaction
to man turning away.
You may by weakest of analogy
appreciate a semblance when you watch
your children with one another...
Be still. Just listen. Do not try so hard.

You are to tell my people, (my children, the world):
to love me,
to keep my commandments, my word.
Above all, love their God above all things,
and their neighbor as themselves.
I am within each of you.
My light is only extinguished in each soul
as they make their final choice—
should they choose not to accept
my/our Father's invitation
to divine eternal life.
They enter the void of hell
with full knowledge of what they have missed
and no hope of experiencing it.
All manner of help is available to each soul
in making this choice.
Not all will/can be saved,
only those who choose to be.
Those who have not heard my word,
my work of salvation,
will be helped in different ways
and judged accordingly.
I am the only way,
the only path to salvation.
No one comes to the Father but through me.
Concern yourself not with how
I bring men of all creeds/faith under one tent.
Accept it as divine mystery.
Respect one another's differences.
(meaning: that of all true religions)
Religions of truth are those which revere life—
human life above all.
The remainder are the work and influence of the devil.
Reverence/respect for human life
is the common thread
which binds my many faces (true religions)
together on earth.
It is beyond your ken, my child or that of any man.

*We are to respect other religions of Truth,*
*bound by mutual respect for life.*


There is much to do, my child.
It is impossible for any one man to accomplish,
but nothing is impossible with God.
Simply allow me to work through you and
all will come to pass as I have told you.
"Jesus, I have so much trouble with my memory; how can I carry out
what you've directed me as with this book?"
Lucky for you, my child;
your memory, it helps you stand less in my way.
I laughed aloud, glowing in the warmth of such loving acceptance that
even limitation was transformed into endearing quality.
The things man finds the most troubling/vexing
are in God's eyes their greatest assets.
Pain and suffering are not all bad of themselves
and joy and good fortune not all good.
It all depends on how truly one follows
the will of God in each—
how much each individual allows God
to come into their life with each experience.
The values (and words) of God are not the values of man.
Do not try to understand the divine
and the ways of the divine;
merely accept what is given you as it is shared.
Look not for more, nor for less
just/simply be open, open to receive...
Go, my child. Go forth to love and serve me.
Take me with you wheresoever you go.
Live in my name.
Do all in my name—
all your joys, suffering, thought, acts,
every deed, every intention.
Bring me ever into your conscious awareness,
my presence, and all will naturally
follow suit/fall into place.

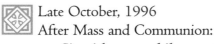 Late October, 1996
After Mass and Communion:

Sit with me a while, pen in hand. Be still, my child.
Do not try so hard. Allow me to work through you.
All is according to our Father's plan. All is in place.
All is to be as it has been directed before the dawn of time.
Be open to my direction. Do not question. Do not plan...
All will be well. Yes, this is the time
to draw your/our book to its conclusion.
It is not the end; it is a new beginning...


Do not be afraid, my child.
Not all is discrepant between heaven above and Earth below.
Only remember to use wisely and in accordance with God's will
all good fortune which comes your way.
"It is a great responsibility, Lord. What if I fail? Please help me not to."
My child, it is simple.
Keep me ever present in your conscious awareness*
and you cannot fail.
"I love you Jesus. I so want to please you. Please help me. It is so hard to
find the stillness, the silence in which to meet you."
Concern yourself not, my child.
Allow me to show you the way.
You try too hard.
In so doing you make it more difficult
to see my way, my help,
my/our Father's will.
It is all to come to pass as my/our Father's plan directs.
Acquiesce your will to me/our Father
and you have done your part.
Will it, and it will be so.
Do not be concerned at how, when, where,
or why it will be so.
It is not important that you know these things.
It is important that your heart's desire
is to do the will of God.

*Meaning: awareness of Christ's presence within me, others, and all creation.

Allow me/our Father to see to the rest.

There is much to do today, my child.

Be up and about your day's work.

Take me with you wheresoever you go.

Your life is a prayer. I love you, my child.

"I love you, Jesus."

 November 20, 1996

After Mass and Communion:

Follow Mary, my child. Fast.

Fast, to make you strong in body, mind and spirit...

All must be strong to most fully do my/our Father's will.

"Jesus, please help me with this book. What am I to include or not of your words?"

Do not rush, my child.

It has already been told to you (given you), but

you are yet unable/unwilling to see it.

"Please help me. Do I continue to be so willful?"

In a manner, my child, though I know it is not your intention.

You are blind to it because you have not yet

fully emptied yourself to do my will.

"Jesus, I do not understand."

My child, I have already told you, eliminate personal details

*except those which further my message...*

You do not yet grasp/see your unimportance in my message.

My message stands alone.

Intruding yourself upon it

only makes it more inaccessible to others.

Make it universal.

Remove yourself from it...

You cannot grasp yet your unimportance.

"I am so sorry Jesus. I am so sorry I have not sufficiently humbled myself before you."

My child, this is man's weakness.

This is man's original sin:

placing himself as false god before himself,

not fully acknowledging his place before God his Creator,

not recognizing his place in the order of all creation.

Your (and every man's) importance
derives solely and directly from God.
Into eternity the measure to which each man
shares in divine life is directly measured by
the extent to which he followed,
*in the intentions of his heart,*
God's will.
The result, my child, is not important—
it is the intention,
it is the choice *which is.*
It is the use of your free will;
how you use that choice *which matters.*
You have yet to more fully learn/accept
these lessons in humility (fully emptying yourself)
for you to be prepared to complete this book...
"I am apprehensive at what that may mean Lord."
My child, it is a matter of faith.
Trust in me, that I am leading you where you need to be.
Trust in me and see. Risk believing. I will not abandon you.
You will see and your faith will grow—just as does grow
the love of parent and child,
and in the most ideal between husband and wife...
...allow your mind blank and
allow me to be present and guide you.
You have all that you need for my/the book,
you have only to remove yourself further from it.
Trust in me, my child. Do this and it will be
as it should, *in accordance with God's plan.*

Regarding persons who had deceived me for their own gain:
Be forgiving toward them. They have sinned against you.
They have been selfish, greedy. It is your task to forgive them,
be there for them, offer them love...
I will guide you. I will draw good from all.
Concern yourself not with how to do my will,
just will it in the depths of your heart
and it will be so. Desire it, my child.
Desire it from the depths of your heart.

Risk trusting in me more deeply that I will not lead you astray.
I will never abandon you.
Do not try to have everything make sense/be logical...

"Forgive me Jesus in my persistence on my children's welfare."
Your concerns as a mother are well understood.
Turn to Mary.
She wants you to turn to her more often.
Your children, as are you, are held safely in her arms...
You are a family, my child.
Enjoy one another's successes.
Be there for one another in your sadness,
your disappointments, rejoice in your triumphs.
Share your love.
This is my command to you.
Love one another as I have loved you.
Begin first in your family. Go on from there.

Regarding the persons who had deceived me for their own gain:
...I am teaching them as well.
Your role is presently only to be tolerant, patient.
Allow life to unfold as my/our Father's plan directs.
They will see the *truth/light*
when it is time; when they are ready.
Your love and forgiveness in this regard
is an important element in both their path and yours.
'Forgive us our trespasses
as we forgive those who trespass against us.'
Remember this often, my child.
Forgiveness is love. Make it available.
Recognize forgiveness offered
is a completed act when it is received.
This requires awareness
before remorse enters their consciousness.
They have no awareness. Judge them accordingly,
as you would not expect a blind man to see;
similarly bear no anger toward them
for that which is beyond their ken.

They will be brought to their own realization of the truth
in their own time (in God's plan). Concern yourself not.
Do not allow yourself to fall prey/be abused by their avarice.
I will help you in this and all things.
I/Mary hold you, your children and your loved ones
safely in our care and protection.
Be not afraid. Live and enjoy life.
I place the people and opportunities about you for a reason.
There are no coincidences. Nothing happens of accident/chance.
"Jesus, this is so bewildering to me then with respect to man's free will."
Do not try to comprehend it, my child.
It is divine mystery, my child, beyond your comprehension.
Each man is master of his/her own soul's destiny,
master of the eternal fate of their soul.
Do they choose to align their own will with God's
or turn away?
It is that simple.
God's plan is immutable,
man's individual participation in it (and the extent of it)
is entirely within the choice of his own free will.
Tell the world to love me, love their fellow man.
It is not too late, though time grows short for all mankind
to turn to me/my Father, their Creator.
Time grows short to humble themselves
before their Creator,
emptying themselves
of their own willfulness/selfishness.
It is long time to stop worshipping
the many false gods you place before yourselves.
Recognize the first false god
is the one of self—your own wills,
placing yourselves above our Father, our Creator.
This is what is meant by original sin.
It is not only the first sin of all mankind
and one in which all men,
with the exception of Mary and myself, shared;
it is the sin from which
all others originate.

Original sin—the first sin
and the one from which all others originate.
Empty yourselves, my children.
Humble yourselves before your Creator.
Take your proper place in the order of creation.
Rejoice and glorify God's name
in all your works, thoughts, and deeds.
Have faith, my child.
Nurture it.
Allow it to grow.
Trust in me.
Risk believing and your faith
will grow in plenitude...

Regarding Christopher's family:
Let them know Christopher continues to look down upon them
with such great love. He does not feel sadness
but rather great joy as he knows one day
they will all be together.
His eyes are open to seeing God's plan unfold on earth.
He knows the pain, disappointments, success, and joys
are all part of God's plan—
all leading his family to more fully share
in the eternal bliss he already lives each day.
He is very close to his little brother
(born four months after his death)
and loves him very much
as well as Jacob (his younger brother).
He has a very special place in his heart for them.
Your people are with me as well, my child.
They pray and long for you to continue
on the path to do God's will.
Be up now, my child. Be about your day's tasks.
There is much to do. I will make you ready.
I love you, my child. Take me with you wheresoever you go.
"It is so peaceful here, Jesus. I just don't want to leave the closeness and
peace of your presence."
Remember, my child, I do not leave you.

It is only your conscious awareness
that does not acknowledge me.
Practice my presence.
Bring my presence within you and others
into your consciousness/awareness
and all will naturally follow.
Do this at every moment of the day,
from the small to the large/grand,
the happy to the sad.
Make awareness of my presence a habit.
Your life will flow more smoothly.
It will be easier.
You will more readily perceive
and then follow the will of God, our Father.
I love you, my child.
Go now, your life is a prayer—
each act, thought, word and deed.
Every intention of your heart's desire, my child, is a prayer.
Begin there, my child.
Will the intentions of your heart's desire.
Actively will it.
Say the words to me throughout your day.
Will it, my child, and it will be so
(meaning: following God's will).
Go now, remember your life is a prayer.
I do not leave you. Take me with you.
Allow me to be present
(meaning: in your conscious awareness)
within and all around you.
I love you. I will make you strong
to do all that is asked of you.
All will be provided you and more.
Keep Mary's presence close to your heart.
She is always there for you
and wants you to turn more often to her
for help, consolation, encouragement, advice.
Follow her example.
Follow her lead.

That which was asked of her she did not
comprehend, find logical, or possible.
Respond as did she: 'Thy will be done.'
'Let it be done unto me according to thy word.'
Pray to her for her special grace, that is what you need.
Your (man's) role in my/our Father's plan
is more of mother (that is, like Mary).
It is a complementary/essential role.
I am the Redeemer.
Follow Mary to more fully comprehend how you (and all men)
are to participate/share in my redemption of all mankind.
Go now, my love. I do not fault you for your reluctance
to leave the beautiful peace of my presence and friendship
but there is other work you must do for me today.
You have been away from me in Mass.
Do not stay away from me or Mary, your Mother.
Attend Mass and receive Communion daily.
Referring to Sunday Mass, children now willingly attending.
Make this the number one priority with your children.
You are loved. Take my love with you
and shine my love on others
in all that you do.
Let my light shine from your eyes,
emanate from your being...

Go forth in my love, peace and protection.
I am always with you. I will never abandon you...
"Thank you, Jesus, I love you."
I love you, my child.

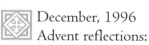 December, 1996
Advent reflections:

Christ's birth did not happen only two thousand years ago. Its mystery, wonder, simplicity, and joy remain—a living legacy—a drama unfolding. The choice is ours. Turning Christ away, as did the innkeeper; or as Mary, allowing Jesus to be born and grow within us—that God become manifest to us, and through us, to all whom we touch.

The first meaning of Christmas is not about giving. It is about receiving—receiving Christ's living presence within us. In this we reach our own greatest giving as we reflect the love of God upon our fellow man.

Christmas is but a season till its Spirit lives in the heart. Allowing Christ to be born and grow in our hearts is to live the Christmas Spirit the year through.

December 16, 1996
After Mass and Communion:
On correcting and disciplining children:

Be kind.

Have I ever spoken to you in anger, my child?

Replace all anger with kindness, patience and compassion.

Let them always know you are open to forgiveness.

Forgiveness reserved for true repentance;

but always there, always available.

Practice my presence within you

and all those about you,

my presence in all creation.

Do this and allow me to speak

and act through you and you will find

this will (naturally) remove

the sharpness from your tongue

and any harshness of anger.

Demonstrating love to your children in discipline

is more healing (productive) than anger.

This is what they need—love.

This is what all souls (humans/persons) need.

Set my world afire with my love and

a transformation you will see...


You will bring many souls to the Father

if you follow his will, *submitting yours to his.*

This is how all souls are most pleasing to their Creator,

each in his (their) own unique way

in keeping with God's plan.

I love you. Be up now, my child.

December 25, 1996

Late evening, I felt Mary's close presence and heard her speak. She anticipated my first thought's question before I could ask it. Mary spoke:

**When you speak with my Son you speak with me.**
**My Son and I are one...**

**It is with great sadness that I weep for the world**
**and the wickedness which holds it fast;**
**but I will vanquish evil and**
**Satan's grip upon mankind and the world.**
**The hour is soon to come, my child.**
**Do not be afraid.**
**It is to be a time of God's great mercy**
**and outpouring of grace upon mankind and all creation...**
**It is with great urgency that you must write and**
**convey my Son's message to all mankind.**

Referring to what had been the moon in the vision of Mary (June 21, 1995) depicted on this book's cover:

**Yes, my child, the round, luminous *Presence was my Son*.**
**Yes, my child, it was the Holy Eucharist—**
**the sacred Presence of my Son.**
**It is from thence all illumination, all life derive.**
**This is it—distinct from none,**
*a part of everyone*
*and all creation.*

(Meaning: Christ is intrinsically part of every human life and all creation.)

There were multiple levels of meaning in the moon's image: moon, sun's reflection, Son's reflection, Son, Eucharist.

**There are many mysteries which man cannot,**
**in his human state, behold.***
**(You're only recently appreciating my Son in my arms**
**is only one mystery, though it was right before you,**
**as simply and plainly as can be seen.)**

---

* Initially I thought Mary had appeared around the moon, but the moon was transformed becoming her Son, in the form of the Holy Eucharist.

Tell more souls to turn to me.

Turn to me more often yourself, my child.

We have hardly made one another's acquaintance;

though I have always been there for you, rejoicing at your birth.

My child, say my Rosary daily.

I will show you better how.

Teach your children the same.

The Eucharist, my child, receive it every day.

You need the full grace my Son can bring to you

in his own Presence.

Difficult times are ahead for all mankind.

The hour is soon at hand for Satan to be cast out.

Be not afraid, you and your loved ones

are safely in my care and protection.

"Help me please, Mary, Mother. I love you. I am sorry I have not turned to you for more help. I am sorry I have not made more effort to know you."

My child, I understand.

You have my full mercy and compassion.

You are forgiven. Accept it and allow me

to be more fully present in your life;

that I may act through you.

Follow my example.

See how I observe our heavenly Father's will.

Observe my faith in our God.

I will help you follow me/my example.

It is time to rest your body to be strong for tomorrow—

the work our Father has planned for you.

You are good, my child.

Go in my Son's peace to love and serve the Lord.

Do this by loving and serving your fellow man.

Referring to a reconciliation with someone, for which I had long prayed: "Thank you all for the beautiful Christmas gift of peace."

My child, our help is yours.

Do not be concerned...

Simply love them as we have loved you.

We are their constant protection as yours.

**Rest your eyes now, my child, and sleep safely in my arms.**
**Rest your heart knowing your loved ones are also**
**safely in my care and protection. I love you.**
"I love you  Mary, Mother, thank you."
**Prepare for sleep now, my child, and lie in my arms.**
**When you awake tomorrow morning you will feel whole**
**and your right shoulder pain will be gone,**
**its use restored.**

This referred to moderately severe right shoulder tendonitis which had developed that day, and resulted in significant limitation in range of motion, pain and decreased strength. The next day my shoulder was at baseline "normal," while past episodes had taken weeks to months of additional treatment to resolve.

Late December, 1996
Aspects of illness or its ramifications, were never far from the moment in reminding me of my own helplessness in some form of humbling experience.

My children and I were walking briskly to the train. I turned to look for the sign indicating our train's platform, at the same time my foot brushed against something on the floor. Suddenly I was airborne, careening forward, positioned for a belly flop. It was like a dream in which you try to help yourself but cannot move. I knew in theory what to do to right myself, but my body refused, as if frozen. It was by no means my first fall but the most dramatic in my children's presence. I landed with a thud, sliding in the thick residue of dried mud and gravel tracked through on winter boots. "Oh! Mom, are you all right?" both of the girls cried, running to my side.

I caught my breath and took stock of myself, grateful for a large soft bag, long winter coat and thick gloves which had cushioned my landing.

"Yes, I am fine."

"Here, let me help you get up." they offered, squatting down beside me. I stood up and brushed myself off.

"What happened to you? Why did you fall?"

"I bumped my foot on something."

"What?" they asked.

"I am not sure." I looked back and saw nothing, but upon closer inspection identified a small metal device imbedded in the floor. Its purpose was to hold open a door. "That." I said pointing at the floor.

"What? I don't see anything."

"Right there." I said pointing more closely to it.

"That little thing! How could that make you fall?"

"If I had not been turning at the same time my foot tapped it I don't think I would have. But it was just enough to throw me off balance and I couldn't adjust."

"Are you sure you're OK?"

"Yes, my gloves are not in too good a shape, but I am fine."

"That was kind of scary, Mom. What if you had fallen on the street or something?"

Her sister added, "Yeah, and then a car came. Oh, please be careful!"

December 28, 1996

I asked guidance in how to say the Rosary. Beyond rote recitation and acknowledging the Glorious, Sorrowful and Joyful Mysteries, I never knew how really to pray the rosary. I was inspired to do it now in an entirely different way. I said the Rosary picturing Mary there as a living presence, and calling to mind that this was what she asked me to pray and how she asked me to speak to her in prayer. I said and pictured each line, emphasizing one line at a time. I prayed for Mary's intentions, my own children, and world peace.* During the Rosary I was given the following:

*So saying the Rosary was about*
*establishing a relationship with Mary, a bonding,*
*in the simplicity of merely spending some time in her presence,*
*devoted to her solely, exclusively in those moments.*

Saying the Rosary this way was unlike my prior experience of bored monotony; instead, it brought me to a state of detachment and sharper awareness. I was left with peace. Later in the day I concretely experienced Mary's grace in managing a situation to which I had repeatedly been unable to bring more.

---

* Post script, August, 1997: In an earlier locution I had been asked to pray for Mary's intentions during the Rosary; though I did, I could not help but add my own. I had not recognized my partial compliance was lack of trust.

*In praying for Mary's intentions when we pray the rosary*
*we pray God's will be done, and we pray for all that is good.*
*There is no need to ask beyond that—all is done.*
*When we pray for Mary's intentions*
*we pray for the world, for all her children.*

January 9, 1997
After Mass and Communion:

In addition to Christ, the divine Presence I experienced also dominantly included Mary.

> Be still, my child. Concern yourself not
> with how you are to accomplish our Father's will.
> Just know that I/we are there with you always,
> constantly at your side.
> All will be there for you and more,
> already prepared, in advance of your need.
> Go, my child, make the rest of your day a prayer.
> Bring my very close presence to you (in your writing) today.
> I will guide your path, your writing, your editing, your way.
> Go in my peace. I love you.

January 13, 1997
During the rosary before Mass I received several insights on the meaning and importance of saying the Rosary.

> *A time to draw closer to Mary,*
> *just to be in her presence, with her company.*
> *A time to receive her strength, consolation, guidance, grace.*

During the Rosary I varied how I pictured Mary: the church statue, stained glass image, Miraculous Medal pose among others. Mary spoke:

> Picture me as you saw me appear about the moon.
> Call me,
> Our Lady of the End Times.
> I bring you (the world), my Son again,
> for his Second Coming.
> This is our second Advent.
> Prepare the way
> by opening your hearts to my Son
> in the Eucharist...

After Communion I felt a strong presence of Christ and Mary...
Mary spoke:

> Allow him to be born and grow within you.
> The End Times are a second Advent
> preparing the world for my Son's Second Coming in great glory,

after which time a great peace will reign upon the earth
*for many years/for a long age* before the end of time.
The End Times are not the end of the world.
They are a second Advent,
a preparation for my Son
to come again in glory.
Each man prepare his heart
for my Son to reside within him
as did I receive our Lord, Jesus, into my womb.
Meet him in the Eucharist,
his living Presence.
Prepare the way, my children.
He is coming.
All who know him;
he will know them.
Know him in your hearts
through the grace he so desires to pour out/forth
upon each of you in the Blessed Sacrament of the Eucharist.
Carry the light of his Presence forth from that Sacrament
and set the world afire/ablaze
with the love he has brought/enkindled in you.


Be not afraid, my child...Be in my peace and protection.
Know that you are safely in my arms...

Christ and Mary spoke:
I love you, my child.
"Thank you. I love you both so much."...
Mary spoke:

I am Mother of all mankind,
*all faiths, and non-believers alike,*
Our Lady of the End Times,
Mother of all mankind.


January 14, 1997
After Mass and Communion:

The intensity of yesterday's spiritual experience and the tenor of
Mary's words left me overwhelmed. In their enormity I realized with
finality that I could not ignore what I had been asked to do in sharing

my journal. Now I found myself struggling to focus on the moment, but unable to tolerate the silence in which to listen and be aware of Christ's presence. I felt myself trying to flee, yet was firmly held back. I was like a moth inextricably drawn to God's love, then too close for comfort, as if singed—unable to endure the intensity of heat and light.
Amidst this turmoil I heard:

**Do not fear the intensity of closeness in a relationship with me.**

"I am sorry, Jesus. Thank you. It's hard for me to allow myself to feel so close to you right now." Though grateful and reassured at Christ's words I could not bear the stillness in which I usually found so much peace after Communion. I rose quickly, left the church and welcomed the frigid air outside. I walked home briskly, perhaps wanting to feel numb myself.

January 24, 1997
After Mass and Communion:

I continued to have great difficulty tolerating the inner quiet necessary to feel Christ's presence.
"Forgive me, Jesus, I can't bear the intensity. I am sorry. I don't understand."

**The intensity of my absence is greater, my child.**
**Persevere and know that I am with you always.**

February 28, 1997
I tried to pray though with continued difficulty. The inner stillness was too uncomfortable, though I was improving. I felt Christ's presence and to a lesser degree Mary's.

**I will place you in my womb and there you will heal.**

Though the feeling which accompanied this image was one of soothing protection, the words challenged part of me, I asked, "Who? Your womb, or do you mean Mary?"

**We are one, my child.**
**I will place you in my womb and there you will heal**
**till you are born on the other side.**

I felt comforted and understood the words in graphic analogy:
*In the circumstances and travails of our own lives we grow and develop*
*by learning better how to love during our earthly existence;*
*in this we are each like a developing fetus within the womb*
*awaiting birth into true and eternal life.*

*The essence of healing is in reconciling our wills with God's.*
*Praying with the greatest purity of heart is to make our deepest intention:*
*"God's will be done."*
*Any additional healing in any other form flows from God.*

> For you have died, and your life is hid with Christ
> in God. When Christ who is our life appears, then
> you also will appear with him in glory.
> Colossians 3:3-4, RSV

 Fall, 1997

> For she is a reflection of eternal light,
> a spotless mirror of the working of God,
> and an image of his goodness.
> Wisdom of Solomon 7:26, RSV

As asked, I had begun praying the rosary picturing Mary as she appeared to me about the moon. It was not until I had the painting for the cover of this book before me that I was able to focus separately on the images of Christ and Mary individually, and then together—as a whole. In viewing the painting during The Hail Mary my eyes would focus back and forth between Mary's face and the light of Christ. To my surprise it helped me concentrate on the words of The Hail Mary more easily. I began to see the power in the simplicity of its phrases, humbly announcing greater depths of meaning and mystery.

| **Mary** | **Christ** |
|---|---|
| *Hail Mary, full of grace;* | *the Lord is with thee:* |
| *blessed art thou among women,* | *and blessed is the fruit* |
| | *of thy womb, Jesus.* |

The first few lines drew me back and forth twice between Mary and Christ—her face illuminated from within (by the light and love of God's grace), and Christ, his light at the center of her being.

| **Mary** | **Christ** |
|---|---|
| *Holy Mary,* | *Mother of God,* |

These words swiftly, intimately move yet again from Mary to Christ as she transcends mortality, time, and all natural laws as she is born and gives birth—becoming Mother of God and is herself born into divine eternal life.

*pray for us sinners, now and at the hour of our death. Amen.*

The glow of light in the painting which surrounds and emanates from Mary, is a fusion of Christ and Mary—their prayer, grace, and love pouring out upon mankind and all creation. It is the full consent of Mary's will which perfectly allows Christ's light to shine through and reflect from her. Unimpeded by her free will, Mary, is a pure reflection of God's love.

Mary and Christ are inseparable. She gives his light bodily form; she is created through his light, even her garments are made of his light. At the center of Mary's being is Christ—pure light, pure love, her essence, our essence, and the essence of all creation. Mary holds Christ in her arms, and he surrounds and holds her in his light. In the consent of Mary's will Christ shines through her, becoming one with her, perfectly reflecting God's love; she is then glorified in union with the divine Presence. Mary, through the power of the Holy Spirit, exists through Christ, with Christ and in Christ.*

Mary is holding what she is created through; she is Mother of what created her. The mystery of Mary's relationship with God the Father, God the Son, God the Holy Spirit, and her connection with each of us, becoming Mother of all mankind, is incomprehensible when logic is bound by human frames of reference. God's ways are not our ways; spiritual reality is not physical reality.

Though only Mary and Christ, free from original sin, can perfectly reflect God's love, we are called to follow their example. Mary brings us her Son and shows us how to draw closer to him; she shows us how to live our priesthood—identification with Christ—by allowing him to be born within us. As loving Mother, she is there to help all her children love Christ and one another.

---

\* It was during Mass that words of the Eucharistic prayer stood out in bold relief, crystallizing what I saw in Mary holding Christ's sacred presence in the form of the Eucharist—the intimate eternal bond between Mary, Christ, the Holy Spirit, God the Father and all creation.

> Through him,
> with him,
> in him,
> in the unity of the Holy Spirit,
> all glory and honor is yours,
> almighty Father,
> for ever and ever.

The image of Our Lady of the End Times celebrates The Hail Mary, and the sacred Presence of Christ in the Eucharist. It beckons us to join Mary in the mystery of the Annunciation, making it ours, a Second Advent—creating a place for Christ in our hearts—preparation for his Second Coming in Glory. The image shows us what we are to do: abandon our will to God's, and accept Christ's presence within us, allowing his light to shine through us (unimpeded by our own free will) upon all whom we meet, all to reflect the love of God as purely as we are able. In saying "yes," we, as Mary, are elevated to divine eternal life, forever glorified and existent in God's presence, without beginning or end—existent with God even prior to our temporal creation on earth and living on into infinity—God our Alpha and Omega.

"Before I formed you in the womb I knew you,
and before you were born I consecrated you..."
                                        Jeremiah 1:5, RSV

# DECEMBER 8, 1997

When Jesus saw his mother, and the disciple whom he loved standing near, he said to his mother, "Woman, behold, your son!" Then he said to the disciple, "Behold, your mother!" And from that hour the disciple took her to his own home.

John 19:26-27, RSV
(spoken from the cross)

It was the feast of the Immaculate Conception*. It was also the anniversary of my father's death. As a child, my mother would remind us on our way to Mass to pray for him. In later life, for twenty-one years as a "lapsed Catholic," my Mass attendance was sporadic but this day, besides Christmas and Easter, I never missed Mass. It always just seemed I should be there. Over the years my feelings at the Mass had varied from numbness to sadness, sometimes grief, and finally peaceful acceptance once I came to faith. Today was different; for the first time I felt happy, extremely happy.

After Communion I felt the close presence of Christ and Mary; with them was my father. His presence was unmistakable and communicated depths of love. Unlike the few other times he had been included in my spiritual experience, this time, I was content with just what was given me. I felt no sadness to be in his presence, no longing for more—that he should speak to me or not leave. It was pure joy, as if all time were contained in that moment; it was complete. Time is passing and timeless eternity is true reality.

---

*The feast of the Immaculate Conception, a holy day of obligation celebrated with a Mass, honors Mary's freedom from original sin from the moment of her conception in the womb.

In a mood of celebration and rejoicing I silently addressed my father, "I am so happy for you, that you're there." I condensed my reaction to his absence from my life and the peace I now felt, "It's OK, Dad; I understand." I was momentarily taken aback at having said his name— said it so naturally. It was the first time since he had died. "I can say it! I can say it! I can finally say it!" I was surprised at how much this elated me. I never realized how much it meant.

Mary's presence now predominated in my awareness. "Mary, thank you for taking him to you on one of your feast days." Part of me asked myself, "What are you saying? What is coming over you? Thank you?" Another first, and a far cry from my childhood wish that I could have shot the angels who took him away."

Mary spoke. The first line referred to my father but in the sense of "everyman."

I am holding him in my arms.
(I am holding him with Christ.)
(referring to the vision of Mary,
as Our Lady of The End Times)
(Picture me holding him
as you saw me hold Christ, my Son.
He is there with Christ in my arms.
He is united with Christ.
They are inseparable;
their light and spirits are commingled as one.
Their light shines through me,
pouring love upon all creation,
just as do all those who have chosen
to align their wills
with God our Father
and so exist in God's presence;
the Communion of Saints,
those who said 'yes'
to God's invitation to divine eternal life,
are united in Christ—
the Mystical Body of Christ.)

# Insights and reflections December 8-18, 1997:

Christ's salvation is universal; it is for every man for all time. I was reminded of several things I had heard: **I am not a God of exclusion. All come to me...** (December 4, 1995) **Leave the mystery of bringing all men to salvation to me** (March 14, 1996) **Knowing me through the person of Jesus Christ is the most direct path by which to reach me; yet I am here for all, regardless of how they have come to know me—their Creator. To know and love Christ, my Son, is to know life made simple.** (November 30, 1995) **No one comes to the Father but through me. Concern yourself not with how I bring men of all creeds/faith under one tent. Accept it as divine mystery. Respect one another's differences.** (meaning: that of all true religions) **Religions of truth are those which revere life—human life above all. The remainder are the work and influence of the devil. Reverence/respect for human life is the common thread which binds my many faces** (true religions) **together on earth.** (October 18, 1996)

I was reminded that the risen Christ was not always recognized even by his closest followers and friends. Mary Magdalen, on the day of Christ's resurrection did not at first know him, mistaking him for a gardener. The disciples on the road to Emmaus mistook Christ for a stranger until they recognized him at dinner in the breaking of the bread—the Eucharist.

Christ reaches all mankind, though they may not recognize him for who he is. All mankind is offered salvation through Christ whether people know him as such or not. This redemption is our link to sharing divine eternal life as God's children, but we must say yes to complete the gift. The question each soul must answer is whether they will accept God's will as their own—yes, or no.

All souls while still bound in their human forms share in the Mystical Body of Christ, because Christ's light exists within each. In this, Mary is Mother of all mankind. Beyond our earthly lives however, Mary remains our Mother only if we choose to share divine life as God's children. When we allow ourselves to be born in Christ and Christ to be born within us, we are like Christ—we are born of Mary and accept that we are children of God.

With the consent and submission of his own divine will to the Father's, Christ humbled himself in taking human form that we might come to share in his divinity. Our last chance to participate in Christ's salvation of all mankind and receive God's mercy and forgiveness is at the moment of physical death, a reckoning of how we have chosen to use the gift of free will over a lifetime. The full burden of responsibility accompanying free will comes due; it culminates in that last moment when we are required to make a final, permanent choice between God's will and our own. How one has lived—favoring God's will or one's own—predisposes one's final choice, but there is hope for all.

For those who turn away from God, Christ's light is forever extinguished in and around them. God is forever absent to them. Like the chaff separated from the wheat they are cast out but exist forever in perpetual darkness and inescapable, unimaginable suffering.

Those who choose God's will over their own are glorified in Christ, forever part of his Mystical Body, and part of the light of God's divine eternal life. The souls who chose to enter God's kingdom offer their Creator a cup—their life's work. Its capacity depends upon how fully they abandoned their own will to God's. Christ and Mary are perfect examples in accepting God's will as their own. The cup we offer our Creator, he fills to overflowing with divine life—eternal light.

Mary holds these souls—the Communion of Saints—with Christ in her arms. They are all distinct, but inseparable in the union of their wills with God's. They radiate all the light they contain. Their light shines forth as one fusion of love upon all creation, giving honor and glory to one God, our Creator.

We are one, joined in the Mystical Body of Christ, united across time and space; unified in Christ we all belong to the same Mother—reborn of Mary—the new Eve. Christ is the renewal of our creation—the fulfillment of salvation from our sin in turning away from God and his will. When we chose our own will over God's, we elevated ourselves to false gods in his place. It is the original sin we all share.

Paradise lost, poor banished children of Eve, our fallen lives are recreated: through Christ, with Christ, and in Christ,* forever alive in God's resplendent eternal light.

Mary weeps in sorrow for us, the world, and the wickedness which ensnares us. As loving Mother, it is her anguish to watch her children suffer, in particular when we hurt one another. Her pain is sweet of knowing that God has used even the suffering created by the chaff cast out to purify in love those souls who remain. Her pain is sweet because it is a Mother's travail in giving birth—to the new creation in Christ.

> For he has made known to us in all wisdom and insight the mystery of his will, according to his purpose which he set forth in Christ as a plan for the fullness of time, to unite all things in him, things in heaven and things on earth.
>
> Ephesians 1:9-10, RSV

*Again the Eucharistic prayer embodied for me the intimate bond between Christ and Mary. My understanding of this bond now broadened to include all who would accept Christ, all who would accept God's will as their own. All creation exists in Christ; he is its summation and renewal. The transforming effect of his living presence remains with us in pure form in the Eucharist—food for our souls. Receiving the Eucharist we are assimilated in Christ, and Christ in us.

"Amen, amen, I say to you, unless a grain of wheat falls to the ground and dies, it remains just a grain of wheat; but if it dies, it produces much fruit. Whoever loves his life loses it, and whoever hates his life in this world will preserve it for eternal life. Whoever serves me must follow me, and where I am, there also will my servant be. The Father will honor whoever serves me.

"I am troubled now. Yet what should I say? 'Father, save me from this hour'? But it was for this purpose that I came to this hour."

John 12:24-27

# December 9, 1997

Jesus looked at them and said, "For human beings it is impossible, but not for God. All things are possible for God."

Mark 10:27

A flood of memories were unlocked in having "Dad" and "Daddy" returned to my vocabulary as natural expressions. More amazing was my reaction. I was happy, not ridden with the ache of loss. It was as if some part of me had been restored, a deeper healing I had not realized was missing.

I remembered my father in a dark suit coming through the door after work. He was slim, and handsome, with black hair, fair skin, blue eyes, high cheek bones and firm jaw. His face would light with a sparkle in his eyes and wide smile upon seeing me running toward him. He would stretch out his arms, leaning forward, knees slightly bent, preparing to catch me. "Daddy! You're home!" I would call as I ran to him. He would catch me with both hands and lift me high into the air as he turned a half circle, prolonging my airborne glide. I shook with my own laughter. He hugged me to him before gently placing me down. Crouching, he came closer to my eye level and spoke with me. Often times he would reach into his jacket and produce a small surprise, a penny candy, a pencil, an eraser, a trinket, and once an ice cream on a stick from the Good Humor truck which regularly jingled to a stop on our block. I best remembered the ice cream. I knew, even at the time, that he had planned it to make me laugh, and laugh we did together. Such a fond memory; how nice to have it back all these years later! There were more.

"Daddy, take me to the park. Daddy teach me how to swing." When I grew tired or frustrated, unable to coordinate the rhythm needed to propel myself I would call, "Daddy, swing me. Get me started. Daddy, push me more, Higher, higher, I want to go higher. Wheee!" I can still feel the wind as the swing sailed, loose strands of hair flying about my face. His firm hand reassuringly there at the end of each arc, gently meeting the small of my back encouraging me forward and upward. Off the swing I ran to the slide, scaling its stairs, midway calling "Daddy, watch me." as I looked, delighted that his eyes were already following me up the ladder. I started down the slide, "Daddy, catch me."

"Daddy, read me a story." When it was through I reached up to hug him about the neck, burying my face in its warmth. I felt his secure arms about me, hugging me back. I kissed him on the cheek, as he lay me down in my bed to sleep. Bringing the covers about my shoulders, he wished me good night and sweet dreams, then kissed me on the forehead. "Daddy, I love you."

"And I love you," he would say with one last affectionate squeeze of my shoulder.

I remembered once speaking to him on the phone while he was in the hospital, "Daddy, when are you coming home?...Why can't you come home now?...But I want you to come home now."

This milestone in healing and the spiritual insight which accompanied it seemed part of the book, though I debated including it and latter entries. I had been long convinced that January 13, 1997 was the book's close. I had been mistaken before, for years telling my family, "It's almost finished." I felt Mary's close presence and with it a strong intuition to include these parts. Her presence intensified. I understood:

*Mary is our gateway to heaven,*
*and Christ is the bridge.*

We were plunged into darkness, cast in human physical form, all time began, death and loss entered the world—all with original sin. We are surrounded by a swirling sea of darkness. Christ is our bridge of light, with rays spanning in every direction into the darkness, reaching every man—like a tunnel through the sea. Mary is gateway, she brings us the bridge. She is our mediator, intercessor, and model. I was directed to the image of Our Lady of the End Times. The blackness of the night was like our sea of darkness, in which Mary brings us Christ, the bridge of light, our salvation.

"Is the book finished now?" I asked Mary.
Yes, my child.


Say the Rosary, my children.
Meet my Son's living presence in the Eucharist.
Receive him into your hearts and
let him grow to full strength within you.
Love one another.
Love your God above all.
I love you, my children.
Come to me.
Come home.

## Prayer With My Children

O Holy Father,
in the name of your Son, our Lord Jesus Christ,
and through the power of the Holy Spirit
please protect us from all evil.

Please heal us.
Please increase our faith and trust in you,
forgive us our sins,
and help us always and in every way
to do your most holy will.

Mary and Jesus, please guide us,
watch over us and protect us.

Please give us your special grace
to always do God's will and be ever faithful.

# AFTERWORD

Do not try so hard.
You impede my/our Father's work.
You (in so doing) interfere with my/our Father's plan.
You confuse yourself as to your will and mine/our Father's.
All will be made ready for you and more as you need it.
I/my Father look after all our creatures and creation.

October 1, 1996

How many times had I heard and not understood: **Do not try so hard?** I did not see it until the book's completion, upon reading it straight through for the first time. "Oh!" I said aloud, astounded at the obvious, The emphasis is not trying actively to do God's will, or even to know God's will, but to accept God's will. The doing is in being "actively receptive." How characteristic this was of my slowly coming to understand and believe—God's gentle patience unfolding, never forcing his truth upon me, allowing me to see and accept it in my time, always there waiting for me.

When I was seventeen, a number of friends and relatives died; the most beloved was my grandfather. I turned to my religion for comfort at his death and was startled to find I had no faith. I could not reconcile the pain of grief, among other sorrows and the outright cruelty in the world, with the concept of a loving God. I wanted to believe in the God I had been taught existed since my childhood, or failing that, a loving God in any religion. No amount of effort, desire, need, or reasoning brought me a shade closer to faith. I was appalled to admit to myself, that I was an agnostic; though I still cherished the values of Christian teaching. I continued to hope God existed, sporadically attending church, sometimes almost believing, though I remained, in the last analysis, agnostic by default—until my first mystical experience.

Now in retrospect, I have had to wonder. In all the time I spent analyzing—searching for God, I never once asked God to give me faith. If God had been trying to grant me faith, anticipating the question I could not myself ask, I would never have heard him. I made too much noise thinking—trying to figure it out my way.

When I was an agnostic trying to reason my way to faith I was like a person pushing mightily on a door that opened in the opposite direction. Logic assured me that I was correct because the door had no handle; surely that meant push because one could not pull. But our frames of reference, like past experience, or logical inference do not encompass God's ways. It is God who opens the door to us from the other side, and determines the manner and timing in which each of us is brought to know him. We all come to know God in different ways. Our part is best accomplished in stepping back, out of the door's way—actively receptive to what God gives us. I was not doing that. In my case when the door swung open first it knocked me down, as if to say, "Now, pay attention."

Someone who considered himself devout told me he could not understand or relate to my experience, because in all his life-long years of religious observance he never had anything like it. "So why should you?" he asked me, as if to imply I was claiming some kind of sanctity.

"Did you ever think it was just the opposite?" I responded. "Maybe I was just so strong willed that God first slowed me down to listen, while you've been listening all along." I am not holy; I am reluctant. My tendency, at times, is still to run the other way, but now I accept that to grow in faith is to sometimes doubt. Why else would we need trust, hope, or courage?

The spiritual gifts I have received are not by virtue or merit, but in many ways in spite of myself. I did not plan or intend them; it was an offer I couldn't refuse—mystic by draft. Even though these extraordinary spiritual things have happened, my life remains full of trials. It is difficult some days to place one foot before the other. Whatever our phase of spiritual development is, it is a struggle trying to turn away from self and turn towards God. Life is a struggle. It is our human condition. Heroism, merit, and the sacred lie in the small acts of kindness we show one another as we each travel our own way of the cross against the tedium of our lives. It is the opportunity we are given to grow in learning to love.

Would my life have been different had I been more humbly receptive of God earlier? I do not know. It is incomprehensible to entertain the notion that I was following God's will as an agnostic, but now I accept the entire course of my life as God's will. I am in awe at the seeming paradox of man's free will, and the infinite complexity, mystery and supremacy of God's will and divine plan: always giving each of us a path back to him, and always ultimately drawing good from bad.

The work of God is perfect, the work of man is not. Man's imperfections do not negate the work of God performed through man as an instrument of God's love. I used to think our part was to strive and aspire to do good—to strive to do God's will. I have come to realize it is presumptuous to think "I" had the ability to "do" God's will. I have glimpsed another level of man's true humility and powerlessness before God and his all-pervasive, immutable will. Man's role is "actively accepting" God's will; it is more a process of keeping our own will out of the way—participating, not impeding God's work. Goodness naturally follows and the barrier between ourselves and Christ falls away within and around us.

I have recorded my experience and the words I have heard, and been asked to share; God's will be done.

> For perfection does not consist in lacerating or killing the body, but in killing our perverse self-will.
> *God's word to Catherine:*
> **Do you know, daughter,**
> **who you are and who I am?**
> **If you know these two things**
> **you have beatitude in your grasp.**
> **You are she who is not, and**
> **I AM WHO IS.**
> St. Catherine of Siena

"And I tell you, ask and you will receive;
seek and you will find; knock and the
door will be opened to you. For everyone
who asks, receives; and the one who
seeks, finds; and to the one who knocks,
the door will be opened. What father
among you would hand his son a snake
when he asks for a fish? Or hand him a
scorpion when he asks for an egg? If you
then, who are wicked, know how to give
good gifts to your children, how much
more will the Father in heaven give the
holy Spirit to those who ask him?"

Luke 11:9-13

# ACKNOWLEDGMENTS

# BIBLIOGRAPHY

*Quotable Saints* by Ronda De Sola Chervin; Servant Publications, Ann Arbor, Michigan. Copyright © 1992 Ronda De Sola Chervin.

*Prayers of the Women Mystics* by Ronda De Sola Chervin; Servant Publications, Ann Arbor, Michigan. Copyright © 1992 Ronda De Sola Chervin.

# TO ORDER

*MY CHILDREN, LISTEN*

phone toll free  1(888) 301-4673

visit our web site at http://www.caritasinc.com